Standards Practice

For Home or School

Grade 6

INCLUDES:
- Home or School Practice
- Lesson Practice and Test Preparation
- English and Spanish School-Home Letters
- Getting Ready for Grade 7 Lessons

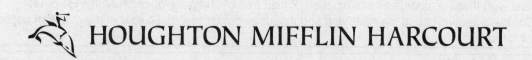

HOUGHTON MIFFLIN HARCOURT

Printed in the U.S.A.

ISBN 978-0-547-58811-7

20 21 0928 20 19 18 17

4500694902   B C D E F G

CRITICAL AREA THE NUMBER SYSTEM

COMMON CORE **Critical Area** Completing understanding of division of fractions and extending the notion of number to the system of rational numbers, which includes negative numbers

1 WHOLE NUMBERS AND DECIMALS

Domain The Number System
Common Core Standards CC.6.NS.2, CC.6.NS.3, CC.6.NS.4

2 FRACTIONS

Domain The Number System
Common Core Standards CC.6.NS.1, CC.6.NS.4, CC.6.NS.6c

3 RATIONAL NUMBERS

Domain The Number System

Common Core Standards CC.6.NS.5, CC.6.NS.6a, CC.6.NS.6b, CC.6.NS.6c, CC.6.NS.7a, CC.6.NS.7b, CC.6.NS.7c, CC.6.NS.7d, CC.6.NS.8

 RATIOS AND RATES

4 RATIOS AND RATES

Domain Ratios and Proportional Relationships
Common Core Standards CC.6.RP.1, CC.6.RP.2, CC.6.RP.3a, CC.6.RP.3b

5 PERCENTS

Domain Ratios and Proportional Relationships
Common Core Standards CC.6.RP.3c

6 UNITS OF MEASURE

Domain Ratios and Proportional Relationships
Common Core Standards CC.6.RP.3d

 **EXPRESSIONS AND EQUATIONS**

 COMMON CORE **Critical Area** Writing, interpreting, and using expressions and equations

7 ALGEBRA: EXPRESSIONS

Domain Expressions and Equations
Common Core Standards CC.6.EE.1, CC.6.EE.2a, CC.6.EE.2b, CC.6.EE.2c, CC.6.EE.3, CC.6.EE.4, CC.6.EE.6

© Houghton Mifflin Harcourt Publishing Company

COMMON CORE **Critical Area** Solve real-world and mathematical problems involving area, surface area, and volume; and developing understanding of statistical thinking

10 AREA

Domain Geometry
Common Core Standards CC.6.G.1, CC.6.G.3

11 SURFACE AREA AND VOLUME

Domain Geometry
Common Core Standards CC.6.G.2, CC.6.G.4

12 DATA DISPLAYS AND MEASURES OF CENTER

Domain Statistics and Probability
Common Core Standards CC.6.SP.1, CC.6.SP.4, CC.6.SP.5a, CC.6.SP.5b, CC.6.SP.5c, CC.6.SP.5d

13 VARIABILITY AND DATA DISTRIBUTIONS

Domain Statistics and Probability
Common Core Standards CC.6.SP.2, CC.6.SP.3, CC.6.SP.4, CC.6.SP.5c, CC.6.SP.5d

End-of-Year Resources

Getting Ready for Grade 7

These lessons review prerequisite skills and prepare you for Grade 7.

School-Home
Letter

© Houghton Mifflin Harcourt Publishing Company

Vocabulary

greatest common factor (GCF)
The greatest factor that two or more numbers have in common.

least common multiple (LCM)
The least number that is a common multiple of two or more whole numbers.

prime factorization A number written as a product of all its prime factors.

Dear Family,

Throughout the next few weeks, our math class will be learning about division, multiples, and factors. We will also be learning how to operate with decimals.

You can expect to see homework that involves addition, subtraction, multiplication, and division of decimals.

Here is a sample of how your child was taught to divide decimals.

🔑 MODEL Divide Decimals

Divide. $44.8 \div 3.2$

STEP 1	**STEP 2**	**STEP 3**
Estimate.	Make the divisor a whole number by multiplying the divisor and dividend by 10.	Divide.
$45 \div 3 = 15$	$3.2\overline{)44.8}$	$\begin{array}{r} 14 \\ 32\overline{)448} \\ -32 \\ \hline 128 \\ -128 \\ \hline 0 \end{array}$

Tips

Estimating with Decimals

When estimating, it may be helpful to round the numbers in the problem to compatible numbers. Compatible numbers are pairs of numbers that are easy to compute with mentally.

For example, to estimate $19.68 \div 4.1$, use the compatible numbers 20 and 4: $20 \div 4 = 5$.

Activity

A trip to the gas station is a perfect opportunity to practice decimal operations. For example, "We bought 8.2 gallons of gasoline that costs $2.90 per gallon. What was the total cost?" Work together to write an operation with decimals that represents the situation. Then estimate before computing the answer.

Carta para la casa

Vocabulario

Máximo factor común (MCF)
El factor mayor que dos o más números tienen en común.

Mínimo común múltiplo (MCM)
El número menor que es un múltiplo común de dos o más números enteros

Factorización en primos Un número escrito como un producto de todos sus factores primos.

Querida familia,

Durante las próximas semanas, en la clase de matemáticas aprenderemos sobre división, múltiplos y factores. También aprenderemos a operar con decimales.

Llevaré a la casa tareas con actividades que incluyen suma, resta, multiplicación y división de decimales.

Este es un ejemplo de la manera como aprenderemos a dividir decimales.

🔑 MODELO   Dividir decimales

Divide. $44.8 \div 3.2$

PASO 1

Estima.

$45 \div 3 = 15$

PASO 2

Convierte el divisor en un número entero multiplicando el divisor y el dividendo por 10.

$3.2\overline{)44.8}$

PASO 3

Divide.

$$
\begin{array}{r}
14 \\
32\overline{)448} \\
-32 \\
\hline
128 \\
-128 \\
\hline
0
\end{array}
$$

Pistas

Estimar con decimales

Para estimar, puede ser útil redondear los números del problema a números compatibles. Los números compatibles son pares de números que son fáciles de calcular mentalmente.

Por ejemplo, para estimar $19.68 \div 4.1$, usa los números compatibles 20 y 4: $20 \div 4 = 5$.

Actividad

Un viaje a la gasolinera es una gran oportunidad para practicar operaciones con decimales. Por ejemplo: "Compramos 8.2 galones de gasolina que cuesta $2.90 por galón. ¿Cuál fue el costo total?" Trabajen juntos para escribir una operación con decimales que represente la situación. Luego estimen antes de computar la respuesta.

Divide Multi-Digit Numbers

COMMON CORE STANDARD CC.6.NS.2

Compute fluently with multi-digit numbers and find common factors and multiples.

Estimate. Then find the quotient. Write the remainder, if any, with an r.

1. $\begin{array}{r} 13 \\ 55\overline{)715} \\ \underline{55} \\ 165 \\ \underline{165} \\ 0 \end{array}$

    Estimate:
    $700 \div 50 = 15$

2. $19\overline{)800}$

3. $68\overline{)1,025}$

Estimate. Then find the quotient. Write the remainder, if any, as a fraction.

4. $32\overline{)1,504}$

5. $20\overline{)1,683}$

6. $35\overline{)955}$

7. $1,034 \div 22$

8. $14,124 \div 44$

9. $11,629 \div 29$

Find the least whole number that can replace ▉ **to make the statement true.**

10. ▉ $\div 7 > 800$

11. ▉ $\div 21 > 13$

12. $15 < $ ▉ $\div 400$

Problem Solving REAL WORLD

13. A plane flew a total of 2,220 miles. Its average speed was 555 miles per hour. How many hours did the plane fly?

14. A van is carrying 486 pounds. There are 27 boxes in the van. What is the average weight of each box in the van?

Lesson Check (CC.6.NS.2)

1. When 1,187 is divided by 74, what is the remainder?

   (A) 0

   (B) 1

   (C) 2

   (D) 3

2. Marco must pay a total of $1,596 for some home repairs. If he divides the cost into 28 equal payments, what will each payment be?

   (A) $56

   (B) $57

   (C) $58

   (D) $59

Spiral Review (CC.5.NBT.2, CC.5.NBT.3b, CC.5.NBT.7)

3. Layla used 0.482 gram of salt in her experiment. Maurice used 0.51 gram of salt in his experiment. Which of the following amounts is greater than Layla's but less than Maurice's? (Previous course)

   (A) 0.48 gram

   (B) 0.6 gram

   (C) 0.505 gram

   (D) 0.12 gram

4. Gavin bought 4 packages of cheese. Each package weighed 1.08 kilograms. How many kilograms of cheese did Gavin buy? (Previous course)

   (A) 4.302 kilograms

   (B) 4.32 kilograms

   (C) 43.2 kilograms

   (D) 432 kilograms

5. Hank bought 2.4 pounds of apples. Each pound cost $1.89. How much did Hank spend on the apples? (Previous course)

   (A) $0.45

   (B) $4.54

   (C) $4.56

   (D) $45.36

6. Mr. Thompson received a water bill for $85.98. The bill covered three months of service. How much does Mr. Thompson pay for water each month? (Previous course)

   (A) $28.66

   (B) $28.67

   (C) $28.76

   (D) $28.77

Prime Factorization

COMMON CORE STANDARD CC.6.NS.4
Compute fluently with multi-digit numbers and find common factors and multiples.

Find the prime factorization.

1. 44

$$2 \times 2 \times 11$$

2. 90

_____

3. 48

_____

4. 204

_____

5. 400

_____

6. 112

_____

Write the number whose prime factorization is given.

7. $3 \times 3 \times 11$

8. $2 \times 2 \times 7 \times 13$

9. $2 \times 3 \times 3 \times 3$

Problem Solving REAL WORLD

10. A computer code is based on the prime factorization of 160. Find the prime factorization of 160.

11. The combination for a lock is a 3-digit number. The digits are the prime factors of 42 listed from least to greatest. What is the combination for the lock?

_____

_____

Lesson Check (CC.6.NS.4)

1. The prime factorization of 60 is the same as the prime factorization of 30 except that the prime factorization of 60 has one more factor. What is that factor?

Ⓐ 2

Ⓑ 3

Ⓒ 5

Ⓓ 6

2. Millicent's password for a website is a 5-digit number. The digits are the prime factors of 2,205 listed from least to greatest. What is Millicent's password?

Ⓐ 33357

Ⓑ 33557

Ⓒ 33577

Ⓓ 35577

Spiral Review (CC.5.OA.2, CC.5.NBT.1, CC.5.NBT.6)

3. Piano lessons cost $15 each. Which expression could be used to find the cost in dollars of 5 lessons? **(Previous course)**

Ⓐ 15 + 5

Ⓑ 15 − 5

Ⓒ 15 × 5

Ⓓ 15 ÷ 5

4. A museum has 13,486 butterflies, 1,856 ants, and 13,859 beetles. Which list shows the insects in order from least number to greatest number? **(Previous course)**

Ⓐ butterflies, beetles, ants

Ⓑ butterflies, ants, beetles

Ⓒ ants, beetles, butterflies

Ⓓ ants, butterflies, beetles

5. A jet airplane costs an airline $69,500,000. What is the place value of the digit 5 in this number? **(Previous course)**

Ⓐ hundred thousands

Ⓑ millions

Ⓒ hundred millions

Ⓓ billions

6. Juan is reading a 312-page book for school. He reads 12 pages each day. How long will it take him to finish the book? **(Previous course)**

Ⓐ 21 days

Ⓑ 26 days

Ⓒ 31 days

Ⓓ 35 days

Least Common Multiple

COMMON CORE STANDARD CC.6.NS.4
Compute fluently with multi-digit numbers and find common factors and multiples.

Find the LCM.

1. 2, 7

Multiples of 2: 2, 4, 6, 8, 10, 12, 14
Multiples of 7: 7, 14

LCM: __**14**__

2. 4, 12

LCM: _____

3. 10, 4

LCM: _____

4. 6, 9

LCM: _____

5. 5, 4

LCM: _____

6. 8, 10

LCM: _____

7. 8, 20

LCM: _____

8. 5, 8, 4

LCM: _____

9. 12, 8, 24

LCM: _____

Write the unknown number for the ■.

10. 3, ■   LCM: 21

11. ■, 7   LCM: 63

12. 10, 5   LCM: ■

■ = _____

■ = _____

■ = _____

Problem Solving REAL WORLD

13. Juanita is making necklaces to give as presents. She plans to put 15 beads on each necklace. Beads are sold in packages of 20. What is the least number of packages she can buy to make necklaces and have no beads left over?

_____

14. Pencils are sold in packages of 10, and erasers are sold in packages of 6. What is the least number of pencils and erasers you can buy so that there is one pencil for each eraser with none left over?

_____

Lesson Check (CC.6.NS.4)

1. Alejandro is making hamburgers in batches of 6. Hamburger buns are sold in packs of 8. What is the least number of hamburgers on a bun he can make with no leftovers?

   (A) 24

   (B) 32

   (C) 40

   (D) 48

2. Which is the LCM of 5 and 15?

   (A) 3

   (B) 15

   (C) 30

   (D) 75

Spiral Review (CC.5.NBT.2, CC.5.NBT.6, CC.5.NF.1)

3. Which of the following can be used to find $76 \div 4$? (Previous course)

   (A) $(2 \times 38) + (2 \times 2)$

   (B) $(4 \times 19) + (4 \times 4)$

   (C) $(4 \times 7) + (4 \times 6)$

   (D) $(4 \times 10) + (4 \times 9)$

4. John has 2,456 pennies in his coin collection. He has them in 3 boxes. Which is the best estimate of how many coins are in each box? (Previous course)

   (A) 8,000

   (B) 1,000

   (C) 800

   (D) 700

5. Which of the following is equal to 10?
   (Previous course)

   (A) 10^0

   (B) 10^1

   (C) 10^2

   (D) 10^{10}

6. What is the distance around a triangle that has sides measuring $2\frac{1}{8}$ feet, $3\frac{1}{2}$ feet, and $2\frac{1}{2}$ feet? (Previous course)

   (A) $7\frac{1}{8}$ feet

   (B) $7\frac{9}{24}$ feet

   (C) 8 feet

   (D) $8\frac{1}{8}$ feet

Greatest Common Factor

COMMON CORE STANDARD CC.6.NS.4
Compute fluently with multi-digit numbers and find common factors and multiples.

List the common factors. Circle the greatest common factor.

1. 25 and 10

$1, \text{⑤}$
_____

2. 36 and 90

_____

3. 45 and 60

_____

Find the GCF.

4. 2, 8

_____

5. 6, 15

_____

6. 14, 18

_____

7. 6, 48

_____

8. 20, 50

_____

9. 16, 100

_____

Use the GCF and the Distributive Property to express the sum as a product.

10. 20 + 35

_____

11. 18 + 27

_____

12. 64 + 40

_____

Problem Solving REAL WORLD

13. Jerome is making prizes for a game at the school fair. He has two bags of different candies, one with 15 pieces of candy and one with 20 pieces. Every prize will have one kind of candy, the same number of pieces, and the greatest number of pieces possible. How many candies should be in each prize?

14. There are 24 sixth graders and 40 seventh graders. Mr. Chan wants to divide both grades into groups of equal size, with the greatest possible number of students in each group. How many students should be in each group?

_____

_____

Lesson Check (CC.6.NS.4)

1. What is the greatest common factor of 128 and 96?

- (A) 12
- (B) 16
- (C) 32
- (D) 48

2. Which of the following expresses the sum of $36 + 63$ as a product?

- (A) $6 \times (36 + 63)$
- (B) $9 \times (36 + 63)$
- (C) $6 \times (4 + 7)$
- (D) $9 \times (4 + 7)$

Spiral Review (CC.5.NBT.5, CC.5.NBT.6, CC.5.NF.7c, CC.6.NS.2)

3. Which number is greater than 8,046,890?
(Previous course)

- (A) 9,012,020
- (B) 8,000,000
- (C) 7,999,789
- (D) 7,147,328

4. There are 147 people attending a dinner party. If each table can seat 7 people, how many tables are needed for the dinner party?
(Previous course)

- (A) 22
- (B) 21
- (C) 20
- (D) 12

5. Sammy has 3 pancakes. He cuts each one in half. How many pancake halves are there?
(Previous course)

- (A) 1
- (B) 3
- (C) 6
- (D) 8

6. When a number is divided by 15, the remainder is 3. Which of the following could be the number? **(Lesson 1.1)**

- (A) 105
- (B) 106
- (C) 107
- (D) 108

Name _____

Problem Solving • Apply the Greatest Common Factor

COMMON CORE STANDARD CC.6.NS.4
Compute fluently with multi-digit numbers and find common factors and multiples.

Read the problem and solve.

1. Ashley is bagging 32 pumpkin muffins and 28 banana muffins for some friends. Each bag will hold only one type of muffin. Each bag will hold the same number of muffins. What is the greatest number of muffins she can put in each bag? How many bags of each type of muffin will there be?

GCF: 4

$32 = 4 \times 8$

$28 = 4 \times 7$

$32 + 28 = 4 \times (8 + 7)$

So, there will be __8__ bags of pumpkin muffins and __7__ bags of banana muffins, with __4__ muffins in each bag.

2. Patricia is separating 16 soccer cards and 22 baseball cards into groups. Each group will have the same number of cards, and each group will have only one kind of sports card. What is the greatest number of cards she can put in each group? How many groups of each type will there be?

_____

3. Bryan is setting chairs in rows for a graduation ceremony. He has 50 black chairs and 60 white chairs. Each row will have the same number of chairs, and each row will have the same color chair. What is the greatest number of chairs that he can fit in each row? How many rows of each color chair will there be?

_____

4. A store clerk is bagging spices. He has 18 teaspoons of cinnamon and 30 teaspoons of nutmeg. Each bag needs to contain the same number of teaspoons, and each bag can contain only one spice. How many teaspoons of spice should the clerk put in each bag? How many bags of each spice will there be?

_____

5. A teacher is placing counters in bags for students. There are 24 blue counters and 56 yellow counters. Each bag needs to have the same number of counters, and each bag can only contain one color. How many counters should the teacher place in each bag, and how many bags of each color will there be?

_____

Lesson Check (CC.6.NS.4)

1. Sue is placing cookies in bags. She has 10 peanut butter cookies and 16 oatmeal cookies. She will place the same number of cookies in each bag, and there will be only one type of cookie in each bag. How many bags will she need?

Ⓐ 8

Ⓑ 10

Ⓒ 13

Ⓓ 16

2. Joseph needs to place chairs in equal rows. There are 22 brown chairs and 33 gray chairs. Each row should contain chairs of the same color. How many chairs should he place in each row?

Ⓐ 2

Ⓑ 3

Ⓒ 11

Ⓓ 44

Spiral Review (CC.5.NF.1, CC.5.NF.2, CC.6.NS.4)

3. A rectangle is $6\frac{2}{3}$ feet long and $3\frac{1}{5}$ feet wide. About how many feet is the distance around the rectangle? **(Previous course)**

Ⓐ 9 feet

Ⓑ 10 feet

Ⓒ 18 feet

Ⓓ 20 feet

4. Lowell bought $4\frac{1}{4}$ pounds of apples and $3\frac{3}{5}$ pounds of oranges. How many pounds of fruit did Lowell buy? **(Previous course)**

Ⓐ $\frac{4}{9}$ pound

Ⓑ $\frac{17}{20}$ pound

Ⓒ $7\frac{4}{9}$ pounds

Ⓓ $7\frac{17}{20}$ pounds

5. How much heavier is a $9\frac{1}{8}$-pound box than a $2\frac{5}{6}$-pound box? **(Previous course)**

Ⓐ $6\frac{1}{4}$ pounds

Ⓑ $6\frac{7}{24}$ pounds

Ⓒ $7\frac{1}{2}$ pounds

Ⓓ $7\frac{17}{24}$ pounds

6. What is the prime factorization of 200? **(Lesson 1.2)**

Ⓐ 10×20

Ⓑ $2 \times 0 \times 0$

Ⓒ $2 \times 2 \times 2 \times 5 \times 5$

Ⓓ $2 \times 2 \times 2 \times 2 \times 5 \times 5$

Name _____

Add and Subtract Decimals

COMMON CORE STANDARD CC.6.NS.3
Compute fluently with multi-digit numbers and find common factors and multiples.

Estimate. Then find the sum or difference.

1. $43.53 + 27.67$

$$40 + 30 = 70$$

$$\begin{array}{r} 43.53 \\ + 27.67 \\ \hline 71.20 \end{array}$$

2. $17 + 3.6 + 4.049$

3. $3.49 - 2.75$

4. $5.07 - 2.148$

5. $3.92 + 16 + 0.085$

6. $41.98 + 13.5 + 27.338$

Evaluate using the order of operations.

7. $8.4 + (13.1 - 0.6)$

8. $34.7 - (12.07 + 4.9)$

9. $(24.3 - 1.12) + 5.18$

10. $(32.45 - 4.8) - 2.06$

Problem Solving  REAL WORLD

11. The average annual rainfall in Clearview is 38 inches. This year, 29.777 inches fell. How much less rain fell this year than falls in an average year?

12. At the theater, the Worth family spent $18.00 on adult tickets, $16.50 on children's tickets, and $11.75 on refreshments. How much did they spend in all?

_____

Lesson Check (CC.6.NS.3)

1. Laura gave the clerk $20 for purchases of a $4.25 notebook and a $3.59 set of markers. How much change did she receive?

   (A) $12.16

   (B) $12.26

   (C) $13.16

   (D) $13.26

2. The perimeter of a rectangle is the sum of all four side lengths. What is the perimeter of a rectangle with length of 5.61 centimeters and width of 4.8 centimeters?

   (A) 9.41 centimeters

   (B) 10.41 centimeters

   (C) 18.42 centimeters

   (D) 20.82 centimeters

Spiral Review (CC.5.NBT.5, CC.5.NBT.6, CC.6.NS.4)

3. A 6-car monorail train can carry 78 people. If one train makes 99 trips during the day, what is the greatest number of people the train can carry in one day? (Previous course)

   (A) 177

   (B) 7,524

   (C) 7,623

   (D) 7,722

4. An airport parking lot has 2,800 spaces. If each row has 25 spaces, how many rows are there? (Previous course)

   (A) 100

   (B) 112

   (C) 116

   (D) 70,000

5. Evan bought 6 batteries at $10 apiece and 6 batteries at $4 apiece. The total cost was the same as he would have spent buying 6 batteries at $14 apiece. So, $(6 \times 10) + (6 \times 4) = 6 \times 14$. Which property does the equation illustrate? (Previous course)

   (A) Commutative Property of Multiplication

   (B) Commutative Property of Addition

   (C) Distributive Property

   (D) Associative Property of Multiplication

6. Cups come in packages of 12, and lids come in packages of 15. What is the least number of cups and lids that Corrine can buy if she wants to have the same number of cups and lids? (Lesson 1.3)

   (A) 3

   (B) 5

   (C) 60

   (D) 180

Name _____

Multiply Decimals

COMMON CORE STANDARD CC.6.NS.3
Compute fluently with multi-digit numbers and find common factors and multiples.

Estimate. Then find the product.

1. 5.69×7.8

$$6 \times 8 = 48$$
$$5.69$$
$$\times\ 7.8$$
$$\overline{4552}$$
$$\underline{39830}$$
$$44.382$$

2. 4.8×1.7

3. 3.92×0.051

4. 2.365×12.4

5. 305.08×1.5

6. 61.8×1.7

7. 35.80×5.6

8. 1.9×8.43

Evaluate the expression using the order of operations.

9. $(13.1 \times 3) + 5.21$

10. $4 \times (15 - 4.55)$

11. $20.5 - (2 \times 8.1)$

Problem Solving REAL WORLD

12. Blaine exchanges $100 for yen before going to Japan. If each U.S. dollar is worth 88.353 yen, how many yen should Blaine receive?

13. A camera costs 115 Canadian dollars. If each Canadian dollar is worth 0.952 U.S. dollars, how much will the camera cost in U.S. dollars?

★ TEST PREP

Lesson Check (CC.6.NS.3)

1. Grace bought 4.5 pounds of fish that cost $4.98 per pound. How much did she pay for the fish?

    (A) $21.41

    (B) $22.41

    (C) $24.41

    (D) $25.51

2. Mike's car can go 22.5 miles on 1 gallon of gas. How many miles can the car go on 13.2 gallons of gas?

    (A) 295 miles

    (B) 296 miles

    (C) 297 miles

    (D) 298 miles

Spiral Review (CC.5.NBT.6, CC.5.OA.1, CC.6.NS.4)

3. Last week, a store sold laptops worth a total of $10,885. Each laptop cost $1,555. How many laptops did the store sell last week? **(Previous course)**

    (A) 4

    (B) 5

    (C) 6

    (D) 7

4. Kyle drives his truck 429 miles on 33 gallons of gas. How many miles can Kyle drive on 1 gallon of gas? **(Previous course)**

    (A)   10 miles

    (B)   13 miles

    (C)   429 miles

    (D) 14,157 miles

5. Seven busloads each carrying 35 students arrived at the game, joining the 23 students who were already there. Evaluate the expression $23 + 7 \times 35$ to find the total number of students at the game. **(Previous course)**

    (A)   268

    (B)   406

    (C)   812

    (D) 1,050

6. The GCF of which two numbers is 8? **(Lesson 1.4)**

    (A) 2 and 4

    (B) 8 and 1

    (C) 50 and 64

    (D) 32 and 56

Name _____

Divide Decimals by Whole Numbers

COMMON CORE STANDARD CC.6.NS.3
Compute fluently with multi-digit numbers and find common factors and multiples.

Estimate. Then find the quotient.

1. $1.284 \div 12$

$$1.2 \div 12 = 0.1$$

$$\begin{array}{r} 0.107 \\ 12\overline{)1.284} \\ -12 \\ \hline 8 \\ -\ 0 \\ \hline 84 \\ -84 \\ \hline 0 \end{array}$$

2. $24.012 \div 6$

3. $9\overline{)2.43}$

4. $4\overline{)1.52}$

5. $6.51 \div 3$

6. $25.65 \div 15$

7. $12\overline{)2.436}$

8. $11\overline{)46.2}$

Evaluate using the order of operations.

9. $(8 - 2.96) \div 3$

10. $(7.772 - 2.38) \div 8$

11. $(53.2 + 35.7) \div 7$

Problem Solving REAL WORLD

12. Jake earned $10.44 interest on his savings account for an 18-month period. What was the average amount of interest Jake earned on his savings account per month?

13. Gloria worked for 6 hours a day for 2 days at the bank and earned $114.24. How much did she earn per hour?

_____   _____

Lesson Check (CC.6.NS.3)

1. The weight of Lyle's dog increased from 29.7 pounds to 48.9 pounds in an 8-month period. What was the dog's average weight increase per month?

- (A) 2.4 pounds
- (B) 2.5 pounds
- (C) 24 pounds
- (D) 25 pounds

2. The cost of one pizza rose from $8.95 to $9.70 over a 5-week period. What was the average increase in the price of pizza per week?

- (A) $0.015
- (B) $0.15
- (C) $1.05
- (D) $1.50

Spiral Review (CC.5.NBT.1, CC.5.NBT.6, CC.6.NS.2, CC.6.NS.4)

3. Which is the correct value of the underlined digit in 9<u>6</u>8,743,220? **(Previous course)**

- (A) six hundred million
- (B) sixty thousand
- (C) sixty-eight million
- (D) sixty million

4. The Tama, Japan, monorail carries 92,700 riders each day. If the monorail usually carries 5,150 riders per hour, how many hours does the monorail run each day? **(Previous course)**

- (A) 1.8
- (B) 18
- (C) 108
- (D) 180

5. Ray paid $812 to rent music equipment that costs $28 per hour. How many hours did he have the equipment? **(Lesson 1.1)**

- (A) 28 hours
- (B) 29 hours
- (C) 280 hours
- (D) 290 hours

6. Jan has 35 teaspoons of chocolate cocoa mix and 45 teaspoons of french vanilla cocoa mix. She wants to put the same amount of mix into each jar, and she only wants one flavor of mix in each jar. How many jars of french vanilla cocoa mix will Jan fill? **(Lesson 1.5)**

- (A) 5
- (B) 7
- (C) 8
- (D) 9

Divide with Decimals

COMMON CORE STANDARD CC.6.NS.3
Compute fluently with multi-digit numbers and find common factors and multiples.

Estimate. Then find the quotient.

1. $43.18 \div 3.4$ **2.** $4.185 \div 0.93$ **3.** $6.3\overline{)25.83}$ **4.** $0.8\overline{)1.008}$

$$\underline{44 \div 4 = 11}$$

$$
\begin{array}{r}
12.7 \\
34\overline{)431.8} \\
-34 \\
\hline
91 \\
-68 \\
\hline
238 \\
-238 \\
\hline
0
\end{array}
$$

_____   _____   _____

Find the quotient.

5. $9.12 \div 0.4$ **6.** $0.143 \div 0.55$ **7.** $0.6\overline{)3.558}$ **8.** $0.24\overline{)1.8}$

_____   _____   _____   _____

Evaluate using the order of operations.

9. $4.92 \div (0.8 - 0.12 \div 0.3)$ **10.** $0.86 \div 5 - 0.3 \times 0.5$ **11.** $17.28 \div (1.32 - 0.24) \times 0.6$

_____   _____   _____

Problem Solving REAL WORLD

12. If Amanda walks at an average speed of 2.72 miles per hour, how long will it take her to walk 6.8 miles?

13. Chad cycled 62.3 miles in 3.5 hours. If he cycled at a constant speed, how far did he cycle in 1 hour?

_____   _____

Lesson Check (CC.6.NS.3)

1. Greg earned $45.76 in 6.4 hours. How much did he earn per hour?

   (A) $7.15
   (B) $7.25
   (C) $7.45
   (D) $8.40

2. Alison wants to buy a mountain bike for $339.12. If she saves $28.26 each month, in how many months will she be able to buy the bike?

   (A) 9
   (B) 10
   (C) 11
   (D) 12

Spiral Review (CC.5.NBT.5, CC.5.NF.3, CC.6.NS.3, CC.6.NS.4)

3. Four bags of pretzels were divided equally among 5 people. How much of a bag did each person get? (Previous course)

   (A) $\frac{5}{4}$
   (B) $\frac{4}{5}$
   (C) $\frac{4}{20}$
   (D) 20

4. A zebra ran at a speed of 20 feet per second. Which operation should you use to find the distance the zebra ran in 10 seconds? (Previous course)

   (A) addition
   (B) multiplication
   (C) subtraction
   (D) division

5. Which of the following has a prime factorization of $2 \times 2 \times 3 \times 5$? (Lesson 1.2)

   (A) 4
   (B) 12
   (C) 60
   (D) 235

6. Nira has $13.50. She receives a paycheck for $55. She spends $29.40. How much money does she have now? (Lesson 1.6)

   (A) $31.04
   (B) $31.40
   (C) $39.01
   (D) $39.10

Chapter 1 Extra Practice

Lesson 1.1

Estimate. Then find the quotient. Write the remainder, if any, as a fraction.

1. $27\overline{)89,420}$

2. $452\overline{)17,628}$

3. $19\overline{)1,353}$

Lessons 1.2

Find the prime factorization.

4. 250

5. 420

6. 360

Lesson 1.3

Find the LCM.

7. 12, 18

8. 20, 15

9. 8, 3

Lessons 1.4 and 1.5

Find the GCF.

10. 26 and 36

11. 40 and 32

12. 21 and 35

Solve.

13. Mr. Ramirez teaches dance. He has 18 sixth-grade students and 24 seventh-grade students. He wants to put the students in equal groups. Each group will have students of only one grade level. How many students should be in each group? How many of each group will there be?

_____

_____

Lesson 1.6

Estimate. Then find the sum or difference.

14. $6.48 - 3.29$	15. $59.58 + 39.6$	16. $21 - 8.42$	17. $0.95 + 3.409 + 16.7$
_____	_____	_____	_____

Lesson 1.7

Estimate. Then find the product.

18. 3.77×7.19	19. 0.71×12.6	20. 9.2×106.45	21. 1.08×0.8
_____	_____	_____	_____

Lessons 1.8 and 1.9

22. Desean spent $80.85 on 3 video games. If each game was the same price, how much did Desean pay for each?

23. Ted earned $147.20 working for $9.20 per hour. How many hours did he work?

School-Home Letter

© Houghton Mifflin Harcourt Publishing Company

Vocabulary

reciprocal One of two numbers whose product is 1. For example, $\frac{3}{5}$ and $\frac{5}{3}$ are reciprocals.

repeating decimal A decimal representation of a number that has a repeating pattern that continues endlessly.

terminating decimal A decimal representation of a number that eventually ends.

Dear Family,

Throughout the next few weeks, our math class will be learning about multiplying and dividing fractions. We will also be learning how to estimate products and quotients of fractions.

You can expect to see homework with real-world problems that involve these operations.

Here is a sample of how your child was taught to divide two mixed numbers.

🔑 MODEL Divide mixed numbers.

Divide. $2\frac{2}{7} \div 2\frac{2}{3}$

STEP 1

Write the mixed numbers as fractions.

$$2\frac{2}{7} \div 2\frac{2}{3} = \frac{16}{7} \div \frac{8}{3}$$

STEP 2

Use the reciprocal of the divisor to write a multiplication problem.

$$= \frac{16}{7} \times \frac{3}{8}$$

STEP 3

Simplify.

$$= \frac{\overset{2}{\cancel{16}}}{7} \times \frac{3}{\underset{1}{\cancel{8}}}$$

STEP 4

Multiply.

$$= \frac{6}{7}$$

Tips

Checking for Reasonable Answers

When the divisor is less than 1, the quotient is greater than the dividend. When the divisor is greater than 1, the quotient is less than the dividend.

Activity

Find an object in your home, such as a ribbon, that can easily be cut into four equal pieces by folding it upon itself. Measure the object to the nearest eighth of an inch. Work together to predict the length of each of the four pieces after the object is cut. Check your prediction by measuring the length of one of the four equal pieces.

Carta para la casa

Vocabulario

recíproco Uno o dos números cuyos productos dan como resultado 1. Por ejemplo $\frac{3}{5}$ y $\frac{5}{3}$ son recíprocos.

decimal periódico Una representación decimal de un número que tiene un patrón repetitivo que continúa interminablemente.

decimal finito Una representación decimal de un número que con el tiempo llega a su fin.

Querida familia,

Durante las próximas semanas, en la clase de matemáticas aprenderemos a multiplicar y dividir fracciones. También aprenderemos a estimar productos y cocientes de fracciones.

Llevaré a la casa tareas con problemas del mundo real que involucren estas operaciones.

Este es un ejemplo de la manera como aprenderemos a dividir dos números mixtos.

🔒 MODELO   Dividir números mixtos.

Divide. $2\frac{2}{7} \div 2\frac{2}{3}$

PASO 1

Escribe los números mixtos como fracciones.

$$2\frac{2}{7} \div 2\frac{2}{3} = \frac{16}{7} \div \frac{8}{3}$$

PASO 2

Usa los recíprocos del divisor para escribir un problema de multiplicación.

$$= \frac{16}{7} \times \frac{3}{8}$$

PASO 3

Simplifica.

$$= \frac{\overset{2}{\cancel{16}}}{7} \times \frac{3}{\underset{1}{\cancel{8}}}$$

PASO 4

Multiplica.

$$= \frac{6}{7}$$

Pistas

Comprobar la respuestas sea razonable

Cuando el divisor es menor que 1, el cociente es mayor que el dividendo. Cuando el divisor es mayor que 1, el cociente es menor que el dividendo.

Actividad

Encuentre un objeto en su hogar, como un listón, que pueda ser fácilmente cortado en pedazos al doblarlo. Mida el objeto al octavo de pulgada más cercano. Trabajen juntos para predecir la longitud de cada una de los cuatro pedazos después de que el objeto haya sido cortado. Comprueben su predicción al medir la longitud de uno de los cuatro pedazos iguales.

Name _____

Fractions and Decimals

COMMON CORE STANDARD CC.6.NS.6c
Apply and extend previous understandings of
numbers to the system of rational numbers.

Write as a fraction or as a mixed number in simplest form.

1. 0.52

$$0.52 = \frac{52}{100}$$
$$= \frac{52 \div 4}{100 \div 4} = \frac{13}{25}$$

_____

2. 0.02

_____

3. 4.8

_____

4. 6.025

_____

Write as a decimal. Tell whether the decimal terminates or repeats.

5. $\frac{17}{25}$

6. $\frac{7}{9}$

7. $4\frac{13}{20}$

8. $7\frac{8}{11}$

_____   _____   _____   _____

**Identify a decimal and a fraction or mixed number in simplest form
for each point.**

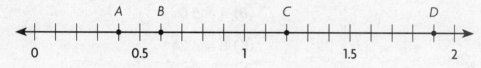

9. Point *A*

10. Point *D*

11. Point *C*

12. Point *B*

_____   _____   _____   _____

Problem Solving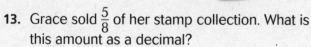

13. Grace sold $\frac{5}{8}$ of her stamp collection. What is
this amount as a decimal?

14. What if you scored a 0.80 on a test? What
fraction of the test, in simplest form, did you
answer correctly?

_____   _____

Lesson Check (CC.6.NS.6c)

1. Devon drank $\frac{5}{6}$ of her juice. What is this amount as a decimal?

Ⓐ $0.\overline{83}$

Ⓑ 1.2

Ⓒ $0.8\overline{3}$

Ⓓ 0.56

2. Jerome lives 4.32 miles from school. What is this distance as a mixed number in simplest form?

Ⓐ $4\frac{8}{25}$

Ⓑ $4\frac{32}{100}$

Ⓒ $4\frac{4}{125}$

Ⓓ $4\frac{4}{25}$

Spiral Review (CC.6.NS.2, CC.6.NS.3, CC.6.NS.4)

3. Mia needs to separate 450 pens into 18 packs. How many pens should she put in each pack? **(Lesson 1.1)**

Ⓐ 24

Ⓑ 25

Ⓒ 26

Ⓓ 27

4. Which pair of numbers has a least common multiple of 12? **(Lesson 1.3)**

Ⓐ 1 and 3

Ⓑ 4 and 6

Ⓒ 8 and 24

Ⓓ 24 and 36

5. Which of the following expressions is equivalent to $42 + 6$? **(Lesson 1.5)**

Ⓐ $6 + 7$

Ⓑ 6×7

Ⓒ $6(7 + 0)$

Ⓓ $6(7 + 1)$

6. Which is the best estimate of the product 8.97×52.47? **(Lesson 1.7)**

Ⓐ 5

Ⓑ 50

Ⓒ 500

Ⓓ 5,000

Compare and Order Fractions and Decimals

COMMON CORE STANDARD CC.6.NS.6c
Apply and extend previous understandings of numbers to the system of rational numbers.

Write <, >, or =.

1. 0.64 ⊘ $\frac{7}{10}$ **2.** 0.48 ◯ $\frac{6}{15}$ **3.** 0.75 ◯ $\frac{7}{8}$ **4.** $7\frac{1}{8}$ ◯ 7.025

$0.64 < 0.7$

Order from least to greatest.

5. $\frac{7}{12}, 0.75, \frac{5}{6}$ **6.** $0.5, 0.41, \frac{3}{5}$ **7.** $3.25, 3\frac{2}{5}, 3\frac{3}{8}$ **8.** $0.9, \frac{8}{9}, 0.86$

_____   _____   _____   _____

Order from greatest to least.

9. $0.7, \frac{7}{9}, \frac{7}{8}$ **10.** $0.2, 0.19, \frac{3}{5}$ **11.** $6\frac{1}{20}, 6.1, 6.07$ **12.** $2\frac{1}{2}, 2.4, 2.35, 2\frac{1}{8}$

_____   _____   _____   _____

Problem Solving  REAL WORLD

13. One day it snowed $3\frac{3}{8}$ inches in Altoona and 3.45 inches in Bethlehem. Which city received less snow that day?

14. Malia and John each bought 2 pounds of sunflower seeds. Each ate some seeds. Malia has $1\frac{1}{3}$ pounds left, and John has $1\frac{2}{5}$ pounds left. Who ate more sunflower seeds?

_____   _____

Lesson Check (CC.6.NS.6c)

1. Samantha bought $\frac{4}{9}$ pound of sunflower seeds, Brittany bought 0.4 pound, and Tia bought $\frac{44}{100}$ pound. List the numbers in order from greatest to least.

Ⓐ $0.4, \frac{44}{100}, \frac{4}{9}$

Ⓑ $\frac{4}{9}, \frac{44}{100}, 0.4$

Ⓒ $\frac{44}{100}, 0.4, \frac{4}{9}$

Ⓓ $\frac{44}{100}, \frac{4}{9}, 0.4$

2. One week Altoona received $6\frac{5}{8}$ inches of snow, Bethlehem received 6.73 inches, and Reading received $5\frac{1}{3}$ inches. List the three cities in order of amount of snowfall received that week from least to greatest.

Ⓐ Bethlehem, Altoona, Reading

Ⓑ Reading, Bethlehem, Altoona

Ⓒ Altoona, Bethlehem, Reading

Ⓓ Reading, Altoona, Bethlehem

Spiral Review (CC.6.NS.3, CC.6.NS.4)

3. What is the prime factorization of 1,575?
(Lesson 1.2)

Ⓐ $3 \times 3 \times 5 \times 5 \times 7$

Ⓑ $3 \times 3 \times 5 \times 5 \times 11$

Ⓒ $3 \times 5 \times 5 \times 7 \times 7$

Ⓓ $5 \times 5 \times 7 \times 9$

4. What is the greatest common factor of 60 and 45? (Lesson 1.4)

Ⓐ 3

Ⓑ 9

Ⓒ 15

Ⓓ 30

5. Which is the best estimate of the sum $17.81 + 0.45 + 5.73$? (Lesson 1.6)

Ⓐ 21

Ⓑ 22

Ⓒ 23

Ⓓ 24

6. The cost of 9 tickets to a concert was $355.50. Which is the best estimate of the cost of 1 ticket? (Lesson 1.8)

Ⓐ $20

Ⓑ $30

Ⓒ $40

Ⓓ $50

Name _____

Multiply Fractions

COMMON CORE STANDARD CC.6.NS.4
Compute fluently with multi-digit numbers and find common factors and multiples.

Find the product. Write it in simplest form.

1. $\frac{4}{5} \times \frac{7}{8} = \frac{28}{40}$

$= \frac{7}{10}$

2. $3 \times \frac{1}{6}$

3. $\frac{5}{9} \times \frac{3}{4}$

4. $\frac{4}{7} \times \frac{1}{2}$

5. $\frac{1}{8} \times 20$

6. $\frac{4}{5} \times \frac{3}{8}$

7. $\frac{6}{7} \times \frac{7}{9}$

8. $1\frac{1}{8} \times \frac{1}{9}$

9. $\frac{1}{14} \times 28$

10. $\frac{3}{4} \times \frac{1}{3} \times \frac{2}{5}$

11. Karen raked $\frac{3}{5}$ of the yard. Minni raked $\frac{1}{3}$ of the amount Karen raked. How much of the yard did Minni rake?

12. $\frac{3}{8}$ of the pets in the pet show are dogs. $\frac{2}{3}$ of the dogs have long hair. What fraction of the pets are dogs with long hair?

Evaluate using the order of operations.

13. $\left(\frac{1}{2} + \frac{3}{8}\right) \times 8$

14. $\frac{3}{4} \times \left(1 - \frac{1}{9}\right)$

15. $4 \times \frac{1}{8} \times \frac{3}{10}$

16. $6 \times \left(\frac{4}{5} + \frac{2}{10}\right) \times \frac{2}{3}$

Problem Solving REAL WORLD

17. Jason ran $\frac{5}{7}$ of the distance around the school track. Sara ran $\frac{4}{5}$ of Jason's distance. What fraction of the total distance around the track did Sara run?

18. A group of students attend a math club. Half of the students are boys and $\frac{4}{9}$ of the boys have brown eyes. What fraction of the group are boys with brown eyes?

Lesson Check (CC.6.NS.4)

1. The length of a rectangle is $4\frac{1}{2}$ centimeters. The width of the rectangle is $2\frac{2}{5}$ centimeters. What is the area of the rectangle?

   (A) $13\frac{4}{5}$ square centimeters

   (B) $10\frac{4}{5}$ square centimeters

   (C) $8\frac{1}{5}$ square centimeters

   (D) $6\frac{9}{10}$ square centimeters

2. Darlene read $\frac{5}{8}$ of a 56-page book. How many pages did Darlene read?

   (A) 30

   (B) 35

   (C) 40

   (D) 45

Spiral Review (CC.6.NS.3, CC.6.NS.4)

3. What is the least common denominator of $\frac{5}{6}$ and $\frac{1}{5}$? (Lesson 1.3)

   (A) 25

   (B) 30

   (C) 45

   (D) 60

4. On an upcoming field trip, 60 sixth graders and 48 seventh graders will be traveling by vans to the museum. Each van will carry the same number of students and carry only sixth graders or only seventh graders. If vans are to carry the greatest possible number of students, how many vans will be needed? (Lesson 1.5)

   (A) 4   (C) 9

   (B) 5   (D) 12

5. Eve has 24 stamps each valued at $24.75. What is the total value of her stamps? (Lesson 1.7)

   (A) $48.75

   (B) $59.40

   (C) $594.00

   (D) $5,940.00

6. Black ink cartridges cost $28.95 each. Which is the best estimate of the number of cartridges you can buy for $600? (Lesson 1.9)

   (A) 2

   (B) 3

   (C) 20

   (D) 30

Simplify Factors

COMMON CORE STANDARD CC.6.NS.4
Compute fluently with multi-digit numbers and find common factors and multiples.

Find the product. Simplify before multiplying.

1. $\dfrac{8}{9} \times \dfrac{5}{12} = \dfrac{^2 8 \times 5}{9 \times 12_3}$

$= \dfrac{10}{27}$

2. $\dfrac{3}{4} \times \dfrac{16}{21}$

_____

3. $\dfrac{15}{20} \times \dfrac{2}{5}$

_____

4. $\dfrac{9}{18} \times \dfrac{2}{3}$

_____

5. $\dfrac{9}{10} \times \dfrac{5}{27}$

_____

6. $\dfrac{3}{4} \times \dfrac{7}{30}$

_____

7. $\dfrac{25}{26} \times \dfrac{1}{5}$

_____

8. $\dfrac{8}{15} \times \dfrac{15}{32}$

_____

9. $\dfrac{12}{21} \times \dfrac{7}{9}$

_____

10. $\dfrac{1}{15} \times \dfrac{5}{8}$

_____

11. $\dfrac{18}{22} \times \dfrac{8}{9}$

_____

12. $\dfrac{2}{7} \times \dfrac{21}{32}$

_____

Problem Solving REAL WORLD

13. Amber has a $\frac{4}{5}$-pound bag of colored sand. She uses $\frac{1}{2}$ of the bag for an art project. How much sand does she use for the project?

_____

14. Tyler has $\frac{3}{4}$ month to write a book report. He finished the report in $\frac{2}{3}$ that time. How much time did it take Tyler to write the report?

_____

Lesson Check (CC.6.NS.4)

1. At a meeting, $\frac{7}{10}$ of the attendees were female. Of the females, $\frac{4}{5}$ wore jeans. What fraction of the attendees were females wearing jeans?

   (A) $\frac{1}{2}$

   (B) $\frac{4}{5}$

   (C) $\frac{7}{10}$

   (D) $\frac{14}{25}$

2. The length of a square is $\frac{5}{6}$ foot. What is the area of the square?

   (A) $1\frac{2}{3}$ square feet

   (B) $3\frac{1}{3}$ square feet

   (C) $\frac{25}{36}$ square feet

   (D) $\frac{5}{6}$ square feet

Spiral Review (CC.6.NS.2, CC.6.NS.3, CC.6.NS.6c)

3. Martin ordered 11 DVDs and paid $154. How much did Martin spend on each DVD? (Lesson 1.1)

   (A) $12

   (B) $13

   (C) $14

   (D) $15

4. Which is the best estimate of the difference $29.702 - 6.89$? (Lesson 1.6)

   (A) 22

   (B) 23

   (C) 24

   (D) 25

5. Gail earned $41.40 interest on her savings account for a 12-month period. What was the average amount of interest she earned per month? (Lesson 1.8)

   (A) $3.40

   (B) $3.45

   (C) $4.40

   (D) $4.45

6. Clara bought 0.8 pound of peaches. How can you write 0.8 as a fraction in simplest form? (Lesson 2.1)

   (A) $\frac{4}{10}$

   (B) $\frac{3}{4}$

   (C) $\frac{4}{5}$

   (D) $\frac{8}{9}$

Name _____

Model Fraction Division

COMMON CORE STANDARD CC.6.NS.1

Apply and extend previous understandings of multiplication and division to divide fractions by fractions.

Use the model to find the quotient.

1. $\frac{1}{4} \div 3 = \frac{1}{12}$

2. $\frac{1}{2} \div \frac{2}{12} = $ _____

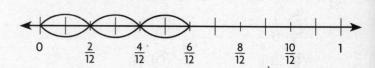

Use fraction strips to find the quotient.

3. $\frac{5}{6} \div \frac{1}{2}$

4. $\frac{2}{3} \div 4$

5. $\frac{1}{2} \div 6$

6. $\frac{1}{3} \div \frac{1}{12}$

_____   _____   _____   _____

Use a number line to find the quotient.

7. How many $\frac{1}{12}$-pint servings of pecans are in $\frac{5}{6}$ pint of pecans?

8. If Jerry runs $\frac{1}{10}$ mile each day, how many days will it take for him to run $\frac{4}{5}$ mile?

_____   _____

Problem Solving REAL WORLD

9. Mrs. Jennings has $\frac{3}{4}$ gallon of paint for an art project. She plans to divide the paint equally into jars. If she puts $\frac{1}{8}$ gallon of paint into each jar, how many jars will she use?

10. If one jar of glue weighs $\frac{1}{12}$ pound, how many jars can Rickie get from $\frac{2}{3}$ pound of glue?

_____   _____

Lesson Check (CC.6.NS.1)

1. There are 2 pounds of clay in the art supplies. If Mrs. Jennings divides the clay evenly into bags and places $\frac{1}{8}$ pound into each bag, how many bags will she use?

   (A) $\frac{1}{8}$ (C) 8

   (B) $\frac{1}{4}$ (D) 16

2. Frank is using butcher paper to make signs advertising the class art show. If he uses $\frac{5}{6}$ yard of butcher paper to make 2 signs, how much paper does he use for each sign?

   (A) $\frac{5}{12}$ yard   (C) 1 yard

   (B) $\frac{1}{2}$ yard   (D) $1\frac{2}{3}$ yards

Spiral Review (CC.6.NS.1, CC.6.NS.3, CC.6.NS.4, CC.6.NS.6c)

3. What is the prime factorization of the number that is equivalent to $3 \times 21 \times 25$?
   (Lesson 1.2)

   (A) $3 \times 5 \times 5 \times 7$

   (B) $2 \times 3 \times 5 \times 7$

   (C) $3 \times 3 \times 3 \times 5 \times 7$

   (D) $3 \times 3 \times 5 \times 5 \times 7$

4. What is the total cost of 0.5 pound of peaches selling for $0.80 per pound and 0.7 pound of oranges selling for $0.90 per pound? (Lesson 1.7)

   (A) $0.51

   (B) $1.02

   (C) $1.03

   (D) $10.30

5. The heights of 4 students are given. Who is tallest? (Lesson 2.2)

   (A) Eduardo, 5.46 feet

   (B) Anton, $5\frac{2}{5}$ feet

   (C) Juan, $5\frac{1}{4}$ feet

   (D) Jesse, $5\frac{9}{20}$ feet

6. Half of a pizza was divided equally among 6 people. What fraction of the whole pizza did each person receive? (Lesson 2.5)

   (A) $\frac{1}{12}$

   (B) $\frac{1}{8}$

   (C) $\frac{1}{6}$

   (D) $\frac{1}{4}$

Estimate Quotients

COMMON CORE STANDARD CC.6.NS.1
Apply and extend previous understandings of
multiplication and division to divide fractions by fractions.

Estimate using compatible numbers.

1. $12\frac{3}{16} \div 3\frac{9}{10}$

  $\downarrow$　　$\downarrow$

  $12 \div 4 = 3$

2. $15\frac{3}{8} \div \frac{1}{2}$

_____

3. $22\frac{1}{5} \div 1\frac{5}{6}$

_____

4. $7\frac{7}{9} \div \frac{4}{7}$

5. $18\frac{1}{4} \div 2\frac{4}{5}$

6. $62\frac{7}{10} \div 8\frac{8}{9}$

_____ _____ _____

7. $\frac{11}{12} \div \frac{1}{5}$

8. $24\frac{3}{4} \div \frac{1}{2}$

9. $\frac{15}{16} \div \frac{1}{7}$

_____ _____ _____

10. $14\frac{7}{8} \div \frac{5}{11}$

11. $53\frac{7}{12} \div 8\frac{11}{12}$

12. $1\frac{1}{6} \div \frac{1}{9}$

_____ _____ _____

Problem Solving REAL WORLD

13. Estimate the number of pieces Sharon will
have if she divides $15\frac{1}{3}$ yards of fabric into
$4\frac{4}{5}$-yard lengths.

14. Estimate the number of $\frac{1}{2}$-quart containers
Ethan can fill from a container with $8\frac{7}{8}$ quarts
of water.

_____

Lesson Check (CC.6.NS.1)

1. A certian dictionary is $3\frac{15}{16}$ inches wide. Which is the best estimate of the number of copies of the dictionary that can be placed side-by-side on a 3 foot shelf?

   (A) 1

   (B) 4

   (C) 9

   (D) 12

2. A CD has $1\frac{1}{4}$ hours of recorded music. Each song lasts an average of $\frac{1}{12}$ hour. Which is the best estimate of the number of songs on the CD?

   (A) 3

   (B) 6

   (C) 10

   (D) 12

Spiral Review (CC.6.NS.3, CC.6.NS.4, CC.6.NS.6c)

3. What is the least common multiple of 9 and 12? **(Lesson 1.3)**

   (A) 3

   (B) 12

   (C) 18

   (D) 36

4. Yvette earned $66.00 for 8 hours of work. Lizbeth earned $68.80 working the same amount of time. How much more per hour did Lizbeth earn than Yvette earned?
   (Lesson 1.8)

   (A) $0.35

   (B) $0.45

   (C) $2.80

   (D) $8.25

5. Of 11 bicycle tires that Keith checked for leaks, 3 were found to be defective. How can you write the fraction of tires that were defective as a repeating decimal? **(Lesson 2.1)**

   (A) $3.\overline{6}$

   (B) $0.\overline{3}$

   (C) $0.\overline{31}$

   (D) $0.\overline{27}$

6. Donny exercised for $\frac{3}{4}$ hour. He lifted weights for $\frac{1}{6}$ of that time. What fraction of an hour did Donny spend lifting weights? **(Lesson 2.3)**

   (A) $\frac{11}{12}$ hour

   (B) $\frac{7}{12}$ hour

   (C) $\frac{2}{5}$ hour

   (D) $\frac{1}{8}$ hour

Divide Fractions

COMMON CORE STANDARD CC.6.NS.1
Apply and extend previous understandings of
multiplication and division to divide fractions by fractions.

Estimate. Then write the quotient in simplest form.

1. $5 \div \frac{1}{6}$

Estimate: 30

$$= 5 \times \frac{6}{1}$$
$$= \frac{30}{1}$$
$$= 30$$

2. $\frac{1}{2} \div \frac{1}{4}$

3. $\frac{4}{5} \div \frac{2}{3}$

4. $\frac{14}{15} \div 7$

5. $\frac{2}{5} \div \frac{7}{10}$

6. $\frac{5}{9} \div \frac{5}{7}$

7. $4 \div \frac{4}{5}$

8. $1 \div \frac{3}{4}$

9. $8 \div \frac{1}{3}$

10. $\frac{12}{21} \div \frac{2}{3}$

11. $\frac{5}{6} \div \frac{5}{12}$

12. $\frac{5}{8} \div \frac{1}{2}$

13. Joy ate $\frac{1}{4}$ of a pizza. If she divides the rest of the pizza into pieces equal to $\frac{1}{8}$ pizza for her family, how many pieces will her family get?

14. Hideko has $\frac{3}{5}$ yard of ribbon to tie on balloons for the festival. Each balloon will need $\frac{3}{10}$ yard of ribbon. How many balloons can Hideko tie with ribbon?

Problem Solving  REAL WORLD

15. Rick knows that 1 cup of glue weighs $\frac{1}{18}$ pound. He has $\frac{2}{3}$ pound of glue. How many cups of glue does he have?

16. Mrs. Jennings had $\frac{5}{7}$ gallon of paint. She gave $\frac{1}{7}$ gallon each to some students. How many students received paint if Mrs. Jennings gave away all the paint?

Lesson Check (CC.6.NS.1)

1. Marsha had $\frac{8}{9}$ yard of fabric. She cut it into 4 pieces of equal length. How long was each piece?

   (A) $\frac{1}{9}$ yard

   (B) $\frac{2}{9}$ yard

   (C) $\frac{4}{9}$ yard

   (D) $3\frac{5}{9}$ yards

2. Which choice has the smallest quotient?

   (A) $2 \div \frac{1}{4}$

   (B) $6 \div \frac{2}{3}$

   (C) $8 \div \frac{4}{5}$

   (D) $4 \div \frac{2}{3}$

Spiral Review (CC.6.NS.1, CC.6.NS.3, CC.6.NS.4)

3. Which is NOT a factor of 144? **(Lesson 1.4)**

   (A) 3

   (B) 9

   (C) 12

   (D) 27

4. During track practice, Chris ran 2.5 laps in 81 seconds. Find his average time per lap. **(Lesson 1.9)**

   (A) 0.03 second

   (B) 3.24 seconds

   (C) 32.4 seconds

   (D) 202.5 seconds

5. Which expression has the same product as $\frac{4}{9} \times \frac{3}{14}$? **(Lesson 2.4)**

   (A) $\frac{2}{3} \times \frac{1}{7}$

   (B) $\frac{2}{3} \times \frac{1}{10}$

   (C) $\frac{4}{3} \times \frac{9}{14}$

   (D) $\frac{1}{5} \times \frac{1}{11}$

6. Sonya has $\frac{2}{3}$ pound of pistachios that she wants to divide into 6 servings. What fraction of a pound will be in each serving? **(Lesson 2.5)**

   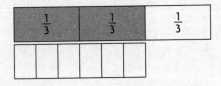

   (A) $\frac{1}{9}$ pound

   (C) $\frac{1}{4}$ pound

   (B) $\frac{2}{9}$ pound

   (D) $\frac{5}{6}$ pound

Model Mixed Number Division

COMMON CORE STANDARD CC.6.NS.1
Apply and extend previous understandings of multiplication and division to divide fractions by fractions.

Use the model to find the quotient.

1. $4\frac{1}{2} \div \frac{1}{2} =$ ___9___

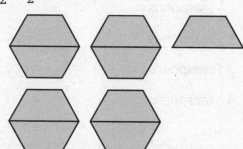

2. $3\frac{1}{3} \div \frac{1}{6} =$ _____

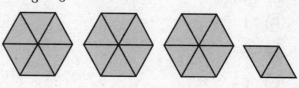

Use pattern blocks to find the quotient. Then draw the model.

3. $2\frac{1}{2} \div \frac{1}{6} =$ _____

4. $1\frac{1}{2} \div \frac{1}{2} =$ _____

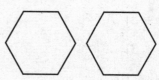

Draw a model to solve.

5. $2\frac{3}{4} \div 2 =$ _____

6. $3\frac{1}{3} \div 3 =$ _____

Problem Solving REAL WORLD

7. Marty has $2\frac{4}{5}$ quarts of juice. He pours the same amount of juice into 2 bottles. How much does he pour into each bottle?

_____

8. How many $\frac{1}{3}$-pound servings are in $4\frac{2}{3}$ pounds of cheese?

_____

Lesson Check (CC.6.NS.1)

1. Sumaya needs $5\frac{1}{2}$ cups of broth to make soup, but she only has a measuring cup that holds $\frac{1}{2}$ cup. How many times will she fill the $\frac{1}{2}$ cup?

   (A) 1

   (B) 5

   (C) $5\frac{1}{2}$

   (D) 11

2. Len uses $3\frac{1}{4}$ teaspoons of chili powder for a batch of chili. He wants to divide this recipe by 2. How much chili powder should he use?

   (A) $1\frac{1}{4}$ teaspoons

   (B) $1\frac{5}{8}$ teaspoons

   (C) $3\frac{1}{8}$ teaspoons

   (D) $6\frac{1}{2}$ teaspoons

Spiral Review (CC.6.NS.1, CC.6.NS.4, CC.6.NS.6c)

3. Which of the following expressions is equivalent to $50 + 30$? (Lesson 1.5)

   (A) $10(5 + 3)$

   (B) $80(5 + 3)$

   (C) $30(20 + 0)$

   (D) $80(50 + 30)$

4. Four students did hospital volunteer work. Which student spent the most time doing volunteer work? (Lesson 2.1)

   (A) Casey, 20.7 hours

   (B) Danielle, $20\frac{3}{4}$ hours

   (C) Javier, $18\frac{9}{10}$ hours

   (D) Forrest, $20\frac{18}{25}$ hours

5. Lily's basketball team won $\frac{4}{5}$ of their games. Lily scored points in $\frac{2}{3}$ of the games her team won. In what fraction of her team's winning games did Lily score points? (Lesson 2.3)

   (A) $\frac{2}{15}$

   (B) $\frac{8}{15}$

   (C) $\frac{3}{4}$

   (D) $\frac{5}{6}$

6. Elaine has $14\frac{3}{4}$ cups of flour. She divides the flour into equal portions of $2\frac{7}{8}$ cups. Which is the best estimate for the number of portions she can make? (Lesson 2.6)

   (A) 3

   (B) 5

   (C) 7

   (D) 15

Divide Mixed Numbers

COMMON CORE STANDARD CC.6.NS.1
Apply and extend previous understandings of multiplication and division to divide fractions by fractions.

Estimate. Then write the quotient in simplest form.

1. $2\frac{1}{2} \div 2\frac{1}{3}$

2. $2\frac{2}{3} \div 1\frac{1}{3}$

3. $2 \div 3\frac{5}{8}$

Estimate: $2 \div 2 = 1$

$$2\frac{1}{2} \div 2\frac{1}{3} = \frac{5}{2} \div \frac{7}{3}$$

$$= \frac{5}{2} \times \frac{3}{7}$$

$$= \frac{15}{14} \text{ or } 1\frac{1}{14}$$

4. $1\frac{13}{15} \div 1\frac{2}{5}$

5. $10 \div 6\frac{2}{3}$

6. $2\frac{3}{5} \div 1\frac{1}{25}$

7. $2\frac{1}{5} \div 2$

8. Sid and Jill hiked $4\frac{1}{8}$ miles in the morning and $1\frac{7}{8}$ miles in the afternoon. How many times as far did they hike in the morning as in the afternoon?

9. Kim has $2\frac{1}{2}$ cups of peaches. How many $\frac{1}{4}$-cup servings can she make?

Problem Solving REAL WORLD

10. It takes Nim $2\frac{2}{3}$ hours to weave a basket. He worked Monday through Friday, 8 hours a day. How many baskets did he make?

11. A tree grows $1\frac{3}{4}$ feet per year. How long will it take the tree to grow from a height of $21\frac{1}{4}$ feet to a height of 37 feet?

Lesson Check (CC.6.NS.1)

1. Barney drove 210 miles in $3\frac{3}{4}$ hours. What was his average speed?

   Ⓐ $44\frac{1}{5}$ miles per hour

   Ⓑ 52 miles per hour

   Ⓒ 56 miles per hour

   Ⓓ $58\frac{3}{4}$ miles per hour

2. One dollar is worth $3\frac{1}{2}$ kruneros. What is the value of $43\frac{3}{4}$ kruneros?

   Ⓐ $7\frac{1}{2}$ dollars

   Ⓑ $12\frac{1}{2}$ dollars

   Ⓒ 15 dollars

   Ⓓ $153\frac{1}{8}$ dollars

Spiral Review (CC.6.NS.1, CC.6.NS.3, CC.6.NS.6c)

3. The three sides of a triangle measure 9.97 meters, 10.1 meters, and 0.53 meter. What is the distance around the triangle?

   (Lesson 1.6)

   Ⓐ 19.5 meters

   Ⓑ 20.6 meters

   Ⓒ 29.6 meters

   Ⓓ 115.1 meters

4. Four numbers are plotted on a number line. Which number is farthest to the left?

   (Lesson 2.2)

   Ⓐ $\frac{4}{9}$

   Ⓑ $\frac{9}{20}$

   Ⓒ 0.43

   Ⓓ $\frac{2}{5}$

5. Fiona starts at the beginning of a hiking trail and walks $\frac{4}{5}$ mile. She counts the mileage markers that are placed every $\frac{1}{10}$ mile along the trail. How many markers does she count?

   (Lesson 2.7)

   Ⓐ 0.08

   Ⓑ 4

   Ⓒ 8

   Ⓓ 10

6. Mr. Ramirez made 5 sandwiches. He cut each sandwich in half. How many half sandwiches does he have? (Lesson 2.8)

   Ⓐ $\frac{1}{2}$

   Ⓑ $2\frac{1}{2}$

   Ⓒ 5

   Ⓓ 10

Name _____

Problem Solving • Fraction Operations

COMMON CORE STANDARD CC.6.NS.1
Apply and extend previous understandings of multiplication and division to divide fractions by fractions.

Read each problem and solve.

1. $\frac{2}{3}$ of a pizza was left over. A group of friends divided the leftover pizza into pieces each equal to $\frac{1}{18}$ of the original pizza. After each friend took one piece, $\frac{1}{6}$ of the leftover pizza remained. How many friends were in the group?

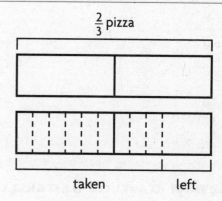

$\frac{2}{3}$ pizza

taken   left

_____ 9

2. Sarah's craft project uses pieces of yarn that are $\frac{1}{8}$ yard long. She has a piece of yarn that is 3 yards long. How many $\frac{1}{8}$-yard pieces can she cut and still have $1\frac{1}{4}$ yards left?

_____

3. Alex opens a 1-pint container of orange butter. He spreads $\frac{1}{16}$ of the butter on his bread. Then he divides the rest of the butter into $\frac{3}{4}$-pint containers. How many $\frac{3}{4}$-pint containers is he able to fill?

_____

4. Kaitlin buys $\frac{9}{10}$ pound of orange slices. She eats $\frac{1}{3}$ of them and divides the rest equally into 3 bags. How much is in each bag?

_____

Lesson Check (CC.6.NS.1)

1. At 9 A.M., a bird bath contained $\frac{7}{8}$ gallon of water. Each hour, $\frac{1}{16}$ gallon evaporated. What time was it when $\frac{1}{4}$ gallon of water remained?

(A) 3 P.M.

(B) 5 P.M.

(C) 6 P.M.

(D) 7 P.M.

2. $\frac{3}{5}$ of Jill's 30-page photo album is full. She wants to set aside $\frac{1}{4}$ of the pages that are left for photos of her vacation. How many pages can she fill before her vacation?

(A) 3

(B) 8

(C) 9

(D) 12

Spiral Review (CC.6.NS.1, CC.6.NS.2, CC.6.NS.3, CC.6.NS.4)

3. A number is multiplied by 26 to get a product of 650. What is the number? (Lesson 1.1)

(A) 25

(B) 26

(C) 27

(D) 28

4. A machine produces 1,000 bowling pins per hour, each valued at $8.37. What is the total value of the pins produced in 1 hour?

(Lesson 1.7)

(A) $8.37

(B) $83.70

(C) $837.00

(D) $8,370.00

5. Henry has $\frac{2}{3}$ of a bag of popcorn. He eats half of the popcorn during a movie. What fraction of a bag of popcorn does Henry eat during the movie? (Lesson 2.3)

(A) $\frac{1}{3}$

(B) $\frac{2}{5}$

(C) $\frac{1}{2}$

(D) $\frac{3}{4}$

6. Jackson spent $2\frac{2}{3}$ hours skateboarding at 4 different parks this week. He spent the same amount of time at each park. How long did he skateboard at each park? (Lesson 2.9)

(A) $\frac{1}{3}$ hour

(B) $\frac{2}{3}$ hour

(C) $5\frac{1}{3}$ hours

(D) $10\frac{2}{3}$ hours

Chapter 2 Extra Practice

Lessons 2.1 and 2.2

Write as a decimal. Tell whether the decimal terminates or repeats.

1. $\frac{3}{8}$

2. $\frac{5}{6}$

3. $1\frac{13}{20}$

4. $\frac{5}{9}$

_____ _____ _____ _____

Order from least to greatest.

5. $\frac{2}{3}, \frac{7}{10}, \frac{3}{5}$

6. $\frac{5}{12}, \frac{1}{3}, \frac{1}{4}$

7. $1\frac{1}{5}, 1.15, 1\frac{3}{25}$

_____ _____ _____

Lessons 2.3 and 2.4

Find the product. Simplify before multiplying.

8. $6 \times \frac{2}{3}$

9. $\frac{5}{6} \times \frac{3}{5}$

10. $\frac{8}{9} \times \frac{3}{10}$

11. $3\frac{2}{5} \times 1\frac{2}{3}$

_____ _____ _____ _____

Evaluate using the order of operations.

12. $\left(\frac{8}{9} - \frac{1}{3}\right) \times \frac{2}{3}$

13. $\left(\frac{1}{4} + \frac{2}{7}\right) \times \frac{4}{5}$

14. $\frac{5}{6} \times \left(\frac{3}{10} + \frac{1}{2}\right) - \frac{2}{5}$

_____ _____ _____

Lesson 2.5

Use the model to find the quotient.

15. $\frac{3}{4} \div 6 =$ _____

16. $\frac{9}{10} \div \frac{2}{5} =$ _____

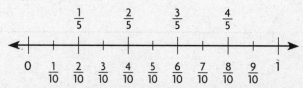

Lessons 2.6 and 2.7

Estimate. Then write the quotient in simplest form.

17. $1 \div \frac{1}{5}$

18. $\frac{5}{9} \div \frac{5}{7}$

19. $\frac{2}{5} \div \frac{7}{10}$

20. $\frac{13}{16} \div \frac{3}{8}$

_____ _____ _____ _____

Lessons 2.8 and 2.9

Use the model to find the quotient.

21. $2\frac{2}{3} \div \frac{1}{3} =$ _____

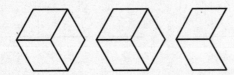

22. $3\frac{1}{2} \div \frac{1}{6} =$ _____

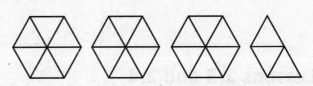

Estimate. Then write the quotient in simplest form.

23. $1\frac{5}{8} \div 2\frac{1}{2}$

24. $3\frac{3}{5} \div 2\frac{1}{4}$

25. $8 \div 5\frac{1}{3}$

26. $5\frac{4}{9} \div 3\frac{1}{2}$

_____ _____ _____ _____

Lesson 2.10

Solve.

27. Tom ate $\frac{1}{4}$ of a pizza. He divided the leftover pizza into pieces each equal to $\frac{1}{12}$ of the original pizza. After he gave some friends one piece each, $\frac{1}{6}$ of the original pizza remained. How many friends got pizza?

28. Bobcat Park is a rectangular park with an area of $5\frac{1}{5}$ square miles. Its width is $1\frac{19}{20}$ miles. How long is the park?

_____ _____

School-Home Letter

Throughout the next few weeks, our math class will be learning about rational numbers and the coordinate plane. We will also be learning how to compare numbers and find the distance between points.

You can expect to see homework with real-world problems that involve the coordinate plane.

Here is a sample of how your child was taught to find the distance between two points.

Vocabulary

absolute value The distance from 0 to a number on the number line.

integers The set of whole numbers and their opposites.

quadrants The four regions of the coordinate plane that are separated by the x- and y-axes.

rational number Any number that can be written as a ratio $\frac{a}{b}$, where a and b are integers and $b \neq 0$.

🔑 MODEL Distance Between Points

Find the distance from the market to the school.

STEP 1	STEP 2	STEP 3
Find the vertical distance from the market to the x-axis.	Find the vertical distance from the school to the x-axis.	Add to find the total distance.
The distance from (2, 3) to (2, 0) is $|3| = 3$.	The distance from (2, ⁻2) to (2, 0) is $|⁻2| = 2$.	$3 + 2 = 5$ So, the distance from the market to the school is 5 units.

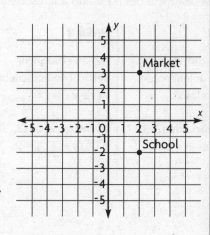

Activity

Find a map of the downtown area of a city that has parallel and perpendicular streets. Take turns finding the number of blocks between two points of interest on the same street. Then find a point of interest given its distance in blocks from another point of interest.

Carta para la casa

Vocabulario

valor absoluto La distancia de 0 a un número en la recta numérica.

enteros El conjunto de números enteros y sus opuestos.

cuadrantes Las cuatro regiones del plano de coordenadas que están separadas por el eje de las *x* y el eje de las *y*.

número racional Todo número que se pueda escribir como una razón $\frac{a}{b}$, donde *a* y *b* son enteros y $b \neq 0$.

Querida familia,

Durante las próximas semanas, en la clase de matemáticas aprenderemos sobre números racionales y el plano de coordenadas. También aprenderemos a comparar números y a hallar la distancia entre dos puntos.

Llevaré a la casa tareas con problemas de la vida real relacionados con el plano de coordenadas.

Este es un ejemplo de la manera como aprendimosa hallar la distancia entre dos puntos.

🔑 MODELO   Distancia entre dos puntos

Calcula la distancia del mercado a la escuela.

PASO 1

Halla la distancia vertical del mercado al eje de las *x*.

La distancia de (2, 3) a (2, 0) es $|3| = 3$.

PASO 2

Halla la distancia vertical de la escuela al eje de las *x*.

La distancia de (2, ⁻2) a (2, 0) es $|{}^{-}2| = 2$.

PASO 3

Suma para hallar la distancia total.

$3 + 2 = 5$

Por tanto, la distancia del mercado a la escuela es 5 unidades.

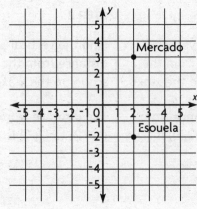

Actividad

Consiga un mapa del centro de una ciudad que tenga calles paralelas y perpendiculares. Túrnense para hallar el número de cuadras entre dos puntos de interés en la misma calle. Luego, busquen un punto de interés dando la distancia en cuadras que lo separa de otro punto de interés.

Understand Positive and Negative Numbers

COMMON CORE STANDARDS CC.6.NS.5, CC.6.NS.6a

Apply and extend previous understandings of numbers to the system of rational numbers.

Graph the integer and its opposite on a number line.

1. ⁻6   opposite: __$+6$__

2. 3   opposite: _____

3. 10   opposite: _____

4. ⁻8   opposite: _____

Name the integer that represents the situation, and tell what 0 represents in that situation.

Situation	Integer	What Does 0 Represent?
5. Michael withdrew $60 from his checking account.		
6. Raquel gained 12 points while playing a video game.		
7. Juan went up 25 feet during a climb on a rock climbing wall.		

Write the opposite of the opposite of the integer.

8. ⁻20 _____   9. 4 _____   10. 95 _____   11. ⁻63 _____

Problem Solving

12. Dakshesh won a game by scoring 25 points. Randy scored the opposite number of points as Dakshesh. What is Randy's score?

13. When Dakshesh and Randy played the game again, Dakshesh scored the opposite of the opposite of his first score. What is his score?

_____   _____

Lesson Check (CC.6.NS.5, CC.6.NS.6a)

1. During their first round of golf, Imani was 7 strokes over par and Peter was 8 strokes below par. What integers represent their scores?

Ⓐ 7 and 8

Ⓑ 7 and ⁻8

Ⓒ ⁻7 and 8

Ⓓ ⁻7 and ⁻8

2. Which situation could be represented by the integer ⁻30?

Ⓐ Wyatt rose 30 feet to the surface.

Ⓑ Divya gained 30 points in a game.

Ⓒ Maci was paid $30 for her artwork.

Ⓓ Ricardo spent $30 for a coat.

Spiral Review (CC.6.NS.1, CC.6.NS.3, CC.6.NS.4)

3. Mr. Nolan's code for his ATM card is a 4-digit number. The digits of the code are the prime factors of 84 listed from least to greatest. What is the code for Mr. Nolan's ATM card? (Lesson 1.2)

Ⓐ 2237

Ⓑ 2337

Ⓒ 2347

Ⓓ 2379

4. Over a four-year period, a tree grew 2.62 feet. If the tree grows at a constant rate, how many feet did the tree grow each year? (Lesson 1.8)

Ⓐ 0.5 feet

Ⓑ 0.655 feet

Ⓒ 6.62 feet

Ⓓ 10.48 feet

5. Omarion has $\frac{9}{10}$ of the pages in a book remaining to read for school. He reads $\frac{2}{3}$ of the remaining pages over the weekend. What fraction of the book does Omarion read over the weekend? (Lesson 2.4)

Ⓐ $\frac{1}{3}$ book

Ⓑ $\frac{3}{5}$ book

Ⓒ $\frac{3}{4}$ book

Ⓓ $\frac{1}{4}$ book

6. Marianne has $\frac{5}{8}$ package of peas. She cooks $\frac{2}{3}$ of those peas for 5 people. If each person is served an equal amount, what fraction of the peas did each person get? (Lesson 2.10)

Ⓐ $\frac{1}{4}$ package

Ⓑ $\frac{1}{5}$ package

Ⓒ $\frac{1}{12}$ package

Ⓓ $\frac{2}{15}$ package

Name _____

Compare and Order Integers

COMMON CORE STANDARDS CC.6.NS.7a, CC.6.NS.7b

Apply and extend previous understandings of numbers to the system of rational numbers.

Compare the numbers. Write < or >.

1. $^-4$ ⟩ $^-5$ Think: $^-4$ is to the ___**right**___ of $^-5$ on the number line,

   so $^-4$ is ___**greater than**___ $^-5$.

2. 0 ◯ $^-1$

3. 4 ◯ $^-6$

4. $^-9$ ◯ $^-8$

5. 2 ◯ $^-10$

6. $^-12$ ◯ $^-11$

7. 1 ◯ $^-10$

Order the numbers from least to greatest.

8. $3, ^-2, ^-7$

9. $0, 2, ^-5$

10. $^-9, ^-12, ^-10$

____ < ____ < ____   ____ < ____ < ____   ____ < ____ < ____

11. $^-2, ^-3, ^-4$

12. $1, ^-6, ^-13$

13. $5, 7, 0$

____ < ____ < ____   ____ < ____ < ____   ____ < ____ < ____

Order the numbers from greatest to least.

14. $0, 13, ^-13$

15. $^-11, 7, ^-5$

16. $^-9, ^-8, 1$

____ > ____ > ____   ____ > ____ > ____   ____ > ____ > ____

17. $32, 10, ^-22$

18. $^-2, ^-4, 0$

19. $^-25, 19, 26$

____ > ____ > ____   ____ > ____ > ____   ____ > ____ > ____

Problem Solving REAL WORLD

20. Meg and Derek played a game. Meg scored $^-11$ points, and Derek scored 4 points. Write a comparison to show that Meg's score is less than Derek's score.

21. Misha is thinking of a negative integer greater than $^-4$. What number could she be thinking of?

_____   _____

Lesson Check (CC.6.NS.7a, CC.6.NS.7b)

1. Which of the following shows numbers in order from least to greatest?

(A) 4, 5, ⁻8

(B) 5, 4, ⁻8

(C) ⁻8, 4, 5

(D) ⁻8, 5, 4

2. Which of the following numbers is less than 1 but greater than ⁻2?

(A) ⁻4

(B) ⁻2

(C) 3

(D) 0

Spiral Review (CC.6.NS.1, CC.6.NS.3, CC.6.NS.4, CC.6.NS.5)

3. What is the least common multiple of 10 and 15? (Lesson 1.3)

(A) 5

(B) 20

(C) 30

(D) 150

4. If Amanda hikes at an average speed of 2.72 miles per hour, how long will it take her to hike 6.8 miles? (Lesson 1.9)

(A) 0.4 hour

(B) 1.5 hours

(C) 2.5 hours

(D) 4.08 hours

5. The area of a rectangle is $5\frac{4}{5}$ square meters. The width of the rectangle is $2\frac{1}{4}$ meter. Which is the best estimate for the length of the rectangle? (Leson 2.6)

(A) 1 meter

(B) 3 meters

(C) 10 meters

(D) 12 meters

6. Which situation could be represented by the integer ⁻4? (Lesson 3.1)

(A) The temperature rose 4 degrees.

(B) Rochelle has $4 left on her gift card.

(C) Harold saved $4 in pennies.

(D) Ellen lost 4 points in a game.

Rational Numbers and the Number Line

COMMON CORE STANDARDS CC.6.NS.6a, CC.6.NS.6c

Apply and extend previous understandings of numbers to the system of rational numbers.

Graph the number on the number line.

1. $-2\frac{3}{4}$

   The number is between the integers  -3 and -2.

   It is closer to the integer -3.

   -3 -2 -1 0 1 2 3

2. $-\frac{1}{4}$

   -2 -1 0 1

3. -0.5

   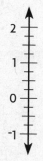

   2

   1

   0

   -1

4. 1.75

   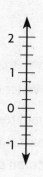

   2

   1

   0

   -1

5. $1\frac{1}{2}$

   -2 -1 0 1 2

State whether the numbers are on the same or opposite sides of zero.

6. -2.4 and 2.3

7. $-2\frac{1}{5}$ and -1

8. -0.3 and 0.3

9. 0.44 and $-\frac{2}{3}$

_____ _____ _____ _____

Write the opposite of the number.

10. -5.23

11. $\frac{4}{5}$

12. -5

13. $-2\frac{2}{3}$

_____ _____ _____ _____

Problem Solving REAL WORLD

14. The outdoor temperature yesterday reached a low of $-4.5°F$. Between what two integers was the temperature?

15. Jacob needs to graph $-6\frac{2}{5}$ on a horizontal number line. Should he graph it to the left or right of -6?

_____ _____

Lesson Check (CC.6.NS.6a, CC.6.NS.6c)

1. Which of the following shows the opposite of 0.2?

   Ⓐ $^-0.2$

   Ⓑ $\frac{1}{5}$

   Ⓒ $^-2.0$

   Ⓓ $\frac{5}{1}$

2. Which number lies between $^-3$ and $^-4$ on a number line?

   Ⓐ 0

   Ⓑ $^-2.8$

   Ⓒ $^-3.4$

   Ⓓ $^-4.2$

Spiral Review (CC.6.NS.1, CC.6.NS.6c, CC.6.NS.7a)

3. To pass a math test, students must correctly answer at least 0.6 of the questions. Donald's score is $\frac{5}{8}$, Karen's score is 0.88, Gino's score is $0.\overline{6}$, and Sierra's score is $\frac{4}{5}$. How many of the students passed the test? **(Lesson 2.1)**

   Ⓐ 1

   Ⓑ 2

   Ⓒ 3

   Ⓓ 4

4. Jonna mixes $\frac{1}{4}$ gallon of orange juice and $\frac{1}{2}$ gallon of pineapple juice to make punch. Each serving is $\frac{1}{16}$ gallon. How many servings can Jonna make? **(Lesson 2.7)**

   Ⓐ 4 servings

   Ⓑ 8 servings

   Ⓒ 12 servings

   Ⓓ 16 servings

5. Yemi used these pattern blocks to solve a division problem. He found a quotient of 7. Which division problem was he solving?

   (Lesson 2.8)

   Ⓐ $3\frac{1}{2} \div \frac{1}{2}$

   Ⓑ $7\frac{1}{2} \div 2$

   Ⓒ $3\frac{1}{2} \div 2$

   Ⓓ $7\frac{1}{2} \div 3$

6. Which of the following shows integers in order from least to greatest? **(Lesson 3.2)**

   Ⓐ $^-6, ^-8, 0, 2$

   Ⓑ $0, ^-5, ^-2, 3$

   Ⓒ $^-8, ^-7, 0, 3$

   Ⓓ $^-3, ^-4, ^-5, ^-6$

Compare and Order Rational Numbers

COMMON CORE STANDARDS CC.6.NS.7a, CC.6.NS.7b

Apply and extend previous understandings of numbers to the system of rational numbers.

Compare the numbers. Write < or >.

1. $-1\frac{1}{2}$ $\bigcirc$< $-\frac{1}{2}$ Think: $-1\frac{1}{2}$ is to the ___left___ of $-\frac{1}{2}$ on the number line,

   so $-1\frac{1}{2}$ is ___less than___ $-\frac{1}{2}$.

2. 0.1 $\bigcirc$ -1.9

3. 0.4 $\bigcirc$ $-\frac{1}{2}$

4. $\frac{2}{5}$ $\bigcirc$ 0.5

5. -1.1 $\bigcirc$ 0

6. $\frac{3}{4}$ $\bigcirc$ $\frac{9}{10}$

7. -2.5 $\bigcirc$ $-\frac{3}{1}$

Order the numbers from least to greatest.

8. $0.2,\ -1.7,\ -1$

9. $-2\frac{3}{4},\ -\frac{3}{5},\ -1\frac{3}{4}$

10. $-0.5,\ -1\frac{2}{3},\ -2.7$

_____ < _____ < _____   _____ < _____ < _____   _____ < _____ < _____

Order the numbers from greatest to least.

11. $-1,\ -\frac{5}{6},\ 0$

12. $1.82,\ -\frac{2}{5},\ \frac{4}{5}$

13. $-2.19,\ -2.5,\ 1.1$

_____ > _____ < _____   _____ > _____ > _____   _____ > _____ > _____

Write a comparison using < or > to show the relationship between the two values.

14. an elevation of -15 m and an elevation of -20.5 m

15. a balance of $78 and a balance of $-$42$

16. a score of -31 points and a score of -30 points

_____   _____   _____

Problem Solving REAL WORLD

17. The temperature in Cold Town on Monday was 1°C. The temperature in Frosty Town on Monday was -2°C. Which town was colder on Monday?

18. Stan's bank account balance is less than $-$20.00$ but greater than $-$21.00$. What could Stan's account balance be?

_____   _____

Lesson Check (CC.6.NS.7a, CC.6.NS.7b)

1. Which of the following shows numbers in order from greatest to least?

   Ⓐ $\frac{1}{2}$, ⁻1.2, $\frac{3}{5}$

   Ⓑ ⁻1.2, $\frac{1}{2}$, $\frac{3}{5}$

   Ⓒ ⁻1.2, $\frac{3}{5}$, $\frac{1}{2}$

   Ⓓ $\frac{3}{5}$, $\frac{1}{2}$, ⁻1.2

2. Which statement is NOT true?

   Ⓐ $\frac{^{-}1}{8} > \frac{^{-}1}{4}$

   Ⓑ ⁻4.8 < 0.01

   Ⓒ ⁻0.23 > ⁻0.2

   Ⓓ $^{-}1\frac{7}{8} < \frac{^{-}1}{4}$

Spiral Review (CC.6.NS.1, CC.6.NS.4, CC.6.NS.6a, CC.6.NS.6c)

3. For an upcoming field trip, there will be 36 fifth graders and 48 sixth graders. Each van will carry the same number of students, and only students from one grade. If each van will carry the greatest possible number of students, how many vans will be needed? **(Lesson 1.5)**

   Ⓐ 6 vans

   Ⓑ 7 vans

   Ⓒ 12 vans

   Ⓓ 14 vans

4. Four students took an exam. Monica's score was $\frac{22}{25}$, Lily's score was $\frac{17}{20}$, Nikki's score was $\frac{4}{5}$, and Sydney's score was $\frac{3}{4}$. Which student had the highest score? **(Lesson 2.2)**

   Ⓐ Monica

   Ⓑ Lily

   Ⓒ Nikki

   Ⓓ Sydney

5. While ice skating, Brian spun around $6\frac{1}{4}$ times in $2\frac{1}{2}$ seconds. How many spins did Brian complete in one second? **(Lesson 2.9)**

   Ⓐ $1\frac{1}{2}$ spins

   Ⓑ $2\frac{1}{2}$ spins

   Ⓒ $12\frac{1}{2}$ spins

   Ⓓ $15\frac{5}{8}$ spins

6. Which number lies between ⁻2 and ⁻1 on the number line? **(Lesson 3.3)**

   Ⓐ $^{-}2\frac{1}{4}$

   Ⓑ 0

   Ⓒ $^{-}1\frac{4}{5}$

   Ⓓ 1

Name _____

Absolute Value

COMMON CORE STANDARD CC.6.NS.7c

Apply and extend previous understandings of numbers to the system of rational numbers.

Find the absolute value.

1. $|7|$ Graph 7 on the number line.

7 is __**7**__ units from 0.

$|7| =$ __**7**__

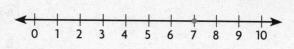

2. $|^-8|$ **3.** $|16|$ **4.** $|^-100|$ **5.** $|0|$ **6.** $|^-5,000|$

_____ _____ _____ _____ _____

7. $|^-15|$ **8.** $\left|-\frac{1}{10}\right|$ **9.** $|8.65|$ **10.** $\left|4\frac{3}{20}\right|$ **11.** $|^-0.06|$

_____ _____ _____ _____ _____

Find all numbers with the given absolute value.

12. 12   **13.** 1.7   **14.** $\frac{3}{5}$ **15.** $3\frac{1}{6}$ **16.** 0

_____ _____ _____ _____ _____

_____ _____ _____ _____ _____

Find the number or numbers that make the statement true.

17. $\left|\right| = 17$ **18.** $\left|\right| = 2.04$ **19.** $\left|\right| = 1\frac{9}{10}$ **20.** $\left|\right| = \frac{19}{24}$

_____ _____ _____ _____

_____ _____ _____ _____

Problem Solving REAL WORLD

21. Which two numbers are 7.5 units away from 0 on a number line?

22. Emilio is playing a game. He just answered a question incorrectly, so his score will change by $^-10$ points. Find the absolute value of $^-10$.

_____   _____

Lesson Check (CC.6.NS.7c)

1. What is the absolute value of $\frac{8}{9}$?

Ⓐ $\frac{8}{9}$

Ⓑ $-\frac{8}{9}$

Ⓒ $\frac{9}{8}$

Ⓓ $-\frac{9}{8}$

2. Which two numbers have an absolute value of $\frac{4}{5}$?

Ⓐ $\frac{4}{5}$ and $\frac{5}{4}$

Ⓑ $\frac{4}{5}$ and 0

Ⓒ $\frac{4}{5}$ and $-\frac{4}{5}$

Ⓓ $-\frac{4}{5}$ and $-\frac{5}{4}$

Spiral Review (CC.6.NS.1, CC.6.NS.3, CC.6.NS.4, CC.6.NS.7b)

3. Rachel earned $89.70 on Tuesday. She spent $55.89 at the grocery store. How much money does she have left? **(Lesson 1.6)**

Ⓐ $33.80

Ⓑ $33.81

Ⓒ $34.19

Ⓓ $34.81

4. Maggie jogged $\frac{7}{8}$ mile on Monday and $\frac{1}{2}$ of that distance on Tuesday. How far did she jog on Tuesday? **(Lesson 2.3)**

Ⓐ $\frac{3}{8}$ mile

Ⓑ $\frac{7}{16}$ mile

Ⓒ $1\frac{3}{8}$ mile

Ⓓ $1\frac{3}{4}$ mile

5. Trygg has $\frac{3}{4}$ package of marigold seeds. He plants $\frac{1}{6}$ of those seeds in his garden and divides the rest equally into 10 flower pots. What fraction of a package of seeds is planted in each flower pot? **(Lesson 2.10)**

Ⓐ $\frac{1}{16}$ package

Ⓑ $\frac{1}{8}$ package

Ⓒ $\frac{1}{10}$ package

Ⓓ $\frac{7}{12}$ package

6. Which temperature is hottest? **(Lesson 3.4)**

Ⓐ $^-32°C$

Ⓑ $^-34°C$

Ⓒ $33°C$

Ⓓ $31°C$

Compare Absolute Values

COMMON CORE STANDARD CC.6.NS.7d
Apply and extend previous understandings of
numbers to the system of rational numbers.

Solve.

1. Jamie scored $^-5$ points on her turn at a trivia
game. In Veronica's turn, she scored more
points than Jamie. Use absolute value to
describe Veronica's score as a loss.

    In this situation, $|^-5|$ represents a loss of
    _____**5**_____ points. Veronica lost ___**fewer**___
    than 5 points.

2. The low temperature on Friday was $^-10°F$. The
low temperature on Saturday was colder. Use
absolute value to describe the temperature on
Saturday as a temperature below zero.

    The temperature on Saturday was _____
    than 10 degrees below zero.

3. The table shows changes in the savings
accounts of five students. Which student had
the greatest increase in money? By how much
did the student's account increase?

    _____

    _____

Student	Account Change ($)
Brett	$^-12$
Destiny	$^-36$
Carissa	15
Rylan	10

Compare. Write <, >, or =.

4. $^-16$ ◯ $|^-16|$

5. 20 ◯ $|20|$

6. 3 ◯ $|^-4|$

7. $|^-12|$ ◯ $|^-11|$

8. $|25|$ ◯ $|27|$

9. $|^-9|$ ◯ $|9|$

Problem Solving REAL WORLD

10. On Wednesday, Miguel's bank account balance
was $^-\$55$. On Thursday, his balance was less
than that. Use absolute value to describe
Miguel's balance on Thursday as a debt.

    In this situation, $^-\$55$ represents a debt of

    _____. On Thursday, Miguel had a debt

    of _____ than $55.

11. During a game, Naomi lost points. She
lost fewer than 3 points. Use an integer to
describe her possible score.

    _____

Lesson Check (CC.6.NS.7d)

1. It is colder than 5°F below zero. Which could be the temperature?

(A) ⁻6°F

(B) ⁻5°F

(C) ⁻4°F

(D) 0°F

2. Which of the following statements is NOT true?

(A) |⁻3| = |3|

(B) |⁻5| > |3|

(C) |⁻17| < 18

(D) |⁻4| < 4

Spiral Review (CC.6.NS.3, CC.6.NS.4, CC.6.NS.6a, CC.6.NS.7c)

3. Etta bought 11.5 yards of fabric selling for $0.90 per yard. What was the total cost?

(Lesson 1.7)

(A) $10.35

(B) $11.35

(C) $12.40

(D) $103.50

4. Yen needs to find the product of $\frac{5}{8} \times \frac{24}{25}$. Before he multiplies, he simplifies the factors. Which of the following is an equivalent expression? **(Lesson 2.4)**

(A) $\frac{1}{1} \times \frac{3}{25}$

(B) $\frac{5}{8} \times \frac{22}{25}$

(C) $\frac{1}{1} \times \frac{3}{5}$

(D) $\frac{5}{3} \times \frac{1}{1}$

5. What is the opposite of 5? **(Lesson 3.1)**

(A) $\frac{5}{1}$

(B) $\frac{1}{5}$

(C) ⁻5

(D) 0.5

6. Which of the following has the least value?

(Lesson 3.5)

(A) ⁻9

(B) |⁻9|

(C) 0

(D) $\frac{1}{9}$

Name _____

Rational Numbers and the Coordinate Plane

COMMON CORE STANDARD CC.6.NS.6c

Apply and extend previous understandings of numbers to the system of rational numbers.

Write the ordered pair for the point. Give approximate coordinates when necessary.

1. A

3. C

5. E

2. B

4. D

6. F

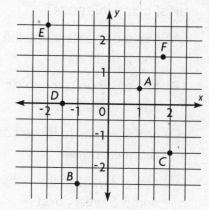

Graph and label the point on the coordinate plane.

7. $G\left(-\frac{1}{2}, 1\frac{1}{2}\right)$

8. $H(0, 2.50)$

9. $J\left(-1\frac{1}{2}, \frac{1}{2}\right)$

10. $K(1, 2)$

11. $L\left(-1\frac{1}{2}, -2\frac{1}{2}\right)$

12. $M(1, {}^-0.5)$

13. $N\left(\frac{1}{4}, 1\frac{1}{2}\right)$

14. $P(1.25, 0)$

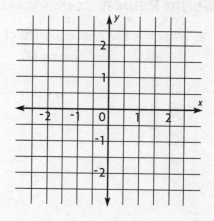

Problem Solving REAL WORLD

Use the map for 15–16.

15. What is the ordered pair for the city hall?

_____

16. The post office is located at $\left(-\frac{1}{2}, 2\right)$. Graph and label a point on the map to represent the post office.

Map of Elmwood

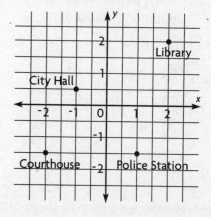

Lesson Check (CC.6.NS.6c)

1. An artist uses a coordinate plane to create a design. As part of the design, the artist wants to graph the point ($^-$6.5, 2). How should the artist graph this point?

   (A) Move 6.5 units to the left of the origin and 2 units up.

   (B) Move 6.5 units to the right of the origin and 2 units up.

   (C) Move 2 units to the left of the origin and 6.5 units down.

   (D) Move 2 units to the right of the origin and 6.5 units down.

2. What are the coordinates of the campground?

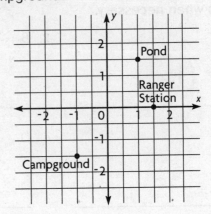

   (A) ($^-$1.5, $^-$1)   (C) ($^-$1, $^-$1.5)

   (B) ($^-$1.5, 1)   (D) (1, $^-$1.5)

Spiral Review (CC.6.NS.1, CC.6.NS.3, CC.6.NS.7a, CC.6.NS.7d)

3. Which is the best estimate of the quotient 14.98 ÷ 2.984? **(Lesson 1.8)**

   (A) 0.5

   (B) 0.7

   (C) 5

   (D) 7

4. Cam has a piece of plywood that is $6\frac{7}{8}$ feet wide. He is going to cut shelves from the plywood that are each $1\frac{1}{6}$ feet wide. Which is the best estimate for the number of shelves Cam can make? **(Lesson 2.6)**

   (A) 1

   (B) 2

   (C) 4

   (D) 7

5. Which of the following is NOT a true statement? **(Lesson 3.2)**

   (A) $0 > ^-3$

   (B) $^-2 < ^-1$

   (C) $^-5 > 0$

   (D) $^-9 > ^-10$

6. Which of the following is a true statement? **(Lesson 3.6)**

   (A) $|^-15| = ^-15$

   (B) $|^-12| > ^-15$

   (C) $|^-12| > |15|$

   (D) $|15| > |^-15|$

Name _____

Ordered Pair Relationships

COMMON CORE STANDARD CC.6.NS.6b

Apply and extend previous understandings of numbers to the system of rational numbers.

Identify the quadrant where the point is located.

1. (10, ⁻2) Quadrant: **IV** ____

2. (⁻5, ⁻6) Quadrant: _____

3. (3, 7) Quadrant: _____

4. (⁻4, 9) Quadrant: _____

5. (8, ⁻1) Quadrant: _____

6. (⁻11, 6) Quadrant: _____

The two points are reflections of each other across the x- or y-axis. Identify the axis.

7. (5, 3) and (⁻5, 3)

8. (⁻7, 1) and (⁻7, ⁻1)

9. (⁻2, 4) and (⁻2, ⁻4)

axis: _____

axis: _____

axis: _____

Give the reflection of the point across the given axis.

10. (⁻6, ⁻10), y-axis

11. (⁻11, 3), x-axis

12. (8, 2), x-axis

_____

_____

_____

Problem Solving REAL WORLD

13. A town's post office is located at the point (7, 5) on a coordinate plane. In which quadrant is the post office located?

14. The grocery store is located at a point on a coordinate plane with the same y-coordinate as the bank but with the opposite x-coordinate. The grocery store and bank are reflections of each other across which axis?

_____

_____

Lesson Check (CC.6.NS.6b)

1. In which quadrant does the point
(⁻4, 15) lie?

Ⓐ Quadrant I

Ⓑ Quadrant II

Ⓒ Quadrant III

Ⓓ Quadrant IV

2. What are the coordinates of the point
(10, ⁻4) if it is reflected across the y-axis?

Ⓐ (⁻10, ⁻4)

Ⓑ (⁻10, 4)

Ⓒ (10, 4)

Ⓓ (10, ⁻4)

Spiral Review (CC.6.NS.1, CC.6.NS.3, CC.6.NS.6a, CC.6.NS.6c)

3. Alison saves $29.26 each month. How many
months will it take her to save enough money
to buy a stereo for $339.12? **(Lesson 1.9)**

Ⓐ 10

Ⓑ 11

Ⓒ 12

Ⓓ 13

4. Tours of the art museum are offered every
$\frac{1}{3}$ hr from 10:00 A.M. until closing at 4:00 P.M.
How many tours are offered each day?

(Lesson 2.7)

Ⓐ 6

Ⓑ 9

Ⓒ 12

Ⓓ 18

5. Which point is located at $^-1\frac{3}{4}$ on the number
line? **(Lesson 3.3)**

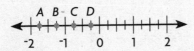

Ⓐ point A

Ⓑ point B

Ⓒ point C

Ⓓ point D

6. Jermaine graphs a point on the y-axis. Which
of these must be true about the ordered pair
for the point? **(Lesson 3.7)**

Ⓐ The x-coordinate is 0.

Ⓑ The y-coordinate is 0.

Ⓒ The x-coordinate is negative.

Ⓓ The y-coordinate is negative.

Name _____

Distance on the Coordinate Plane

COMMON CORE STANDARD CC.6.NS.8
Apply and extend previous understandings of numbers to the system of rational numbers.

Find the distance between the pair of points.

1. (1, 4) and (⁻3, 4)

$|1| = 1; |{}^-3| = 3;$
$1 + 3 = 4$

____4____ units

2. (7, ⁻2) and (11, ⁻2)

_____ units

3. (6, 4) and (6, ⁻8)

_____ units

4. (8, ⁻10) and (5, ⁻10)

_____ units

5. (⁻2, ⁻6) and (⁻2, 5)

_____ units

6. (⁻5, 2) and (⁻5, ⁻4)

_____ units

Write the coordinates of a point that is the given distance from the given point.

7. 5 units from (⁻1, ⁻2)

$\left(\text{▢}, {}^-2 \right)$

8. 8 units from (2, 4)

$\left(2, \text{▢} \right)$

9. 3 units from (⁻7, ⁻5)

$\left({}^-7, \text{▢} \right)$

10. 6 units from (4, ⁻1)

$\left(4, \text{▢} \right)$

11. 10 units from (⁻1, 9)

$\left(\text{▢}, 9 \right)$

12. 7 units from (⁻3, 2)

$\left(\text{▢}, 2 \right)$

Problem Solving REAL WORLD

The map shows the locations of several areas in an amusement park. Each unit represents 1 kilometer.

13. How far is the Ferris wheel from the rollercoaster?

_____

14. How far is the water slide from the restrooms?

_____

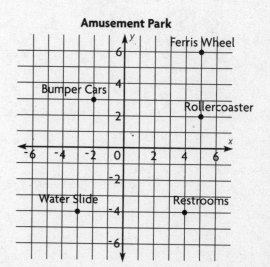

Amusement Park

Lesson Check (CC.6.NS.8)

1. What is the distance between the points (4, ⁻7) and (⁻5, ⁻7)?

(A) 1 unit

(B) 3 units

(C) 7 units

(D) 9 units

2. Which of the following values could be the *y*-coordinate of the point (10, ▨) that is 13 units from (10, 6)?

(A) 17

(B) 3

(C) ⁻1

(D) ⁻7

Spiral Review (CC.6.NS.1, CC.6.NS.6b, CC.6.NS.6c, CC.6.NS.7a)

3. An apple is cut into 10 pieces. 0.8 of the apple is eaten. Which fraction, in simplest form, represents the amount of apple that is left? (Lesson 2.1)

(A) $\frac{1}{10}$

(B) $\frac{2}{10}$

(C) $\frac{1}{5}$

(D) $\frac{2}{5}$

4. A carton contains soup cans weighing a total of 20 pounds. Each can weighs $1\frac{1}{4}$ pounds. How many cans does the carton contain? (Lesson 2.9)

(A) 16 cans

(B) 18 cans

(C) 25 cans

(D) 30 cans

5. Which shows numbers in order from greatest to least? (Lesson 3.4)

(A) $-1\frac{2}{3} > -1 > \frac{1}{4}$

(B) $-1 > \frac{1}{4} > -1\frac{2}{3}$

(C) $\frac{1}{4} > -1 > -1\frac{2}{3}$

(D) $-1 > -1\frac{2}{3} > \frac{1}{4}$

6. What will be the new coordinates of (3, ⁻1) if it is reflected across the *y*-axis? (Lesson 3.8)

(A) (⁻3, ⁻1)

(B) (3, 1)

(C) (⁻3, 1)

(D) (⁻1, ⁻3)

Name _____

Problem Solving • The Coordinate Plane

COMMON CORE STANDARD CC.6.NS.8
Apply and extend previous understandings of
numbers to the system of rational numbers.

Read each problem and solve.

1. On a coordinate map of Clifton, an electronics store is located
   at (6, ⁻7). A convenience store is located 7 units north of the
   electronics store on the map. What are the map coordinates of
   the convenience store?

   (6, 0)

2. Sonya and Lucas walk from the school to the library. They walk
   5 blocks south and 4 blocks west to get to the library. If the
   school is located at a point (9, ⁻1) on a coordinate map, what
   are the map coordinates of the library?

3. On a coordinate map, Sherry's house is at the point
   (10, ⁻2) and the mall is at point (⁻4, ⁻2). If each unit on
   the map represents one block, what is the distance between
   Sherry's house and the mall?

4. Arthur left his job at (5, 4) on a coordinate map and walked to
   his house at (5, ⁻6). Each unit on the map represents 1 block.
   How far did Arthur walk?

5. A fire station is located 2 units east and 6 units north of a
   hospital. If the hospital is located at a point (⁻2, ⁻3) on a
   coordinate map, what are the coordinates of the fire station?

6. Xavier's house is located at the point (4, 6). Michael's house is
   10 blocks west and 2 blocks south of Xavier's house. What are
   the coordinates of Michael's house?

7. On a coordinate map, a pizzeria is located at (9, 3). A pizza
   is being delivered to a house located at (9, ⁻3). Each unit
   represents 1 mile. How far is the pizzeria from the house?

Lesson Check (CC.6.NS.8)

1. The points (⁻4, ⁻4), (⁻4, 4), (4, 4), and (4, ⁻4) form a square on a coordinate plane. How long is a side length of the square?

   Ⓐ 4 units

   Ⓑ 8 units

   Ⓒ 10 units

   Ⓓ 12 units

2. Which point is 10 units from (2, 5)?

   Ⓐ (12, 5)

   Ⓑ (⁻7, 5)

   Ⓒ (2, ⁻6)

   Ⓓ (2, ⁻10)

Spiral Review (CC.6.NS.1, CC.6.NS.6c, CC.6.NS.7c, CC.6.NS.8)

3. Which of the following shows numbers in order from least to greatest? (Lesson 2.2)

   Ⓐ $2\frac{1}{5}$, $2\frac{1}{6}$, $2\frac{1}{7}$

   Ⓑ $2\frac{1}{8}$, $2\frac{1}{4}$, 2.4

   Ⓒ 2.4, $2\frac{1}{5}$, 2.6

   Ⓓ 2.2, 2.5, 2.25

4. Jan began with $\frac{5}{6}$ pound of modeling clay and used $\frac{1}{5}$ of the clay to make decorative magnets. She divides the remaining clay into 8 equal portions. What is the weight of the clay in each portion? (Lesson 2.10)

   Ⓐ $\frac{1}{48}$ pound

   Ⓑ $\frac{1}{12}$ pound

   Ⓒ $\frac{1}{8}$ pound

   Ⓓ $\frac{2}{3}$ pound

5. What numbers will make the statement true? (Lesson 3.5)

$$\left|\ \ \right| = \frac{5}{6}$$

   Ⓐ $\frac{5}{6}$ and $\frac{-5}{6}$

   Ⓑ $-\frac{5}{6}$ and $-\frac{6}{5}$

   Ⓒ $\frac{6}{5}$ and $-\frac{6}{5}$

   Ⓓ $-\frac{5}{6}$ and $\frac{6}{5}$

6. Which two points are 3 units away from the point (⁻2, ⁻3)? (Lesson 3.9)

   Ⓐ (⁻2, 3) and (⁻2, 6)

   Ⓑ (5, ⁻3) and (⁻2, 3)

   Ⓒ (⁻2, 0) and (⁻1, ⁻3)

   Ⓓ (⁻5, ⁻3) and (1, ⁻3)

Name _____

COMMON CORE STANDARDS CC.6.NS.5, CC.6.NS.6a, CC.6.NS.6b, CC.6.NS.6c, CC.6.NS.7a, CC.6.NS.7b, CC.6.NS.7c, CC.6.NS.7d, CC.6.NS.8

Chapter 3 Extra Practice

Lesson 3.1

Name the integer that represents the situation.

1. lose 3 points   **2.** 4 questions correct   **3.** spent $25   **4.** dropped 8 degrees

_____   _____   _____   _____

Lesson 3.2 and 3.4

Compare the numbers. Write < or >.

5. 7 ◯ $^-$9   **6.** $^-$5 ◯ $^-$6   **7.** 0 ◯ $^-$10

8. $-\frac{1}{2}$ ◯ $^-$0.1   **9.** $-\frac{3}{5}$ ◯ $-\frac{1}{8}$ **10.** 8 ◯ $^-$9.25

Lesson 3.3

Graph the number on the horizontal number line.

11. $-\frac{2}{3}$ **12.** $-3\frac{1}{4}$ **13.** 2.2

   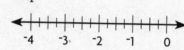 

Lesson 3.5

Find the absolute value.

14. $|^-1|$ **15.** $\left|\frac{3}{10}\right|$ **16.** $|^-0.28|$

_____   _____   _____

Find the number or numbers that make the statement true.

17. $|\ \ | = 29$ **18.** $|\ \ | = 5.3$ **19.** $|\ \ | = 224$

_____   _____   _____

Lesson 3.6

Compare. Write <, >, or =.

20. $^-19$ ◯ $|^-19|$

21. $|^-24|$ ◯ $|24|$

22. $|^-14|$ ◯ $|5|$

23. Yesterday, Jamal scored $^-20$ points on a puzzle. Today he scored more points. Use absolute value to describe today's score as a loss.

Today's score is a loss of _____ than 20 points.

24. The surface of the water in a pool is at an elevation greater than $^-8$ feet. Use absolute value to describe the depth of the surface.

The surface is at a depth _____ than 8 feet.

Lesson 3.7

Graph and label the point on the coordinate plane.

25. $A(0, \ ^-2)$

26. $B\left(2, \ 3\frac{1}{2}\right)$

27. $C\left(^-4\frac{1}{2}, \ ^-1\right)$

28. $D(3, \ ^-2.5)$

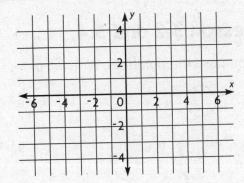

Lesson 3.8

Give the reflection of the point across the given axis.

29. $(2, \ ^-5)$, y-axis

30. $(^-1, 4)$, x-axis

31. $(^-5, 0)$, y-axis

_____

_____

_____

Lesson 3.9

Find the distance between the pair of points.

32. $(7, \ ^-3)$ and $(1, \ ^-3)$

33. $(^-3, 1)$ and $(^-3, \ ^-2)$

34. $(^-2, 8)$ and $(^-7, 8)$

_____

_____

_____

Lesson 3.10

Solve.

35. On a map, the pie shop is located at $(^-4, 5)$. To get from the pie shop to the grocery store, go 3 blocks east and 6 blocks south. What are the coordinates of the grocery store?

36. Lena drew a rectangle with vertices at $(^-1, 1)$, $(^-1, \ ^-2)$, $(4, 1)$, and $(4, \ ^-2)$. What is the perimeter of the rectangle?

_____

_____

School-Home Letter

Vocabulary

equivalent ratios Ratios that name the same comparison.

rate A ratio that compares two quantities that have different units of measure.

ratio A comparison of two quantities by division.

unit rate A rate that compares a quantity to 1 unit.

Dear Family,

Throughout the next few weeks, our math class will be learning about ratios and rates. We will also be learning how to solve problems using equivalent ratios.

You can expect to see homework that provides practice with ratios and rates in a variety of contexts.

Here is a sample of how your child was taught to find an unknown value using equivalent ratios.

🔑 MODEL Use Equivalent Ratios

Solve $\frac{4}{5} = \frac{\blacksquare}{30}$.

STEP 1

Identify a common denominator.

30 is a multiple of 5, so 30 is a common denominator.

STEP 2

Multiply the numerator and denominator of the ratio on the left by 6 to write the ratios with a common denominator.

$$\frac{4 \times 6}{5 \times 6} = \frac{\blacksquare}{30}$$

STEP 3

The denominators are the same, so the numerators are equal.

$$\frac{24}{30} = \frac{\blacksquare}{30}$$

So, $\blacksquare = 24$.

Tips

Equivalent Ratios

You can find equivalent ratios by multiplying or dividing both quantities in a ratio by the same number.

For example,
$\frac{3}{4} = \frac{3 \times 7}{4 \times 7} = \frac{21}{28}$, so $\frac{3}{4}$ and $\frac{21}{28}$ are equivalent ratios.

Activity

Keep track of time and distance data on your next family outing. Use this to write and solve problems that involve rates. For example, "We drove 150 miles in 3 hours. At this rate, how far could we have traveled in 5 hours?"

Carta para la casa

Vocabulario

razones equivalentes Razones que nombran la misma comparación.

tasa Una razón que compara dos cantidades que tienen unidades de medida distintas.

razón Una comparación entre dos cantidades hecha con una división.

tasa unitaria Tasa que compara una cantidad con 1 unidad.

Querida familia,

Durante las próximas semanas, en la clase de matemáticas aprenderemos sobre rezones y tasas. También aprenderemos a resolver problemas usando razones equivalentes.

Llevaré a la casa tareas para practicar razones y tasas en diversos contextos.

Este es un ejemplo de la manera como aprenderemos a calcular un valor desconocido usando razones equivalentes.

🔑 MODELO Usar razones equivalentes

Resuelve $\dfrac{4}{5} = \dfrac{\blacksquare}{30}$.

PASO 1

Identifica un común denominador.

30 es múltiplo de 5, por tanto 30 es un común denominador.

PASO 2

Multiplica el numerador y el denominador de la razón de la izquierda por 6, para escribir las razones con un común denominador.

$$\frac{4 \times 6}{5 \times 6} = \frac{\blacksquare}{30}$$

PASO 3

Los denominadores son iguales, por tanto los numeradores son iguales.

$$\frac{24}{30} = \frac{\blacksquare}{30}$$

Por tanto, $\blacksquare$ = 24.

Pistas

Razones equivalentes

Puedes hallar razones equivalentes multiplicando o dividiendo ambas cantidades en una razón por el mismo número.

Por ejemplo, $\frac{3}{4} = \frac{3 \times 7}{4 \times 7} = \frac{21}{28}$, por tanto $\frac{3}{4}$ y $\frac{21}{28}$ son razones equivalentes.

Actividad

En su siguiente paseo familiar, lleve la cuenta del tiempo y la distancia. Use esto para escribir y resolver problemas que se relacionen con tasas. Por ejemplo, "Viajamos 150 millas en 3 horas. A este paso, ¿cuánto habríamos viajado en 5 horas?"

Model Ratios

COMMON CORE STANDARD CC.6.RP.1
Understand ratio concepts and use ratio reasoning to solve problems.

Write the ratio of gray counters to white counters.

1.

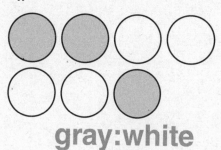

gray:white
3:4

2.

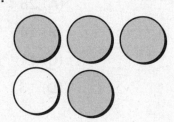

3.

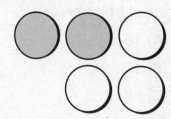

Draw a model of the ratio.

4. 5:1

5. 6:3

Use the ratio to complete the table.

6. Marc is assembling gift bags. For every 2 pencils he places in the bag, he uses 3 stickers. Complete the table to show the ratio of pencils to stickers.

Pencils	2	4	6	8
Stickers	3			

7. Singh is making a bracelet. She uses 5 blue beads for every 1 silver bead. Complete the table to show the ratio of blue beads to silver beads.

Blue	5	10		20
Silver	1		3	

Problem Solving

8. There are 4 quarts in 1 gallon. How many quarts are in 3 gallons?

9. Martin mixes 1 cup lemonade with 4 cups cranberry juice to make his favorite drink. How much cranberry juice does he need if he uses 5 cups of lemonade?

_____

Lesson Check (CC.6.RP.1)

1. Francine is making a necklace that has 1 blue bead for every 6 white beads. How many white beads will she use if she uses 11 blue beads?

- (A) 16
- (B) 17
- (C) 60
- (D) 66

2. There are 7 days in a week. How many days are in 4 weeks?

- (A) 28
- (B) 14
- (C) 11
- (D) 3

Spiral Review (CC.6.NS.4, CC.6.NS.5, CC.6.NS.6a, CC.6.NS.7d, CC.6.NS.8)

3. Of the 24 students in Greg's class, $\frac{3}{8}$ ride the bus to school. How many students ride the bus? **(Lesson 2.3)**

- (A) 6
- (B) 8
- (C) 9
- (D) 12

4. Which of the following shows a pair of opposites? **(Lesson 3.1)**

- (A) 5 and ⁻5
- (B) 8 and $\frac{1}{8}$
- (C) 0.3 and 3.0
- (D) 6 and $-\frac{1}{6}$

5. Which of the following statements is true? **(Lesson 3.6)**

- (A) $9 > |^-9|$
- (B) $|^-10| > |11|$
- (C) $3 > |^-2|$
- (D) $|^-6| > 8$

6. On a coordinate plane, the vertices of a rectangle are (⁻1, 1), (3, 1), (⁻1, ⁻4), and (3, ⁻4). What is the perimeter of the rectangle? **(Lesson 3.10)**

- (A) 9 units
- (B) 14 units
- (C) 18 units
- (D) 20 units

Ratios and Rates

COMMON CORE STANDARD CC.6.RP.1
Understand ratio concepts and use ratio
reasoning to solve problems.

Write the ratio in two different ways.

1. $\frac{4}{5}$

   4 to 5

   4:5

   _____

2. 16 to 3

   _____

3. 9:13

   _____

4. $\frac{2}{11}$

   _____

5. 7:10

   _____

6. $\frac{1}{6}$

   _____

7. 22 to 4

   _____

8. $\frac{15}{8}$

   _____

9. There are 20 light bulbs in 5 packages. Complete the table to find the rate that gives the number of light bulbs in 3 packages. Write this rate in three different ways.

Light Bulbs		8		16	20
Packages	1	2	3	4	5

_____

_____

Problem Solving REAL WORLD

10. Gemma spends 4 hours each week playing soccer and 3 hours each week practicing her clarinet. Write the ratio of hours spent practicing clarinet to hours spent playing soccer three different ways.

11. Randall bought 2 game controllers at Electronics Plus for $36. What is the unit rate for a game controller at Electronics Plus?

_____

_____

Lesson Check (CC.6.RP.1)

1. At the grocery store, Luis bought 10 bananas and 4 apples. Which of the following shows two different ways to write the ratio of apples to bananas?

- (A) 4 to 10 and 4:10
- (B) 10 to 4 and 10:4
- (C) 10:4 and $\frac{4}{10}$
- (D) 4:10 and $\frac{10}{4}$

2. A zoo spends $50 every 2 weeks on each animal it takes care of. What is the unit rate for the money spent each week for an animal?

- (A) $\frac{\$50}{2\text{ weeks}}$
- (B) $\frac{\$25}{1\text{ week}}$
- (C) $\frac{\$20}{1\text{ week}}$
- (D) $\frac{\$50}{1\text{ week}}$

Spiral Review (CC.6.RP.1, CC.6.NS.4, CC.6.NS.6c, CC.6.NS.7a)

3. Pedro has a bag of flour that weighs $\frac{9}{10}$ pound. He uses $\frac{2}{3}$ of the bag to make gravy. How many pounds of flour does Pedro use to make gravy? **(Lesson 2.4)**

- (A) $\frac{3}{5}$ pound
- (B) $\frac{1}{15}$ pound
- (C) $\frac{7}{30}$ pound
- (D) 15 pounds

4. Which of the following shows integers in order from greatest to least? **(Lesson 3.2)**

- (A) ⁻8, 0, 7
- (B) ⁻10, ⁻9, ⁻8
- (C) 0, ⁻5, ⁻4
- (D) ⁻4, ⁻5, ⁻6

5. Gina draws a map of her town on a coordinate plane. The point that represents the town's civic center has a negative x-value and a positive y-value. Which of these could be the ordered pair for the civic center? **(Lesson 3.7)**

- (A) (1, 4)
- (B) (⁻1, 4)
- (C) (1, ⁻4)
- (D) (⁻1, ⁻4)

6. Stefan draws these shapes. What is the ratio of triangles to stars? **(Lesson 4.1)**

- (A) 5:2
- (B) 2:5
- (C) 2:7
- (D) 7:2

Equivalent Ratios and Multiplication Tables

COMMON CORE STANDARD CC.6.RP.3a
Understand ratio concepts and use ratio
reasoning to solve problems.

Write two equivalent ratios.

1. Use a multiplication table to write two ratios that are equivalent to $\frac{5}{3}$.

$$\frac{5}{3} = \frac{10}{6}, \frac{15}{9}$$

2.
6		
7		

3.
3		
2		

4.
9		
2		

5.
7		
10		

6. $\frac{4}{5}$

7. $\frac{1}{9}$

8. $\frac{6}{8}$

9. $\frac{11}{1}$

_____   _____   _____   _____

Determine whether the ratios are equivalent.

10. $\frac{2}{3}$ and $\frac{5}{6}$

11. $\frac{5}{10}$ and $\frac{1}{6}$

12. $\frac{8}{3}$ and $\frac{32}{12}$

13. $\frac{9}{12}$ and $\frac{3}{4}$

_____   _____   _____   _____

Problem Solving REAL WORLD

14. Tristan uses 7 stars and 9 diamonds to make a design. Write two ratios that are equivalent to $\frac{7}{9}$.

15. There are 12 girls and 16 boys in Javier's math class. There are 26 girls and 14 boys in Javier's choir class. Is the ratio of girls to boys in the two classes equivalent? Explain.

_____   _____

Lesson Check (CC.6.RP.3a)

1. Which two ratios are equivalent to $\frac{11}{12}$?

   (A) $\frac{4}{5}$ and $\frac{12}{13}$

   (B) $\frac{22}{24}$ and $\frac{33}{36}$

   (C) $\frac{22}{23}$ and $\frac{33}{34}$

   (D) $\frac{23}{24}$ and $\frac{35}{36}$

2. A pancake recipe calls for 4 cups of flour and 3 cups of milk. Which recipe calls for flour and milk in the same ratio?

   (A) A biscuit recipe that calls for 2 cups of flour and 1 cup of milk

   (B) A scone recipe that calls for 3 cups of flour and 1 cup of milk

   (C) A muffin recipe that calls for 2 cups of flour and 1.5 cups of milk

   (D) A waffle recipe that calls for 1 cup of flour and 1 cup of milk

Spiral Review (CC.6.RP.1, CC.6.NS.1, CC.6.NS.6b, CC.6.NS.6c)

3. Della has $3\frac{5}{8}$ yards of ribbon. About how many $\frac{1}{4}$-yard-long pieces can she cut? (Lesson 2.6)

   (A) 9 pieces

   (B) 12 pieces

   (C) 14 pieces

   (D) 17 pieces

4. Which point is located at $^-1.1$? (Lesson 3.3)

   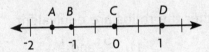

   (A) A

   (B) B

   (C) C

   (D) D

5. In which quadrant is the point $(1, \,^-7)$ located? (Lesson 3.8)

   (A) Quadrant I

   (B) Quadrant II

   (C) Quadrant III

   (D) Quadrant IV

6. There are 20 bandages in one box. How many bandages are in 5 boxes? (Lesson 4.2)

   (A) 4

   (B) 40

   (C) 10

   (D) 100

Name _____

Problem Solving • Use Tables to Compare Ratios

COMMON CORE STANDARD CC.6.RP.3a
Understand ratio concepts and use ratio reasoning to solve problems.

Read each problem and solve.

1. Sarah asked some friends about their favorite colors. She found that 4 out of 6 people prefer blue, and 8 out of 12 people prefer green. Is the ratio of friends who chose blue to the total asked equivalent to the ratio of friends who chose green to the total asked?

Blue			
Friends who chose blue	4	8	12	16
Total asked	6	12	18	24

Green			
Friends who chose green	8	16	24	32
Total asked	12	24	36	48

Yes, $\frac{4}{6}$ is equivalent to $\frac{8}{12}$.

2. Lisa and Tim make necklaces. Lisa uses 5 red beads for every 3 yellow beads. Tim uses 9 red beads for every 6 yellow beads. Is the ratio of red beads to yellow beads in Lisa's necklace equivalent to the ratio in Tim's necklace?

_____

3. Mitch scored 4 out of 5 on a quiz. Demetri scored 8 out of 10 on a quiz. Did Mitch and Demetri get equivalent scores?

_____

4. Chandra ordered 10 chicken nuggets and ate 7 of them. Raul ordered 15 chicken nuggets and ate 12 of them. Is Chandra's ratio of nuggets ordered to nuggets eaten equivalent to Raul's ratio of nuggets ordered to nuggets eaten?

_____

Lesson Check (CC.6.RP.3a)

1. Each ratio represents the number of books to the number of pencils. Which ratio is NOT equivalent to $\frac{2}{10}$?

   Ⓐ $\frac{1}{5}$

   Ⓑ $\frac{7}{15}$

   Ⓒ $\frac{4}{20}$

   Ⓓ $\frac{8}{40}$

2. Keith uses 18 cherries and 3 peaches to make a pie filling. Lena uses an equivalent ratio of cherries to peaches when she makes pie filling. Which ratio could she use?

   Ⓐ 21 cherries to 6 peaches

   Ⓑ 36 cherries to 21 peaches

   Ⓒ 26 cherries to 6 peaches

   Ⓓ 36 cherries to 6 peaches

Spiral Review (CC.6.RP.1, CC.6.NS.1, CC.6.NS.7a, CC.6.NS.8)

3. What is the quotient $\frac{3}{20} \div \frac{7}{10}$? (Lesson 2.7)

   Ⓐ $\frac{3}{14}$

   Ⓑ $\frac{30}{14}$

   Ⓒ $\frac{1}{20}$

   Ⓓ $\frac{21}{200}$

4. Which number is greater than ⁻2.25 but less than ⁻1? (Lesson 3.4)

   Ⓐ 1

   Ⓑ ⁻1.5

   Ⓒ 0

   Ⓓ ⁻2.5

5. Alicia plots a point at (0, 5) and (0, ⁻2). What is the distance between the points? (Lesson 3.9)

   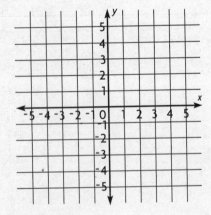

   Ⓐ 7 units

   Ⓑ 3 units

   Ⓒ ⁻3 units

   Ⓓ ⁻7 units

6. Morton sees these stickers at a craft store. What is the ratio of clouds to suns? (Lesson 4.1)

   Ⓐ 2:3

   Ⓑ 2:5

   Ⓒ 3:2

   Ⓓ 3:5

Name _____

Use Equivalent Ratios

COMMON CORE STANDARD CC.6.RP.3a

Understand ratio concepts and use ratio reasoning to solve problems.

Use equivalent ratios to find the unknown value.

1. $\dfrac{4}{10} = \dfrac{\blacksquare}{40}$

$$\dfrac{4 \times 4}{10 \times 4} = \dfrac{\blacksquare}{40}$$

$$\dfrac{16}{40} = \dfrac{\blacksquare}{40}$$

$$\blacksquare = 16$$

2. $\dfrac{3}{24} = \dfrac{33}{\blacksquare}$

_____

3. $\dfrac{7}{\blacksquare} = \dfrac{21}{27}$

_____

4. $\dfrac{\blacksquare}{9} = \dfrac{12}{54}$

_____

5. $\dfrac{3}{2} = \dfrac{12}{\blacksquare}$

6. $\dfrac{4}{5} = \dfrac{\blacksquare}{40}$

7. $\dfrac{\blacksquare}{2} = \dfrac{45}{30}$

8. $\dfrac{8}{\blacksquare} = \dfrac{16}{18}$

_____ _____ _____ _____

9. $\dfrac{45}{\blacksquare} = \dfrac{5}{6}$

10. $\dfrac{\blacksquare}{18} = \dfrac{7}{3}$

11. $\dfrac{36}{50} = \dfrac{18}{\blacksquare}$

12. $\dfrac{32}{12} = \dfrac{\blacksquare}{3}$

Problem Solving

13. Honeybees produce 7 pounds of honey for every 1 pound of beeswax they produce. Use equivalent ratios to find how many pounds of honey are produced when 25 pounds of beeswax are produced.

_____

14. A 3-ounce serving of tuna provides 21 grams of protein. Use equivalent ratios to find how many grams of protein are in 9 ounces of tuna.

_____

Lesson Check (CC.6.RP.3a)

1. Jaron paid $2.70 for 6 juice boxes. How much should Jaron expect to pay for 18 juice boxes?

   (A) $5.40

   (B) $5.70

   (C) $8.10

   (D) $48.60

2. A certain shade of orange paint is made by mixing 3 quarts of red paint with 2 quarts of yellow paint. To make more paint of the same shade, how many quarts of yellow paint should be mixed with 6 quarts of red paint?

   (A) 3 quarts

   (B) 4 quarts

   (C) 9 quarts

   (D) 12 quarts

Spiral Review (CC.6.RP.3a, CC.6.NS.1, CC.6.NS.7c, CC.6.NS.8)

3. What is the quotient $2\frac{4}{5} \div 1\frac{1}{3}$? (Lesson 2.9)

   (A) $1\frac{1}{10}$

   (B) $2\frac{1}{15}$

   (C) $2\frac{1}{10}$

   (D) $3\frac{11}{15}$

4. What is the absolute value of $^-2\frac{2}{3}$? (Lesson 3.5)

   (A) $^-2\frac{2}{3}$

   (B) $\frac{^-8}{3}$

   (C) $\frac{3}{8}$

   (D) $2\frac{2}{3}$

5. On a map, a clothing store is located at $(^-2, ^-3)$. A seafood restaurant is located 6 units to the right of the clothing store. What are the coordinates of the restaurant? (Lesson 3.10)

   (A) $(4, ^-3)$

   (B) $(^-2, 3)$

   (C) $(6, ^-3)$

   (D) $(^-8, ^-3)$

6. Marisol plans to make 9 mini-sandwiches for every 2 people attending her party. Which of the following ratios are equivalent to Marisol's ratio? (Lesson 4.3)

   (A) $\frac{20}{4}$ and $\frac{30}{8}$

   (B) $\frac{10}{3}$ and $\frac{11}{4}$

   (C) $\frac{27}{6}$ and $\frac{45}{10}$

   (D) $\frac{18}{6}$ and $\frac{36}{12}$

Find Unit Rates

COMMON CORE STANDARD CC.6.RP.2

Understand ratio concepts and use ratio reasoning to solve problems.

Write the rate as a fraction. Then find the unit rate.

1. A wheel rotates through 1,800° in 5 revolutions.

$$\frac{1{,}800°}{5 \text{ revolutions}}$$

$$\frac{1{,}800° \div 5}{5 \text{ revolutions} \div 5} = \frac{360°}{1 \text{ revolution}}$$

2. There are 312 cards in 6 decks of playing cards.

_____

3. Bana ran 18.6 miles of a marathon in 3 hours.

_____

4. Cameron paid $30.16 for 8 pounds of almonds.

_____

Compare unit rates.

5. An online game company offers a package that includes 2 games for $11.98. They also offer a package that includes 5 games for $24.95. Which package is a better deal?

_____

6. At a track meet, Samma finished the 200-meter race in 25.98 seconds. Tom finished the 100-meter race in 12.54 seconds. Which runner ran at a faster average rate?

_____

7. Elmer Elementary School has 576 students and 24 teachers. Savoy Elementary School has 638 students and 29 teachers. Which school has the lower unit rate of students per teacher?

_____

8. One cell phone company offers 500 minutes of talk time for $49.99. Another company offers 480 minutes for $44.99. Which company offers the better deal?

_____

Problem Solving  REAL WORLD

9. Sylvio's flight is scheduled to travel 1,792 miles in 3.5 hours. At what average rate will the plane have to travel to complete the trip on time?

_____

10. Rachel bought 2 pounds of apples and 3 pounds of peaches for a total of $10.45. The apples and peaches cost the same amount per pound. What was the unit rate?

_____

Lesson Check (CC.6.RP.2)

1. Cran-Soy trail mix costs $2.99 for 5 ounces, Raisin-Nuts mix costs $3.41 for 7 ounces, Lots of Cashews mix costs $7.04 for 8 ounces, and Nuts for You mix costs $2.40 for 6 ounces. List the trail mix brands in order from the best deal to the worst deal.

Ⓐ Cran-Soy, Lots of Cashews, Raisin-Nuts, Nuts for You

Ⓑ Nuts for You, Raisin-Nuts, Cran-Soy, Lots of Cashews

Ⓒ Raisin-Nuts, Nuts for You, Cran-Soy, Lots of Cashews

Ⓓ Nuts for You, Lots of Cashews, Cran-Soy, Raisin-Nuts

2. Aaron's heart beats 166 times in 120 seconds. Callie's heart beats 88 times in 60 seconds. Emma's heart beats 48 times in 30 seconds. Galen's heart beats 22 times in 15 seconds. Which two students' heart rates are equivalent?

Ⓐ Aaron and Callie

Ⓑ Aaron and Emma

Ⓒ Callie and Galen

Ⓓ Emma and Galen

Spiral Review (CC.6.RP.1, CC.6.RP.3a, CC.6.NS.1, CC.6.NS.7d)

3. Courtlynn combines $\frac{7}{8}$ cup sour cream with $\frac{1}{2}$ cup cream cheese. She then divides the mixture between 2 bowls. How much mixture does Courtlynn put in each bowl? (Lesson 2.10)

Ⓐ $\frac{3}{16}$ cup

Ⓑ $\frac{7}{32}$ cup

Ⓒ $\frac{7}{8}$ cup

Ⓓ $\frac{11}{16}$ cup

4. Which of the following statements is NOT true? (Lesson 3.6)

Ⓐ $\left|\frac{-2}{3}\right| > \frac{-5}{6}$

Ⓑ $|{-1}| > 1\frac{1}{2}$

Ⓒ $0 < \left|{-2}\frac{5}{6}\right|$

Ⓓ $\left|\frac{-7}{10}\right| < 2$

5. There are 18 tires on one truck. How many tires are on 3 trucks of the same type? (Lesson 4.2)

Ⓐ 54 tires

Ⓑ 21 tires

Ⓒ 15 tires

Ⓓ 6 tires

6. Which of the following ratios is equivalent to $\frac{5}{6}$? (Lesson 4.4)

Ⓐ $\frac{4}{5}$

Ⓑ $\frac{6}{7}$

Ⓒ $\frac{10}{6}$

Ⓓ $\frac{15}{18}$

Use Unit Rates

COMMON CORE STANDARD CC.6.RP.3b
Understand ratio concepts and use ratio
reasoning to solve problems.

Use a unit rate to find the unknown value.

1. $\dfrac{34}{17} = \dfrac{\blacksquare}{7}$

$$\dfrac{34 \div 17}{17 \div 17} = \dfrac{\blacksquare}{7}$$

$$\dfrac{2}{1} = \dfrac{\blacksquare}{7}$$

$$\dfrac{2 \times 7}{1 \times 7} = \dfrac{\blacksquare}{7}$$

$$\dfrac{14}{7} = \dfrac{\blacksquare}{7}$$

$$\blacksquare = 14$$

2. $\dfrac{16}{32} = \dfrac{\blacksquare}{14}$

3. $\dfrac{18}{\blacksquare} = \dfrac{21}{7}$

4. $\dfrac{\blacksquare}{16} = \dfrac{3}{12}$

_____   _____   _____

Draw a bar model to find the unknown value.

5. $\dfrac{15}{45} = \dfrac{6}{\blacksquare}$

6. $\dfrac{3}{6} = \dfrac{\blacksquare}{7}$

_____   _____

7. $\dfrac{\blacksquare}{6} = \dfrac{6}{9}$

8. $\dfrac{7}{\blacksquare} = \dfrac{2}{10}$

_____   _____

Problem Solving  REAL WORLD

9. To stay properly hydrated, a person should drink 32 fluid ounces of water for every 60 minutes of exercise. How much water should Damon drink if he rides his bike for 135 minutes?

10. Lillianne made 6 out of every 10 baskets she attempted during basketball practice. If she attempted to make 25 baskets, how many did she make?

_____   _____

Lesson Check (CC.6.RP.3b)

1. Randi's school requires that there are 2 adult chaperones for every 18 students when the students go on a field trip to the museum. If there are 99 students going to the museum, how many adult chaperones are needed?

   (A) 9 chaperones

   (B) 11 chaperones

   (C) 18 chaperones

   (D) 99 chaperones

2. Landry's neighbor pledged $5.00 for every 2 miles he swims in a charity swim-a-thon. If Landry swims 3 miles, how much money will his neighbor donate?

   (A) $15.00

   (B) $12.50

   (C) $7.50

   (D) $6.00

Spiral Review (CC.6.RP.2, CC.6.RP.3a, CC.6.NS.6a, CC.6.NS.6c)

3. Which situation could be represented by ⁻8? (Lesson 3.1)

   (A) Megan made $8 babysitting.

   (B) Kyle scored 8 points.

   (C) The temperature increased by 8°F.

   (D) Carla spent $8.

4. What are the coordinates of G? (Lesson 3.7)

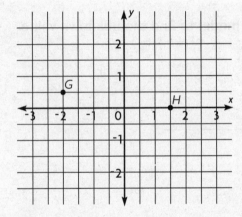

   (A) (⁻2, 0.5)   (C) (⁻4, 0.5)

   (B) (⁻4, 1)   (D) (⁻2, 1)

5. Gina bought 6 containers of yogurt for $4. How many containers of yogurt could Gina buy for $12? (Lesson 4.5)

   (A) 2

   (B) 8

   (C) 14

   (D) 18

6. A bottle containing 64 fluid ounces of juice costs $3.84. What is the unit rate? (Lesson 4.6)

   (A) $0.05 for 1 fluid ounce

   (B) $0.06 for 1 fluid ounce

   (C) $1.92 for 32 fluid ounces

   (D) $3.84 for 64 fluid ounces

© Houghton Mifflin Harcourt Publishing Company

Equivalent Ratios and Graphs

COMMON CORE STANDARD CC.6.RP.3a

Understand ratio concepts and use ratio reasoning to solve problems.

Christie makes bracelets. She uses 8 charms for each bracelet. Use this information for 1–4.

1. Complete the table of equivalent ratios for the first 5 bracelets.

Charms	8	16	24	32	40
Bracelets	1	2	3	4	5

2. Write ordered pairs, letting the *x*-coordinate represent the number of bracelets and the *y*-coordinate represent the number of charms.

   (1, __8__), (2, __16__), (_____ , _____),

   (_____ , _____), (_____ , _____)

4. What does the point (1, 8) represent on the graph?

   _____

   _____

3. Use the ordered pairs to graph the charms and bracelets.

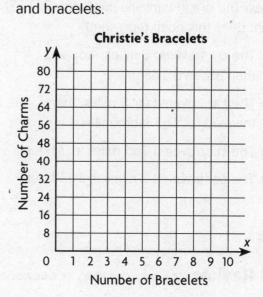

Christie's Bracelets

The graph shows the number of granola bars that are in various numbers of boxes of Crunch N Go. Use the graph for 5–6.

5. Complete the table of equivalent ratios.

Bars				
Boxes	1	2	3	4

6. Find the unit rate of granola bars per box.

   _____

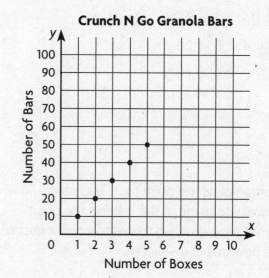

Crunch N Go Granola Bars

Problem Solving REAL WORLD

7. Look at the graph for Christie's Bracelets. How many charms are needed for 7 bracelets?

   _____

8. Look at the graph for Crunch N Go Granola Bars. Stefan needs to buy 90 granola bars. How many boxes must he buy?

   _____

Lesson Check (CC.6.RP.3a)

1. A graph shows the distance a car traveled over time. The *x*-axis represents time in hours, and the *y*-axis represents distance in miles. The graph contains the point (3, 165). What does this point represent?

   Ⓐ The car traveled 3 miles, stopped, then traveled 165 miles.

   Ⓑ The car traveled for 3 miles, then traveled for 165 more miles.

   Ⓒ The car traveled 165 miles in 3 hours.

   Ⓓ The car traveled 3 miles in 165 hours.

2. Maura charges $11 per hour to babysit. She makes a graph comparing the amount she charges (the *y*-coordinate) to the time she babysits (the *x*-coordinate). Which ordered pair is NOT on the graph?

   Ⓐ (3, 33)

   Ⓑ (11, 1)

   Ⓒ (5, 55)

   Ⓓ (2, 22)

Spiral Review (CC.6.RP.3b, CC.6.NS.6b, CC.6.NS.7a, CC.6.NS.7c)

3. Which of the following shows integers in order from least to greatest? (Lesson 3.2)

   Ⓐ $^-5 < {}^-6 < {}^-7$

   Ⓑ $0 < {}^-4 < 3$

   Ⓒ $^-4 < 0 < 2$

   Ⓓ $^-2 < 0 < {}^-6$

4. What numbers can be used in place of the ■ to make the statement true? (Lesson 3.5)

   $$|■| = \frac{8}{9}$$

   Ⓐ $\frac{8}{9}$ and $\frac{^-8}{9}$

   Ⓑ $\frac{8}{9}$ and $\frac{9}{8}$

   Ⓒ $\frac{8}{9}$ and $1\frac{8}{9}$

   Ⓓ $\frac{^-8}{9}$ and $\frac{^-9}{8}$

5. Morgan plots the point (4, ⁻7) on a coordinate plane. If she reflects the point across the *y*-axis, what are the coordinates of the new point? (Lesson 3.8)

   Ⓐ (4, 7)

   Ⓑ (⁻4, 7)

   Ⓒ (⁻4, ⁻7)

   Ⓓ (4, ⁻7)

6. Jonathan drove 220 miles in 4 hours. Assuming he drives at the same rate, how far will he travel in 7 hours? (Lesson 4.7)

   Ⓐ 165 miles

   Ⓑ 223 miles

   Ⓒ 385 miles

   Ⓓ 440 miles

Name _____

COMMON CORE STANDARDS CC.6.RP.1, CC.6.RP.2,
CC.6.RP.3a, CC.6.RP.3b

Chapter 4 Extra Practice

Lessons 4.1 and 4.2

Write the ratio of white counters to gray counters in
two different ways.

1.

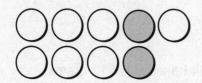

_____

2.

_____

3.

_____

Lesson 4.3

Write two equivalent ratios.

4.

1		
3		

5.

5		
6		

6.

8		
5		

Determine whether the ratios are equivalent.

7. $\frac{3}{4}$ and $\frac{6}{7}$

8. $\frac{12}{5}$ and $\frac{36}{15}$

9. $\frac{24}{54}$ and $\frac{4}{9}$

_____ _____ _____

Lesson 4.4

Solve.

10. The table shows the number of free throws that several people
attempted when playing basketball. Which two people have
equivalent ratios of successes to attempts? Explain how
you know.

Free Throws Attempted and Made	
Person	**Successes**
Corey	3 out of 5
Tess	8 out of 10
Rodney	6 out of 10
Cherie	6 out of 8

_____

_____

_____

© Houghton Mifflin Harcourt Publishing Company

Lesson 4.5

Use equivalent ratios to find the unknown value.

11. $\dfrac{16}{\blacksquare} = \dfrac{4}{5}$

12. $\dfrac{7}{10} = \dfrac{\blacksquare}{30}$

13. $\dfrac{\blacksquare}{18} = \dfrac{8}{3}$

14. $\dfrac{25}{4} = \dfrac{75}{\blacksquare}$

_____   _____   _____   _____

Lesson 4.6

Write the rate as a fraction. Then find the unit rate.

15. A jar containing 14 ounces of jelly costs $3.22.

16. The mass of 4 bananas is 512 grams.

_____   _____

Lesson 4.7

Use equivalent ratios to solve.

17. Ms. Brown biked 35 miles in 2.5 hours. How many miles could she bike in 3 hours at the same rate?

18. There are 180 calories in 4 cheese-flavored rice cakes. Pete eats 3 rice cakes. How many calories does he consume?

_____   _____

Lesson 4.8

The graph shows the money that Charese earns mowing lawns. Use the graph for 19 and 20.

19. Complete the table of equivalent ratios.

Earnings ($)				
Lawns	1	2	3	4

20. What does the point (1, 30) represent?

_____

_____

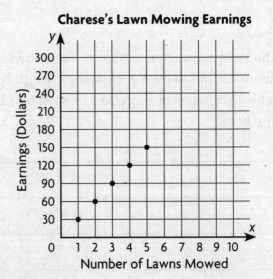

Charese's Lawn Mowing Earnings

School-Home Letter

Dear Family,

Throughout the next few weeks, our math class will be learning about percents. We will also be learning how to solve problems using percents written as ratios.

You can expect to see homework that provides practice with percents, fractions, and decimals in a variety of contexts.

Here is a sample of how your child was taught to solve a percent problem.

Vocabulary

equivalent ratios Ratios that name the same comparison.

percent A ratio, or rate, that compares a number to 100.

rate A ratio that compares two quantities that have different units of measure.

ratio A comparison of two quantities by division.

🔑 MODEL Find the whole.

42 is 30% of what number?

STEP 1

Write the relationship among the percent, part, and whole. The percent is written as a ratio.

$$\text{percent} = \frac{\text{part}}{\text{whole}}$$

$$\frac{30}{100} = \frac{42}{\blacksquare}$$

STEP 2

Simplify the known ratio.

$$\frac{30 \div 10}{100 \div 10} = \frac{42}{\blacksquare}$$

$$\frac{3}{10} = \frac{42}{\blacksquare}$$

STEP 3

Write an equivalent ratio.

$$\frac{3 \times 14}{10 \times 14} = \frac{42}{\blacksquare}$$

$$\frac{42}{140} = \frac{42}{\blacksquare}$$

So, 42 is 30% of 140.

Tips

Equivalent Ratios

You can find equivalent ratios by multiplying or dividing both quantities in a ratio by the same number.

For example,
$\frac{3}{4} = \frac{3 \times 7}{4 \times 7} = \frac{21}{28}$, so $\frac{3}{4}$ and $\frac{21}{28}$ are equivalent ratios.

Activity

Gather loose change from around the house. Count the number of coins (not the value). Ask, "The number of coins is 30% of what number?" Find the answer and then try different percents. See who can get a whole number as their answer.

Capítulo 5

Carta para la casa

Vocabulario

razones equivalentes Razones que nombran la misma comparación.

porcentaje Una razón, o tasa, que compara un número con 100.

tasa Una razón que compara dos cantidades que tienen unidades de medida distintas.

razón Una comparación entre dos cantidades hecha con una división.

Querida familia,

Durante las próximas semanas, en la clase de matemáticas aprenderemos sobre porcentajes. También aprenderemos a resolver problemas usando porcentaje escritos como razones.

Llevaré a la casa tareas para practicar porcentajes, fracciones y decimales en diversos contextos.

Este es un ejemplo de la manera como aprendimos a resolver un problema de porcentajes.

🔑 MODELO Hallar el entero.

¿42 es el 30% de qué número?

PASO 1

Escribe la relación entre porcentaje, la parte y el entero.

El porcentaje se escribe como una razón.

$$porcentaje = \frac{parte}{entero}$$

$$\frac{30}{100} = \frac{42}{\blacksquare}$$

PASO 2

Simplifica la razón conocida.

$$\frac{30 \div 10}{100 \div 10} = \frac{42}{\blacksquare}$$

$$\frac{3}{10} = \frac{42}{\blacksquare}$$

PASO 3

Escribe una razón equivalente.

$$\frac{3 \times 14}{10 \times 14} = \frac{42}{\blacksquare}$$

$$\frac{42}{140} = \frac{42}{\blacksquare}$$

Por lo tanto, 42 es el 30% de 140.

Pistas

Razones equivalentes

Puedes hallar razones equivalentes multiplicando o dividiendo ambas cantidades en una razón entre el mismo número.

Por ejemplo,
$\frac{3}{4} = \frac{3 \times 7}{4 \times 7} = \frac{21}{28}$, por lo tanto $\frac{3}{4}$ y $\frac{21}{28}$ son razones equivalentes.

Actividad

Reúna cambio que encuentre por la casa. Cuente el número de monedas (no su valor). Pregunte: "¿El número de monedas es el 30% de qué número?". Encuentren la respuesta y después practiquen con diferentes porcentajes. Miren quién puede obtener un número entero como respuesta.

Model Percents

COMMON CORE STANDARD CC.6.RP.3c
Understand ratio concepts and use ratio reasoning to solve problems.

Write a ratio and a percent to represent the shaded part.

1.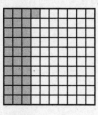

2.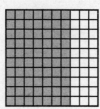

3.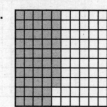

ratio: $\dfrac{31}{100}$ percent: **31%**

ratio: _____ percent: _____

ratio: _____ percent: _____

Model the percent and write it as a ratio.

4. 97%

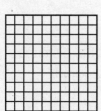

ratio: _____

5. 24%

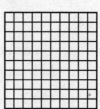

ratio: _____

6. 50%

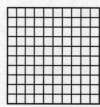

ratio: _____

Problem Solving

The table shows the pen colors sold at the school supply store one week. Write the ratio comparing the number of the given color sold to the total number of pens sold. Then shade the grid.

Pens Sold	
Color	**Number**
Blue	36
Black	49
Red	15

7. Black

_____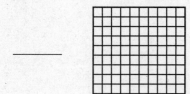

8. Not blue

_____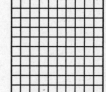

Lesson Check (CC.6.RP.3c)

1. Which percent represents the shaded part?

- (A) 37%
- (B) 40%
- (C) 53%
- (D) 63%

2. Which ratio represents the shaded part?

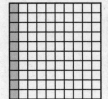

- (A) $\frac{1}{100}$
- (B) $\frac{10}{100}$
- (C) $\frac{90}{100}$
- (D) $\frac{99}{100}$

Spiral Review (CC.6.RP.3a, CC.6.NS.6a, CC.6.NS.6c, CC.6.NS.8)

3. Which number is less than $^-2\frac{4}{5}$ but greater than $^-3\frac{1}{5}$? (Lesson 3.3)

- (A) $^-3\frac{1}{2}$
- (B) $^-3\frac{2}{3}$
- (C) $^-2\frac{1}{2}$
- (D) $^-2\frac{7}{8}$

4. On a coordinate grid, what is the distance between (2, 4) and (2, $^-3$)? (Lesson 3.9)

- (A) 7 units
- (B) 5 units
- (C) 1 unit
- (D) 0 units

5. Each week, Diana spends 4 hours playing soccer and 6 hours babysitting. Which ratio is equivalent to the ratio of the time Diana spends playing soccer to the time she spends babysitting? (Lesson 4.3)

- (A) $\frac{1}{2}$
- (B) $\frac{6}{10}$
- (C) $\frac{8}{12}$
- (D) $\frac{15}{18}$

6. Antwone earns a steady rate of money mowing lawns. The points (1, 25) and (5, 125) appear on a graph of the amount earned over time. Which is another point that will appear on the graph? (Lesson 4.8)

- (A) (2, 26)
- (B) (2, 75)
- (C) (3, 75)
- (D) (3, 100)

Name _____

Write Percents as Fractions and Decimals

COMMON CORE STANDARD CC.6.RP.3c
Understand ratio concepts and use ratio reasoning to solve problems.

Write the percent as a fraction or mixed number.

1. 44%

$$44\% = \frac{44}{100}$$
$$= \frac{11}{25}$$

2. 32%

_____

3. 116%

_____

4. 250%

_____

5. 0.3%

_____

6. 0.4%

_____

7. 1.5%

_____

8. 12.5%

_____

Write the percent as a decimal.

9. 63%

_____

10. 90%

_____

11. 110%

_____

12. 8%

_____

13. 42.15%

_____

14. 2.5%

_____

15. 0.1%

_____

16. 22.1%

_____

Problem Solving  REAL WORLD

17. An online bookstore sells 0.8% of its books to foreign customers. What fraction of the books are sold to foreign customers?

_____

18. In Mr. Klein's class, 40% of the students are boys. What decimal represents the portion of the students that are girls?

_____

Lesson Check (CC.6.RP.3c)

1. The enrollment at Sonya's school this year is 109% of last year's enrollment. What decimal represents this year's enrollment compared to last year's?

    (A)   0.109

    (B)   1.09

    (C)   10.9

    (D) 109.0

2. An artist's paint set contains 30% watercolors and 25% acrylics. What fraction represents the portion of the paints that are watercolors or acrylics?

    (A) $\frac{1}{4}$

    (B) $\frac{3}{10}$

    (C) $\frac{11}{20}$

    (D) $\frac{9}{11}$

Spiral Review (CC.6.RP.3a, CC.6.RP.3c, CC.6.NS.7a, CC.6.NS.7b, CC.6.NS.8)

3. Which of the following statements is true?

    (Lesson 3.4)

    (A) $^-7.4 > {}^-7.39$

    (B) $^-5.25 > {}^-5.3$

    (C) $4.5 < {}^-6$

    (D) $0 < {}^-6.32$

4. On a coordinate plane, the vertices of a rectangle are $(2, 4)$, $(2, {}^-1)$, $({}^-5, {}^-1)$, and $({}^-5, 4)$. What is the perimeter of the rectangle? (Lesson 3.10)

    (A) 11 units

    (B) 12 units

    (C) 16 units

    (D) 24 units

5. The table below shows the ratio of width to length, in feet, for different playgrounds. Which playgrounds have equivalent ratios? (Lesson 4.4)

	A	B	C	D
Width	12	15	20	16.5
Length	20	22.5	25	27.5

    (A) A and C

    (B) A and D

    (C) B and D

    (D) C and D

6. What percent represents the shaded part?

    (Lesson 5.1)

    (A) 15%

    (B) 25%

    (C) 75%

    (D) 85%

Write Fractions and Decimals as Percents

COMMON CORE STANDARD CC.6.RP.3c
Understand ratio concepts and use ratio reasoning to solve problems.

Write the fraction or decimal as a percent.

1. $\frac{7}{20}$

$$\frac{7}{20} = \frac{7 \times 5}{20 \times 5}$$
$$= \frac{35}{100} = 35\%$$

2. $\frac{3}{50}$

3. $\frac{1}{25}$

4. $\frac{5}{5}$

5. 0.622

6. 0.303

7. 0.06

8. 2.45

Write the number in two other forms (fraction, decimal, or percent).

9. $\frac{19}{20}$

10. $\frac{9}{16}$

11. 0.4

12. 0.22

Problem Solving REAL WORLD

13. According to the U.S. Census Bureau, $\frac{3}{25}$ of all adults in the United States visited a zoo in 2007. What percent of all adults in the United States visited a zoo in 2007?

14. A bag contains red and blue marbles. Given that $\frac{17}{20}$ of the marbles are red, what percent of the marbles are blue?

Lesson Check (CC.6.RP.3c)

1. The portion of shoppers at a supermarket who pay by credit card is 0.36. What percent of shoppers at the supermarket do not pay by credit card?

   (A) 0.64%

   (B) 6.4%

   (C) 64%

   (D) 640%

2. About $\frac{23}{40}$ of a lawn is planted with Kentucky bluegrass. Which percent is closest to the percent of the lawn that is planted with Kentucky bluegrass?

   (A) 40%

   (B) 50%

   (C) 60%

   (D) 70%

Spiral Review (CC.6.RP.1, CC.6.RP.2, CC.6.RP.3a, CC.6.RP.3c)

3. A basket contains 6 peaches and 8 plums. What is the ratio of peaches to total pieces of fruit? (Lesson 4.2)

   (A) 6 to 8

   (B) 8 to 6

   (C) 6 to 14

   (D) 8 to 14

4. It takes 8 minutes for 3 cars to move through a car wash. At the same rate, how many cars can move through the car wash in 24 minutes? (Lesson 4.5)

   (A) 6 cars

   (B) 9 cars

   (C) 12 cars

   (D) 48 cars

5. Which box of cereal is sold at a unit rate of $0.15 per ounce? (Lesson 4.6)

   (A) Box A: 16 ounces for $1.92

   (B) Box B: 14 ounces for $2.10

   (C) Box C: 12 ounces for $1.68

   (D) Box D: 11 ounces for $2.09

6. A model railroad kit contains curved tracks and straight tracks. Given that 35% of the tracks are curved, what fraction of the tracks are straight? (Lesson 5.2)

   (A) $\frac{7}{20}$

   (B) $\frac{2}{5}$

   (C) $\frac{3}{5}$

   (D) $\frac{13}{20}$

Percent of a Quantity

COMMON CORE STANDARD CC.6.RP.3c
Understand ratio concepts and use ratio reasoning to
solve problems.

Find the percent of the quantity.

1. 60% of 140

$$60\% = \frac{60}{100}$$

$$\frac{60}{100} \times 140$$

$$= 84$$

2. 55% of 600

3. 4% of 50

4. 50% of 82

_____

_____

_____

5. 10% of 2,350

6. 80% of 40

7. 160% of 30

8. 250% of 2

_____

_____

_____

_____

9. 105% of 260

10. 0.5% of 12

11. 40% of 16.5

12. 75% of 8.4

_____

_____

_____

_____

Problem Solving  REAL WORLD

13. The recommended daily amount of
vitamin C for children 9 to 13 years old is
45 mg. A serving of a juice drink contains
60% of the recommended amount. How much
vitamin C does the juice drink contain?

14. During a 60-minute television program,
25% of the time is used for commercials and
5% of the time is used for the opening and
closing credits. How many minutes remain for
the program itself?

_____

_____

Lesson Check (CC.6.RP.3c)

1. A store has a display case with cherry, peach, and grape fruit chews. There are 160 fruit chews in the display case. Given that 25% of the fruit chews are cherry and 40% are peach, how many grape fruit chews are in the display case?

- (A) 16
- (B) 56
- (C) 65
- (D) 104

2. Kelly has a ribbon that is 60 inches long. She cuts off 40% of the ribbon for an art project. While working on the project, she decides she only needs 75% of the piece she cut off. How much of the ribbon does Kelly end up using in her project?

- (A) 6 inches
- (B) 9 inches
- (C) 18 inches
- (D) 42 inches

Spiral Review (CC.6.RP.3b, CC.6.RP.3c, CC.6.NS.7d)

3. Which of the following statements is NOT true? (Lesson 3.6)

- (A) $|{}^-12| > 11$
- (B) $|0| > {}^-4$
- (C) $|10| < |{}^-20|$
- (D) $6 < |{}^-3|$

4. Miyuki can type 135 words in 3 minutes. How many words can she expect to type in 8 minutes? (Lesson 4.7)

- (A) 270
- (B) 315
- (C) 360
- (D) 405

5. Which percent represents the model? (Lesson 5.1)

- (A) 37%
- (B) 40%
- (C) 63%
- (D) 70%

6. About $\frac{2}{3}$ of the students at Roosevelt Elementary School live within one mile of the school. Which percent is closest to the percent of students who live within one mile of the school? (Lesson 5.3)

- (A) 40%
- (B) 50%
- (C) 60%
- (D) 70%

Problem Solving • Percents

COMMON CORE STANDARD CC.6.RP.3c
Understand ratio concepts and use ratio reasoning to
solve problems.

Read each problem and solve.

1. On Saturday, a souvenir shop had
   125 customers. Sixty-four percent of
   the customers paid with a credit card.
   The other customers paid with cash.
   How many customers paid with cash?

   $$1\% \text{ of } 125 = \frac{125}{100} = 1.25$$

   $$64\% \text{ of } 125 = 64 \times 1.25 = 80$$

   $$125 - 80 = 45 \text{ customers}$$

2. A carpenter has a wooden stick that is
   84 centimeters long. She cuts off 25% from the end
   of the stick. Then she cuts the remaining stick into
   6 equal pieces. What is the length of each piece?

   _____

3. Mike has $136 to spend at the amusement park.
   He spends 25% of that money on his ticket into the
   park. How much does Mike have left to spend?

   _____

4. A car dealership has 240 cars in the parking lot
   and 17.5% of them are red. Of the other 6 colors in
   the lot, each color has the same number of cars. If
   one of the colors is black, how many black cars are
   in the lot?

   _____

5. The utilities bill for the Millers' home in April was
   $132. Forty-two percent of the bill was for gas,
   and the rest was for electricity. How much did the
   Millers pay for gas, and how much did they pay for
   electricity?

   _____

6. Andy's total bill for lunch is $20. The cost of the
   drink is 15% of the total bill and the rest is the cost
   of the food. What percent of the total bill did Andy's
   food cost? What was the cost of his food?

   _____

Lesson Check (CC.6.RP.3c)

1. Milo has a collection of DVDs. Out of 45 DVDs, 40% are comedies and the remaining are action-adventures. How many action-adventure DVDs does Milo own?

   (A) 16 DVDs

   (B) 18 DVDs

   (C) 24 DVDs

   (D) 27 DVDs

2. Andrea and her partner are writing a 12-page science report. They completed 25% of the report in class and 50% of the remaining pages after school. How many pages do Andrea and her partner still have to write?

   (A) 3.5 pages

   (B) 4.5 pages

   (C) 6 pages

   (D) 9 pages

Spiral Review (CC.6.RP.3a, CC.6.RP.3c, CC.6.NS.6c , CC.6.NS.7c)

3. What is the absolute value of $-\frac{4}{25}$? (Lesson 3.5)

   (A) $\frac{-25}{4}$

   (B) $-\frac{4}{25}$

   (C) $\frac{25}{4}$

   (D) $\frac{4}{25}$

4. Ricardo graphed a point by starting at the origin and moving 5 units to the left. Then he moved up 2 units. What is the ordered pair for the point he graphed? (Lesson 3.7)

   (A) (5, 2)

   (B) (5, ⁻2)

   (C) (⁻5, 2)

   (D) (⁻5, ⁻2)

5. The population of birds in a sanctuary increases at a steady rate. The graph of the population over time has the points (1, 105) and (3, 315). What is another point on the graph? (Lesson 4.8)

   (A) (2, 106)

   (B) (3, 110)

   (C) (4, 520)

   (D) (5, 525)

6. Alicia's MP3 player contains 1,260 songs. Given that 35% of the songs are rock songs and 20% of the songs are rap songs, how many of the songs are other types of songs? (Lesson 5.4)

   (A) 252

   (B) 441

   (C) 567

   (D) 693

Find the Whole From a Percent

COMMON CORE STANDARD CC.6.RP.3c
Understand ratio concepts and use ratio reasoning to solve problems.

Find the unknown value.

1. 9 is 15% of ____60____

$$\frac{15}{100} = \frac{9}{\boxed{}}$$

$$\frac{15 \div 5}{100 \div 5} = \frac{3 \times 3}{20 \times 3} = \frac{9}{60}$$

2. 54 is 75% of _____

3. 12 is 2% of _____

4. 18 is 50% of _____

5. 16 is 40% of _____

6. 56 is 28% of _____

7. 5 is 10% of _____

8. 24 is 16% of _____

9. 15 is 25% of _____

10. 11 is 44% of _____

11. 19 is 95% of _____

12. 10 is 20% of _____

Problem Solving REAL WORLD

13. Michaela is hiking on a weekend camping trip. She has walked 6 miles so far. This is 30% of the total distance. What is the total number of miles she will walk?

14. A customer placed an order with a bakery for cupcakes. The baker has completed 37.5% of the order after baking 81 cupcakes. How many cupcakes did the customer order?

_____

_____

Lesson Check (CC.6.RP.3c)

1. Kareem saves his coins in a jar. 30% of the coins are pennies. If there are 24 pennies in the jar, how many coins does Kareem have?

(A) 8

(B) 54

(C) 72

(D) 80

2. A guitar shop has 19 acoustic guitars on display. This is 76% of the total number of guitars. What is the total number of guitars the shop is selling?

(A) 4

(B) 25

(C) 43

(D) 57

Spiral Review (CC.6.RP.3a, CC.6.RP.3c, CC.6.NS.6b)

3. On a coordinate grid, which point is located in Quadrant II? (Lesson 3.8)

(A) (5, ⁻4)

(B) (⁻5, ⁻4)

(C) (⁻5, 4)

(D) (5, 4)

4. A box contains 16 cherry fruit chews, 15 peach fruit chews, and 12 plum fruit chews. Which two flavors are in the ratio 5 to 4? (Lesson 4.3)

(A) cherry to peach

(B) peach to plum

(C) cherry to plum

(D) plum to peach

5. During basketball season, Marisol made $\frac{19}{25}$ of her free throws. What percent of her free throws did Marisol make? (Lesson 5.2)

(A) 76%

(B) 68%

(C) 31%

(D) 19%

6. Landon is entering the science fair. He has a budget of $115. He has spent 20% of the money on new materials. How much does Landon have left to spend? (Lesson 5.5)

(A) $18

(B) $23

(C) $92

(D) $97

Chapter 5 Extra Practice

Lesson 5.1

Write a ratio and a percent to represent the shaded part.

1.

_____

2.

_____

3.

_____

Model the percent.

4. 23%
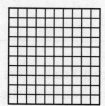

5. 80%
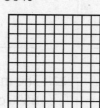

6. 56%
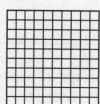

Lesson 5.2

Write the percent as a fraction and as a decimal.

7. 19%

8. 3%

9. 102%

10. 0.5%

_____ _____ _____ _____

Lesson 5.3

Write the fraction or decimal as a percent.

11. 0.08

_____

12. 0.4

_____

13. $\frac{2}{5}$

_____

14. $\frac{19}{20}$

_____

Lessons 5.4 and 5.5

Find the percent of the quantity.

15. 40% of 50

_____

16. 2% of 250

_____

17. 75% of 1,800

_____

18. 120% of 40

_____

19. A cafeteria sold 80 frozen yogurts on Monday, and 55% of these were peach yogurt. How many peach yogurts were sold on Monday?

_____

20. Jamal has 1,240 songs on his MP3 player, and 40% of the songs are rock songs. How many of the songs are NOT rock songs?

_____

21. Rianda bought 32 apples. She set aside 25% to eat and divided the rest equally among 6 pies. How many apples are in each pie?

_____

22. The math class has a set of 40 calculators, and 85% of the calculators have working batteries. How many calculators need new batteries?

_____

Lesson 5.6

Find the unknown value.

23. 63 is 90% of ?

_____

24. 648 is 54% of ?

_____

25. 27 is 50% of ?

_____

26. 6 is 3% of ?

_____

© Houghton Mifflin Harcourt Publishing Company

School-Home Letter

© Houghton Mifflin Harcourt Publishing Company

Vocabulary

capacity The amount a container can hold when filled.

conversion factor A rate in which the two quantities are equivalent, but use different units.

Dear Family,

Throughout the next few weeks, our math class will be learning about units of measure. We will also be learning how to convert between units of measure.

You can expect to see homework that includes customary and metric units of measure for length, capacity, mass, and weight.

Here is a sample of how your child was taught to convert customary units of length.

🔑 MODEL   Convert Units of Length

Convert 60 inches to feet.

STEP 1

Choose a conversion factor.

1 foot = 12 inches

Use the rate $\frac{1\,ft}{12\,in.}$ as the conversion factor.

STEP 2

Multiply 60 inches by the conversion factor.

$60\text{ in.} \times \dfrac{1\text{ ft}}{12\text{ in.}}$

$= \dfrac{\overset{5}{\cancel{60}\text{ in.}}}{1} \times \dfrac{1\text{ ft}}{\underset{1}{\cancel{12}\text{ in.}}}$

$= 5\text{ ft}$

Tips

Conversion Factors

Because a conversion factor is equal to 1, you can convert from one unit to another by multiplying by an appropriate conversion factor.

Activity

Use beverage containers in your home to practice converting units of capacity. For example, orange juice is often sold in cartons that contain 64 fluid ounces. Work together to determine the number of one-cup servings that can be poured from such a container.

Capítulo 6

Carta para la casa

Querida familia,

Durante las próximas semanas, en la clase de matemáticas aprenderemos sobre unidades de medida. También aprenderemos a convertir unidades de medida.

Llevaré a la casa tareas para practicar unidades de medida métricas y usuales para longitud, capacidad, masa y peso.

Este es un ejemplo de la manera como aprenderemos convertir unidades usuales de longitud.

🔑 MODELO Convertir unidades de longitud

Convierte 60 pulgadas a pies

PASO 1

Elige un factor de conversión.

1 pie = 12 pulgadas

Usa la tasa $\frac{1 \text{ pie}}{12 \text{ pulgs.}}$ como el factor de conversión.

PASO 2

Multiplica 60 pulgadas por el factor de conversión.

$$60 \text{ pulgs.} \times \frac{1 \text{ pie}}{12 \text{ pulgs.}}$$

$$= \frac{\overset{5}{\cancel{60}} \text{ pulgs.}}{1} \times \frac{1 \text{ pie}}{\underset{1}{\cancel{12}} \text{ pulgs.}}$$

$$= 5 \text{ pies}$$

Pistas

Factores de conversión

Dado que un factor de conversión es igual a 1, puedes convertir de una unidad a otra multiplicando por el factor de conversión apropiado.

Actividad

Use recipientes de bebidas que tenga en casa para practicar la conversión de unidades de capacidad. Por ejemplo, el jugo de naranja se suele vender en envases que contienen 64 onzas líquidas. Trabajen juntos para determinar el número de vasos que se pueden servir de ese recipiente.

Convert Units of Length

COMMON CORE STANDARD CC.6.RP.3d
Understand ratio concepts and use ratio reasoning
to solve problems.

Convert to the given unit.

1. 42 ft = ▨ yd

conversion factor: $\dfrac{1 \text{ yd}}{3 \text{ ft}}$

42 ft $\times$ $\dfrac{1 \text{ yd}}{3 \text{ ft}}$

42 ft = 14 yd

2. 2,350 m = ▨ km

3. 18 ft = ▨ in.

_____

_____

4. 289 m = ▨ dm

5. 5 mi = ▨ yd

6. 35 mm = ▨ cm

_____

_____

_____

Compare. Write <, >, or =.

7. 1.9 dm $\bigcirc$ 1,900 mm

8. 12 ft $\bigcirc$ 4 yd

9. 56 cm $\bigcirc$ 56,000 km

10. 98 in. $\bigcirc$ 8 ft

11. 64 cm $\bigcirc$ 630 mm

12. 2 mi $\bigcirc$ 10,560 ft

Problem Solving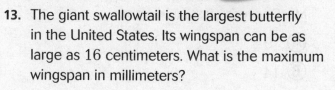

13. The giant swallowtail is the largest butterfly in the United States. Its wingspan can be as large as 16 centimeters. What is the maximum wingspan in millimeters?

14. The 102nd floor of the Sears Tower in Chicago is the highest occupied floor. It is 1,431 feet above the ground. How many yards above the ground is the 102nd floor?

_____

_____

Lesson Check (CC.6.RP.3d)

1. Justin rides his bicycle 2.5 kilometers to school. Luke walks 1,950 meters to school. How much farther does Justin ride to school than Luke walks to school?

   (A) 550 meters

   (B) 55 meters

   (C) 55 kilometers

   (D) 550 kilometers

2. The length of a room is $10\frac{1}{2}$ feet. What is the length of the room in inches?

   (A) 132 inches

   (B) 126 inches

   (C) 121 inches

   (D) $22\frac{1}{2}$ inches

Spiral Review (CC.6.RP.3a, CC.6.RP.3c, CC.6.NS.8)

3. Each unit on the map represents 1 mile. What is the distance between the campground and the waterfall? (Lesson 3.9)

   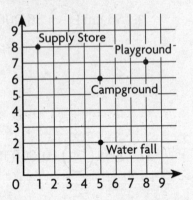

   (A) 2 miles   (C) 5 miles

   (B) 4 miles   (D) 9 miles

4. On a field trip, 2 vans can carry 32 students. How many students can go on a field trip when there are 6 vans? (Lesson 4.5)

   (A) 18

   (B) 36

   (C) 64

   (D) 96

5. According to a 2008 survey, $\frac{29}{50}$ of all teens have sent at least one text message in their lives. What percent of teens have sent a text message? (Lesson 5.3)

   (A) 29%

   (B) 50%

   (C) 58%

   (D) 72%

6. Of the students in Ms. Danver's class, 6 walk to school. This represents 30% of her students. How many students are in Ms. Danver's class? (Lesson 5.6)

   (A) 9

   (B) 14

   (C) 18

   (D) 20

Convert Units of Capacity

COMMON CORE STANDARD CC.6.RP.3d
Understand ratio concepts and use ratio reasoning to solve problems.

Convert to the given unit.

1. 7 gallons = ☐ quarts

conversion factor: $\dfrac{4\ qt}{1\ gal}$

$7\ gal \times \dfrac{4\ qt}{1\ gal}$

$7\ gal = 28\ qt$

2. 5.1 liters = ☐ kiloliters

Move the decimal point **3** places to the left.

5.1 liters = **0.0051** kiloliters

3. 20 qt = ☐ gal

4. 40 L = ☐ mL

5. 16 c = ☐ pt

_____

_____

_____

6. 300 L = ☐ kL

7. 33 pt = ☐ qt ☐ pt

8. 29 cL = ☐ daL

_____

_____

_____

9. 4 pt = ☐ fl oz

10. 7.7 kL = ☐ cL

11. 24 fl oz = ☐ pt ☐ c

_____

_____

_____

Problem Solving REAL WORLD

12. A bottle contains 3.5 liters of water. A second bottle contains 3,750 milliliters of water. How many more milliliters are in the larger bottle than in the smaller bottle?

13. Arnie's car used 100 cups of gasoline during a drive. He paid $3.12 per gallon for gas. How much did the gas cost?

_____

_____

Lesson Check (CC.6.RP.3d)

1. Gina filled a tub with 25 quarts of water. What is this amount in gallons and quarts?

   Ⓐ 12 gallons, 1 quart

   Ⓑ 8 galllons, 1 quart

   Ⓒ 7 gallons, 1 quart

   Ⓓ 6 gallons, 1 quart

2. Four horses are pulling a wagon. Each horse drinks 45,000 milliliters of water each day. How many liters of water will the horses drink in 5 days?

   Ⓐ 9 liters

   Ⓑ 90 liters

   Ⓒ 900 liters

   Ⓓ 9,000 liters

Spiral Review (CC.6.RP.2, CC.6.RP.3c, CC.6.RP.3d, CC.6.NS.8)

3. The map shows Henry's town. Each unit is 1 kilometer. After school, Henry walks to the library. How far does he walk? (Lesson 3.10)

   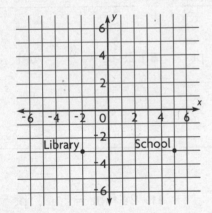

   Ⓐ 2 kilometers   Ⓒ 6 kilometers

   Ⓑ 5 kilometers   Ⓓ 7 kilometers

4. An elevator travels 117 feet in 6.5 seconds. What is the elevator's unit rate? (Lesson 4.6)

   Ⓐ 117 feet per 6.5 seconds

   Ⓑ 117 feet per second

   Ⓒ 18 feet per 6.5 seconds

   Ⓓ 18 feet per second

5. Julie's MP3 player contains 860 songs. If 20% of the songs are rap songs and 15% of the songs are R&B songs, how many of the songs are other types of songs? (Lesson 5.4)

   Ⓐ 129

   Ⓑ 172

   Ⓒ 301

   Ⓓ 559

6. Which length is equivalent to 3,570 meters? (Lesson 6.1)

   Ⓐ 0.0357 kilometer

   Ⓑ 0.357 kilometer

   Ⓒ 3.57 kilometers

   Ⓓ 35.7 kilometers

Convert Units of Weight and Mass

COMMON CORE STANDARD CC.6.RP.3d
Understand ratio concepts and use ratio reasoning to solve problems.

Convert to the given unit.

1. 5 pounds = [ ] ounces

conversion factor: $\dfrac{16 \text{ oz}}{1 \text{ lb}}$

5 pounds = 5 lb × $\dfrac{16 \text{ oz}}{1 \text{ lb}}$ = **80** oz

2. 2.36 grams = [ ] hectograms

Move the decimal point **2** places to the left.

2.36 grams = **0.0236** hectogram

3. 48 oz = [ ] lb

4. 30 g = [ ] dg

5. 5 T = [ ] lb

6. 17.2 hg = [ ] g

7. 400 lb = [ ] T

8. 38,600 mg = [ ] dag

9. 87 oz = [ ] lb [ ] oz

10. 0.0793 kg = [ ] cg

11. 0.65 T = [ ] lb

Problem Solving  REAL WORLD

12. Maggie bought 52 ounces of swordfish selling for $6.92 per pound. What was the total cost?

13. Three bunches of grapes have masses of 1,000 centigrams, 1,000 decigrams, and 1,000 grams, respectively. What is the total combined mass of the grapes in kilograms?

Lesson Check (CC.6.RP.3d)

1. Denise's rock sample weighs 684 grams. Pauline's rock sample weighs 29,510 centigrams. How much heavier is Denise's sample than Pauline's?

   Ⓐ 2,882.6 centigrams

   Ⓑ 3,889 centigrams

   Ⓒ 28,826 centigrams

   Ⓓ 38,890 centigrams

2. A sign at the entrance to a bridge says "Maximum allowable weight 2.25 tons." Jason's truck weighs 2,150 pounds. How much additional weight can he carry?

   Ⓐ 100 pounds

   Ⓑ 1,450 pounds

   Ⓒ 2,350 pounds

   Ⓓ 4,400 pounds

Spiral Review (CC.6.RP.1, CC.6.RP.3b, CC.6.RP.3c, CC.6.RP.3d)

3. There are 23 students in a math class. Twelve of them are boys. What is the ratio of girls to total number of students? (Lesson 4.2)

   Ⓐ 12 to 23

   Ⓑ 11 to 23

   Ⓒ 11 to 12

   Ⓓ 23 to 12

4. Miguel hiked 3 miles in 54 minutes. At this rate, how long will it take him to hike 5 miles? (Lesson 4.7)

   Ⓐ 56 minutes

   Ⓑ 60 minutes

   Ⓒ 72 minutes

   Ⓓ 90 minutes

5. Marco borrowed $150 from his brother. He has paid him back 30% so far. How much money does Marco still owe his brother? (Lesson 5.5)

   Ⓐ $45

   Ⓑ $105

   Ⓒ $120

   Ⓓ $150

6. Which volume is equivalent to 2.7 liters? (Lesson 6.2)

   Ⓐ 0.0027 milliliters

   Ⓑ 270 milliliters

   Ⓒ 2,700 milliliters

   Ⓓ 27,000 milliliters

Name _____

Transform Units

COMMON CORE STANDARD CC.6.RP.3d
Understand ratio concepts and use ratio reasoning to solve problems.

Multiply or divide the quantities.

1. $\dfrac{62\text{ g}}{1\text{ day}} \times 4\text{ days}$

$$\dfrac{62\text{ g}}{1\text{ day}} \times \dfrac{4\text{ days}}{1} = 248\text{ g}$$

2. $322\text{ sq yd} \div 23\text{ yd}$

$$\dfrac{322\text{ sq yd}}{23\text{ yd}}$$

$$\dfrac{322\text{ yd} \times \text{yd}}{23\text{ yd}} = 14\text{ yd}$$

3. $\dfrac{128\text{ kg}}{1\text{ hr}} \times 10\text{ hr}$

4. $136\text{ sq km} \div 8\text{ km}$

5. $\dfrac{88\text{ lb}}{1\text{ day}} \times 12\text{ days}$

_____ _____ _____

6. $154\text{ sq mm} \div 11\text{ mm}$

7. $\dfrac{\$150}{1\text{ sq ft}} \times 20\text{ sq ft}$

8. $234\text{ sq ft} \div 18\text{ ft}$

_____ _____ _____

9. $324\text{ sq yd} \div 9\text{ yd}$

10. $\dfrac{72\text{ km}}{1\text{ gal}} \times 20\text{ gal}$

11. $225\text{ sq dm} \div 5\text{ dm}$

_____ _____ _____

Problem Solving REAL WORLD

12. Green grapes are on sale for \$2.50 a pound. How much will 9 pounds cost?

13. A car travels 32 miles for each gallon of gas. How many gallons of gas does it need to travel 192 miles?

_____ _____

Lesson Check (CC.6.RP.3d)

1. A parking lot has an area of 682 square yards. The lot is 22 yards wide. What is the length of the parking lot, to the nearest yard?

   (A) 28 yards

   (B) 29 yards

   (C) 30 yards

   (D) 31 yards

2. A machine assembles 44 key chains per hour. How many key chains are produced in 11 hours?

   (A) 11

   (B) 55

   (C) 88

   (D) 484

Spiral Review (CC.6.RP.3a, CC.6.RP.3c)

3. Which ratio is NOT equivalent to $\frac{8}{20}$?
   (Lesson 4.3)

   (A) $\frac{2}{5}$

   (B) $\frac{12}{24}$

   (C) $\frac{16}{40}$

   (D) $\frac{40}{100}$

5. Megan answered 18 questions correctly on a test. That is 75% of the total number of questions. How many questions were on the test? (Lesson 5.6)

   (A) 57

   (B) 24

   (C) 14

   (D) 4

4. The graph shows the money that Marco earns for different numbers of days worked. How much money does he earn per day?
   (Lesson 4.8)

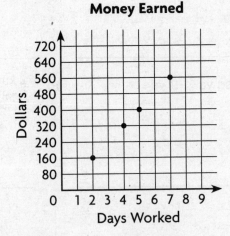

Money Earned

   (A) $80   (C) $240

   (B) $160   (D) $320

Problem Solving • Distance, Rate, and Time Formulas

COMMON CORE STANDARD CC.6.RP.3d
Understand ratio concepts and use ratio reasoning to solve problems.

Read each problem and solve.

1. A downhill skier is traveling at a rate of 0.5 mile per minute. How far will the skier travel in 18 minutes?

$$d = r \times t$$
$$d = \frac{0.5 \text{ mi}}{1 \text{ min}} \times 18 \text{ min}$$
$$d = 9 \text{ miles}$$

2. How long will it take a seal swimming at a speed of 8 miles per hour to travel 52 miles?

3. A dragonfly traveled at a rate of 35 miles per hour for 2.5 hours. What distance did the dragonfly travel?

4. A race car travels 1,212 kilometers in 4 hours. What is the car's rate of speed?

5. A cyclist travels at a rate of 1.8 kilometers per minute. How far will the cyclist travel in 48 minutes?

6. Kim and Jay leave at the same time to travel 25 miles to the beach. Kim drives 9 miles in 12 minutes. Jay drives 10 miles in 15 minutes. If they both continue at the same rate, who will arrive at the beach first?

Lesson Check (CC.6.RP.3d)

1. Mark cycled 25 miles at a rate of 10 miles per hour. How long did it take Mark to cycle 25 miles?

   (A) 3 hours

   (B) 2.5 hours

   (C) 0.4 hour

   (D) 0.25 hour

2. Joy ran 13 miles in $3\frac{1}{4}$ hours. What was her average rate?

   (A) 2 miles per hour

   (B) 3 miles per hour

   (C) 4 miles per hour

   (D) 5 miles per hour

Spiral Review (CC.6.RP.3a, CC.6.RP.3c, CC.6.RP.3d)

3. Which shows two ratios that are equivalent to $\frac{9}{12}$? (Lesson 4.3)

   (A) $\frac{10}{13}$ and $\frac{8}{11}$

   (B) $\frac{3}{4}$ and $\frac{18}{20}$

   (C) $\frac{3}{4}$ and $\frac{27}{36}$

   (D) $\frac{12}{9}$ and $\frac{9}{12}$

4. In the Chang family's budget, 0.6% of the expenses are for Internet service. What fraction of the family's expenses is for Internet service? (Lesson 5.2)

   (A) $\frac{3}{5,000}$

   (B) $\frac{3}{500}$

   (C) $\frac{3}{50}$

   (D) $\frac{3}{5}$

5. Which length is equivalent to 357 centimeters? (Lesson 6.1)

   (A) 0.357 m

   (B) 3.57 m

   (C) 35.7 m

   (D) 3,570 m

6. What is the product of the two quantities shown below? (Lesson 6.4)

   $$\frac{60 \text{ mi}}{1 \text{ hr}} \times 12 \text{ hr}$$

   (A) 5 mi

   (B) 5 hr

   (C) 720 mi

   (D) 720 hr

Name _____

Chapter 6 Extra Practice

Lesson 6.1

Convert to the given unit.

1. 288 in. = [ ] ft

2. 4.1 mm = [ ] cm

3. 5 yd = [ ] in.

4. 20 km = [ ] dam

_____ _____ _____ _____

Lesson 6.2

Convert to the given unit.

5. 184 qt = [ ] gal

6. 180 mL = [ ] L

7. 32 qt = [ ] pt

8. 0.035 kL = [ ] L

_____ _____ _____ _____

Lesson 6.3

Convert to the given unit.

9. 8 lb = [ ] oz

10. 800 mg = [ ] g

11. 8,000 lb = [ ] T

12. 0.004 kg = [ ] mg

_____ _____ _____ _____

Lesson 6.4

Multiply or divide the quantities.

13. $\dfrac{27 \text{ cm}}{1 \text{ min}} \times 3 \text{ min}$

14. 234 sq ft ÷ 9 ft

15. $\dfrac{49 \text{ sq yd}}{1 \text{ hr}} \times 8 \text{ hr}$

_____ _____ _____

Solve.

16. Evan earns $12 per hour. How much does he earn in 5.5 hours?

_____

17. A tile floor costs $8.50 per square foot. How much tile can Brett buy for $93.50?

_____

18. A poster has an area of 1,080 square inches. The poster is 36 inches tall. What is the width of the poster in inches?

_____

19. A machine produces 16 toys per hour. How many hours does it take the machine to make 176 toys?

_____

Lesson 6.5

Choose the appropriate formula. Include the unit in your answer.

20. An Olympic sprinter ran at a rate of 36 feet per second. How far did he run in 12 seconds?

_____

21. Glen hiked 14 miles in 4 hours. What was his average rate of speed?

_____

22. How long will it take a jet airliner to travel 310 kilometers at a speed of 930 kilometers per hour?

_____

23. The track at East Side High School is 440 yards long. It took Maya 10 minutes to jog around the track 4 times. Find her speed in miles per hour.

_____

24. Kim started hiking at 10:40 A.M. She stopped for lunch at 1:10 P.M., having hiked at an average rate of 3 miles per hour. How far did she hike?

_____

School-Home Letter

Vocabulary

algebraic expression A mathematical phrase that includes at least one variable.

order of operations The process for evaluating expressions.

terms The parts of an algebraic expression that are separated by an addition or subtraction sign.

variable A letter or symbol that stands for one or more numbers.

Dear Family,

Throughout the next few weeks, our math class will be learning about operations and algebraic expressions. We will also be learning how to work with exponents.

You can expect to see homework that requires students to write, evaluate, and simplify expressions.

Here is a sample of how your child was taught to evaluate an expression.

🔑 MODEL Evaluate Expressions

This is how we will be evaluating $n^2 - 2m$ for $n = 4$ and $m = 3$.

STEP 1

Write the expression.

$$n^2 - 2m$$

STEP 2

Substitute the given values for the variables.

$$4^2 - 2 \times 3$$

STEP 3

Find the value of the number with an exponent.

$$16 - 2 \times 3$$

STEP 4

Multiply.

$$16 - 6$$

STEP 5

Subtract.

$$10$$

Tips

Order of Operations

To evaluate an expression, first perform the operations in parentheses, then find the values of numbers with exponents, then perform all multiplication and division from left to right, and then perform all addition and subtraction from left to right.

Activity

You can write algebraic expressions to describe family relationships. Be sure to remind your child to explain what the variable in each expression represents. For example, if a child is 3 years older than her sister, the expression $s + 3$ represents the child's age, where s is her sister's age.

Carta para la casa

Vocabulario

expresión algebraica Una frase matemática que incluye al menos una variable.

orden de las operaciones El proceso que se usa para evaluar expresiones.

términos Las partes de una expresión algebraica que están separadas por un signo de suma o resta.

variable Una letra o símbolo que representa uno o más números.

Querida familia,

Durante las próximas semanas, en la clase de matemáticas aprenderemos sobre expresiones algebraicas y operaciones. También aprenderemos a trabajar con exponentes.

Llevaré a la casa tareas actividades que requieren que los estudiantes escriban, evalúen y simplifiquen expresiones.

Este es un ejemplo de la manera como aprenderemos a evaluar una expresión.

🔑 MODELO   Evaluar expresiones

Así evaluamos $n^2 - 2m$ para $n = 4$ y $m = 3$.

PASO 1

Escribe la expresión.

$n^2 - 2m$

PASO 2

Sustituye los valores dados para las variables.

$4^2 - 2 \times 3$

PASO 3

Halla el valor del número que tiene un exponente.

$16 - 2 \times 3$

PASO 4

Multiplica.

$16 - 6$

PASO 5

Resta.

10

Pistas

Orden de las operaciones

Para evaluar una expresión, haz primero las operaciones entre paréntesis. Luego halla los valores de los números con exponentes. Después haz las multiplicaciones y divisiones, de izquierda a derecha. Finalmente, haz las sumas y restas, de izquierda a derecha.

Actividad

Puede escribir expresiones algebraicas para describir relaciones de familia. Asegúrese de recordarles a su niño(a) que expliquen lo que representa la variable en cada expresión. Por ejemplo, si una niña es 3 años mayor que su hermana, la expresión $s + 3$ representa la edad de la niña, donde la s es la edad de su hermana.

Exponents

COMMON CORE STANDARD CC.6.EE.1
Apply and extend previous understandings of
arithmetic to algebraic expressions.

Use one or more exponents to write the expression.

1. 6×6

2. $11 \times 11 \times 11 \times 11$

3. $9 \times 9 \times 9 \times 9 \times 7 \times 7$

$$6^2$$

_____

_____

_____

Find the value.

4. 9^2

5. 6^4

6. 1^6

_____

_____

_____

7. 5^3

8. 10^5

9. 23^2

_____

_____

_____

10. Write 144 with an exponent by using 12 as the base.

11. Write 343 with an exponent by using 7 as the base.

_____

_____

Problem Solving REAL WORLD

12. Each day Sheila doubles the number of push-ups she did the day before. On the fifth day, she does $2 \times 2 \times 2 \times 2 \times 2$ push-ups. Use an exponent to write the number of push-ups Shelia does on the fifth day.

13. The city of Beijing has a population of more than 10^7 people. Write 10^7 without using an exponent.

_____

_____

Lesson Check (CC.6.EE.1)

1. The number of games in the first round of a chess tournament is equal to $2 \times 2 \times 2 \times 2 \times 2 \times 2$. Which is another way of writing the number of games in the first round?

   (A) 2^1

   (B) 2^2

   (C) 2^6

   (D) 6^2

2. The number of gallons of water in a tank at an aquarium is equal to 8^3. How many gallons of water are in the tank?

   (A) 24 gallons

   (B) 64 gallons

   (C) 192 gallons

   (D) 512 gallons

Spiral Review (CC.6.RP.3a, CC.6.RP.3c, CC.6.RP.3d)

3. The table shows the amount of strawberry juice and lemonade needed to make different amounts of strawberry lemonade. Based on the table, which ratio of strawberry juice to lemonade could Keena use to make strawberry lemonade? (Lesson 4.4)

Strawberry juice (cups)	2	3	4
Lemonade (cups)	6	9	12

   (A) 1:4

   (B) 5:15

   (C) 12:4

   (D) 16:6

4. Which percent is equivalent to the fraction $\frac{37}{50}$? (Lesson 5.3)

   (A) 37%

   (B) 50%

   (C) 64%

   (D) 74%

5. Which volume is equivalent to 2.7 liters? (Lesson 6.2)

   (A) 0.0027 milliliter

   (B) 270 milliliters

   (C) 2,700 milliliters

   (D) 27,000 milliliters

6. Use the formula $d = rt$ to find the distance traveled by a car driving at an average speed of 50 miles per hour for 4.5 hours. (Lesson 6.5)

   (A) 9 miles

   (B) 11 miles

   (C) 200 miles

   (D) 225 miles

Evaluate Expressions Involving Exponents

COMMON CORE STANDARD CC.6.EE.1
Apply and extend previous understandings of
arithmetic to algebraic expressions.

Evaluate the expression.

1. $5 + 17 - 10^2 \div 5$

$5 + 17 - 100 \div 5$

$5 + 17 - 20$

$22 - 20$

2

2. $7^2 - 3^2 + 4$

3. $2^4 \div (7 - 5)$

4. $(8^2 + 36) \div (4 \times 5^2)$

5. $12 + 21 \div 3 + 2^5 \times 0$

6. $(12 - 8)^3 - 24 + 3$

Place parentheses in the expression so that it equals the given value.

7. $12 \times 2 + 2^3$; value: 120

8. $7^2 + 1 - 5 \times 3$; value: 135

Problem Solving REAL WORLD

9. Hugo is saving for a new baseball glove. He saves $10 the first week, and $6 each week for the next 6 weeks. The expression $10 + 6^2$ represents the total amount in dollars he has saved. What is the total amount Hugo has saved?

10. A scientist placed fish eggs in a tank. Each day, twice the number of eggs from the previous day hatch. The expression 5×2^6 represents the number of eggs that hatch on the sixth day. How many eggs hatch on the sixth day?

Lesson Check (CC.6.EE.1)

1. Ritchie wants to paint his bedroom ceiling and four walls. Both the ceiling and walls are 8 feet by 8 feet. A gallon of paint covers 40 square feet. Which expression can be used to find the number of gallons of paint Ritchie needs to buy?

   (A) $8^2(4 + 1) \times 40$

   (B) $8^2(4 \times 1) \div 40$

   (C) $8^2(4 + 1) \div 40$

   (D) $8^2(4 \times 1) \times 40$

2. A Chinese restaurant uses about 15^2 pairs of chopsticks each day. The manager wants to order a 30-day supply of chopsticks. The chopsticks come in boxes of 750 pairs. How many boxes should the manager order?

   (A) 9 boxes

   (B) 18 boxes

   (C) 25 boxes

   (D) 100 boxes

Spiral Review (CC.6.RP.3a, CC.6.RP.3c, CC.6.RP.3d, CC.6.EE.1)

3. Annabelle spent $5 to buy 4 raffle tickets. How many tickets can she buy for $20? **(Lesson 4.5)**

   (A) 8 tickets

   (B) 16 tickets

   (C) 25 tickets

   (D) 40 tickets

4. Gavin has 460 baseball players in his collection of baseball cards, and 15% of the players are pitchers. How many pitchers are in Gavin's collection? **(Lesson 5.4)**

   (A) 15

   (B) 31

   (C) 69

   (D) 85

5. Which weight is equivalent to 40 ounces? **(Lesson 6.3)**

   (A) 2.5 pounds

   (B) 3.8 pounds

   (C) 5 pounds

   (D) 6.2 pounds

6. Which expression has the greatest value? **(Lesson 7.1)**

   (A) 1^5

   (B) 3^3

   (C) 4^2

   (D) 8^1

Write Algebraic Expressions

COMMON CORE STANDARD CC.6.EE.2a
Apply and extend previous understandings of
arithmetic to algebraic expressions.

Write an algebraic expression for the word expression.

1. 13 less than p

$$p - 13$$

2. the sum of x and 9

3. 6 more than the difference of b and 5

4. the sum of 15 and the product of 5 and v

5. the difference of 2 and the product of 3 and k

6. 12 divided by the sum of h and 2

7. the quotient of m and 7

8. 9 more than 2 multiplied by f

9. 6 minus the difference of x and 3

10. 10 less than the quotient of g and 3

11. the sum of 4 multiplied by a and 5 multiplied by b

12. 14 more than the difference of r and s

Problem Solving REAL WORLD

13. Let h represent Mark's height in inches. Suzanne is 7 inches shorter than Mark. Write an algebraic expression that represents Suzanne's height in inches.

14. A company rents bicycles for a fee of $10 plus $4 per hour of use. Write an algebraic expression for the total cost in dollars for renting a bicycle for h hours.

Lesson Check (CC.6.EE.2a)

1. The female lion at a zoo weighs 190 pounds more than the female cheetah. Let c represent the weight in pounds of the cheetah. Which expression gives the weight in pounds of the lion?

   (A) $c + 190$

   (B) $c - 190$

   (C) $190 - c$

   (D) $190 \times c$

2. Tickets to a play cost $8 each. Which expression gives the ticket cost in dollars for a group of g girls and b boys?

   (A) $8 + (g + b)$

   (B) $8 \times (g + b)$

   (C) $8 + (g \times b)$

   (D) $8 \times (g \times b)$

Spiral Review (CC.6.RP.2, CC.6.RP.3c, CC.6.RP.3d, CC.6.EE.1)

3. A bottle of cranberry juice contains 32 fluid ounces and costs $2.56. What is the unit rate? (Lesson 4.6)

   (A) $0.08 for 1 fluid ounce

   (B) $1.28 for 16 fluid ounces

   (C) $0.12 for 1 fluid ounce

   (D) $2.56 for 32 fluid ounces

4. There are 32 peanuts in a bag. Elliott takes 25% of the peanuts from the bag. Then Zaire takes 50% of the remaining peanuts. How many peanuts are left in the bag? (Lesson 5.5)

   (A) 4

   (B) 8

   (C) 12

   (D) 24

5. Hank earns $12 per hour for babysitting. How much does he earn for 15 hours of babysitting? (Lesson 6.4)

   (A) 27 hours

   (B) $27

   (C) 180 hours

   (D) $180

6. Which expression represents the area of the figure in square centimeters? (Lesson 7.2)

   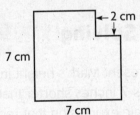

   (A) $7^2 - 2^2$

   (B) $7 - 2$

   (C) 7×2

   (D) $7^2 \times 2^2$

Identify Parts of Expressions

COMMON CORE STANDARD CC.6.EE.2b
Apply and extend previous understandings of
arithmetic to algebraic expressions.

**Identify the parts of the expression. Then write a word
expression for the numerical or algebraic expression.**

1. $(16 - 7) \div 3$

   The subtraction is the difference
   of 16 and 7. The division is the
   quotient of the difference and 3.
   Word expression: the quotient of
   the difference of 16 and 7 and 3

2. $20 + 5 \times 9$

   _____

   _____

   _____

   _____

   _____

3. $2e - f$

   _____

   _____

   _____

   _____

4. $8 + 6q + q$

   _____

   _____

   _____

   _____

**Identify the terms of the expression. Then give the
coefficient of each term.**

5. $11r + 7s$

   _____

   _____

6. $6g - h$

   _____

   _____

Problem Solving REAL WORLD

7. Adam bought granola bars at the store. The
   expression $6p + 5n$ gives the number of bars
   in p boxes of plain granola bars and n boxes
   of granola bars with nuts. What are the terms
   of the expression?

   _____

   _____

8. In the sixth grade, each student will get 4
   new books. There is one class of 15 students
   and one class of 20 students. The expression
   $4 \times (15 + 20)$ gives the total number of
   new books. Write a word expression for the
   numerical expression.

   _____

   _____

Lesson Check (CC.6.EE.2b)

1. A fabric store sells pieces of material for $5 each. Ali bought 2 white pieces and 8 blue pieces. She also bought a pack of buttons for $3. The expression $5 \times (2 + 8) + 3$ gives the cost in dollars of Ali's purchase. Which describes a part of the expression?

   (A) the sum of 8 and 3

   (B) the sum of 2 and 8

   (C) the product of 2 and 8

   (D) the product of 5 and 2

2. A hotel offers two different types of rooms. The expression $k + 2f$ gives the number of beds in the hotel where k is the number of rooms with a king size bed and f is the number of rooms with 2 full size beds. What are the terms of the expression?

   (A) 1 and 2

   (B) k and f

   (C) k and $2f$

   (D) + and ×

Spiral Review (CC.6.RP.3b, CC.6.RP.3c, CC.6.RP.3d, CC.6.EE.2a)

3. Meg paid $9 for 2 tuna sandwiches. At the same rate, how much does Meg pay for 8 tuna sandwiches? (Lesson 4.7)

   (A) .$3

   (B) $15

   (C) $36

   (D) $72

4. Jan is saving for a skateboard. She has saved $30 already, which is 20% of the total price. How much does the skateboard cost?
   (Lesson 5.6)

   (A) $600

   (B) $150

   (C) $50

   (D) $6

5. It took Eduardo 8 hours to drive from Buffalo, NY, to New York City, a distance of about 400 miles. Find his average speed. (Lesson 6.5)

   (A) 32 miles per hour

   (B) 40 miles per hour

   (C) 50 miles per hour

   (D) 64 miles per hour

6. Which expression represents the value, in cents, of n nickels? (Lesson 7.3)

   (A) n

   (B) $n + 5$

   (C) $n - 5$

   (D) $5n$

Evaluate Algebraic Expressions and Formulas

COMMON CORE STANDARD CC.6.EE.2c
Apply and extend previous understandings of
arithmetic to algebraic expressions.

Evaluate the expression for the given values of the variables.

1. $w + 6$ for $w = 11$

$11 + 6$

17

2. $r - 9$ for $r = 20$

_____

3. $17 - 2c$ for $c = 7$

_____

4. $b^2 - 4$ for $b = 5$

5. $(h - 3)^2$ for $h = 5$

6. $x + x^2$ for $x = 6$

_____

7. $m + 2m + 3$ for $m = 12$

8. $9a - 5a$ for $a = 7$

9. $4 \times (21 - 3h)$ for $h = 5$

_____

10. $7m - 9n$ for $m = 7$ and $n = 5$

11. $d^2 - 9k + 3$ for $d = 10$ and $k = 9$

12. $3x + 4y \div 2$ for $x = 7$ and $y = 10$

_____

Problem Solving REAL WORLD

13. The formula $P = 2\ell + 2w$ gives the perimeter P of a rectangular room with length ℓ and width w. A rectangular living room is 26 feet long and 21 feet wide. What is the perimeter of the room?

14. The formula $c = 5(f - 32) \div 9$ gives the Celsius temperature in c degrees for a Fahrenheit temperature of f degrees. What is the Celsius temperature for a Fahrenheit temperature of 122 degrees?

_____

Lesson Check (CC.6.EE.2c)

1. The expression $(p \div 20) \times 4$ gives the time in minutes that a person will have to wait to ride a roller coaster when there are p people in front of him or her. How long will Ty have to wait if there are 60 people in front of him?

   - (A) 12 minutes
   - (B) 15 minutes
   - (C) 80 minutes
   - (D) 120 minutes

2. The distance, in meters, that Kim runs during track practice is equal to $400\ell + 100s$, where ℓ is the number of laps and s is the number of sprints. How far does Kim run when she does 4 laps and 6 sprints?

   - (A) 1,400 meters
   - (B) 1,600 meters
   - (C) 2,200 meters
   - (D) 5,000 meters

Spiral Review (CC.6.RP.3a, CC.6.RP.3d, CC.6.EE.2b)

3. The graph shows the gas usage of Tyrone's car. How many gallons of gas are needed for Tyrone to drive 100 miles?

   (Lesson 4.8)

   - (A) 2 gallons
   - (B) 3 gallons
   - (C) 4 gallons
   - (D) 5 gallons

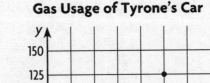
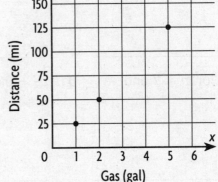

Gas Usage of Tyrone's Car

4. Which length is equivalent to 26 yards? **(Lesson 6.1)**

   - (A) 8.7 feet
   - (B) 13 feet
   - (C) 52 feet
   - (D) 78 feet

5. Which expression shows the sum of 5 and the product of 2 and h? **(Lesson 7.4)**

   - (A) $5 + 2h$
   - (B) $5 + 2 + h$
   - (C) $5 \times 2 \times h$
   - (D) $5(2 + h)$

Name _____

Use Algebraic Expressions

COMMON CORE STANDARD CC.6.EE.6
Reason about and solve one-variable equations and inequalities.

Jeff sold the pumpkins he grew for $7 each at the farmer's market.

1. Write an expression to represent the amount of money Jeff made selling the pumpkins. Tell what the variable in your expression represents.

   7p, where p is the number of pumpkins

2. If Jeff sold 30 pumpkins, how much money did he make?

   _____

An architect is designing a building. Each floor will be 12 feet tall.

3. Write an expression for the number of floors the building can have for a given building height. Tell what the variable in your expression represents.

   _____

4. If the architect is designing a building that is 132 feet tall, how many floors can be built?

   _____

Write an algebraic expression for each word expression.
Then evaluate the expression for these values of the variable: 1, 6, 13.5

5. the quotient of 100 and the sum of b and 24

6. 13 more than the product of m and 5

Problem Solving REAL WORLD

7. In the town of Pleasant Hill, there is an average of 16 sunny days each month. Write an expression to represent the approximate number of sunny days for any number of months. Tell what the variable represents.

8. How many sunny days can a resident of Pleasant Hill expect to have in 9 months?

Lesson Check (CC.6.EE.6)

1. Oliver drives 45 miles per hour. Which expression represents the distance in miles he will travel for *h* hours driven?

(A) $45h$

(B) $45 + h$

(C) $45 - h$

(D) $\frac{45}{h}$

2. Socks cost $5 per pair. The expression $5p$ represents the cost in dollars of *p* pairs of socks. Which best describes the possible values of the variable *p*?

(A) A single unknown number

(B) Any positive number

(C) Any whole number

(D) Any integer

Spiral Review (CC.6.RP.3c, CC.6.RP.3d, CC.6.EE.1, CC.6.EE.2c)

3. Sterling silver consists of 92.5% silver and 7.5% copper. What decimal represents the portion of silver in sterling silver? **(Lesson 5.2)**

(A) 0.925

(B) 9.25

(C) 92.5

(D) 925.0

4. Which of the following is equivalent to 3 gallons? **(Lesson 6.2)**

(A) $\frac{1}{3}$ pint

(B) 6 pints

(C) 18 pints

(D) 24 pints

5. Which of the following should be done first to evaluate $10 + (66 - 6^2)$? **(Lesson 7.2)**

(A) Add 10 and 66.

(B) Subtract 6 from 66.

(C) Multiply 6 and 2.

(D) Square 6.

6. Evaluate the algebraic expression $h(m + n) \div 2$ for $h = 4$, $m = 5$, and $n = 6$. **(Lesson 7.5)**

(A) 13

(B) 17

(C) 22

(D) 27

Name _____

Problem Solving • Combine Like Terms

COMMON CORE STANDARD CC.6.EE.3
Apply and extend previous understandings of
arithmetic to algebraic expressions.

Read each problem and solve.

1. A box of pens costs $3 and a box of markers costs $5. The expression $3p + 5p$ represents the cost in dollars to make p packages that includes 1 box of pens and 1 box of markers. Simplify the expression by combining like terms.

$$3p + 5p = 8p$$

2. Riley's parents got a cell phone plan that has a $40 monthly fee for the first phone. For each extra phone, there is a $15 phone service charge and a $10 text service charge. The expression $40 + 15e + 10e$ represents the total phone bill in dollars, where e is the number of extra phones. Simplify the expression by combining like terms.

_____

3. A radio show lasts for h hours. For every 60 minutes of air time during the show, there are 8 minutes of commercials. The expression $60h - 8h$ represents the air time in minutes available for talk and music. Simplify the expression by combining like terms.

_____

4. A publisher sends 100 books to each bookstore where its books are sold. At each store, about 3 books are sold at a discount to employees and about 40 books are sold during store weekend sales. The expression $100s - 3s - 40s$ represents the approximate number of the publisher's books sold at full price in s stores. Simplify the expression by combining like terms.

_____

5. A sub shop sells a meal that includes an Italian sub for $6 and chips for $2. If a customer purchases more than 3 meals, he or she receives a $5 discount. The expression $6m + 2m - 5$ shows the cost in dollars of the customer's order for m meals, where m is greater than 3. Simplify the expression by combining like terms.

_____

Lesson Check (CC.6.EE.3)

1. For each gym class, a school has 10 soccer balls and 6 volleyballs. All of the classes share 15 basketballs. The expression $10c + 6c + 15$ represents the total number of balls the school has for c classes. Which of the following is a simpler form of the expression?

- **(A)** $2c + 31$
- **(C)** $10c + 21$
- **(B)** $4c + 15$
- **(D)** $16c + 15$

2. A public library wants to place 4 magazines and 9 books on each display shelf. The expression $4s + 9s$ represents the number of items that will be displayed on s shelves. Which of the following is a simpler form of the expression?

- **(A)** $13s$
- **(C)** $5s + 9$
- **(B)** $12s$
- **(D)** $2s + 13$

Spiral Review (CC.6.RP.3c, CC.6.RP.3d, CC.6.EE.2a, CC.6.EE.6)

3. A bag has 8 bagels. Three of the bagels are cranberry. What percent of the bagels are cranberry? (Lesson 5.3)

- **(A)** 37.5%
- **(B)** 30%
- **(C)** 26.7%
- **(D)** 3%

4. Which amount is equivalent to 3,200 grams? (Lesson 6.3)

- **(A)** 3.2 kilograms
- **(B)** 32 kilograms
- **(C)** 320 kilograms
- **(D)** 32,000 kilograms

5. Toni earns \$200 per week plus \$5 for every magazine subscription that she sells. How much, in dollars, will she earn in a week in which she sells s subscriptions? (Lesson 7.3)

- **(A)** $200 + 5s$
- **(B)** $200 + 5 + s$
- **(C)** $1,000s$
- **(D)** $200(s + 5)$

6. At a snack stand, drinks cost \$1.50. Which expression could be used to find the total cost of d drinks? (Lesson 7.6)

- **(A)** $1.5 + d$
- **(B)** $1.5 - d$
- **(C)** $1.5d$
- **(D)** $1.5 \div d$

Name _____

Generate Equivalent Expressions

COMMON CORE STANDARD CC.6.EE.3
Apply and extend previous understandings of
arithmetic to algebraic expressions.

Use properties of operations to write an equivalent expression by combining like terms.

1. $7h - 3h$

4h

2. $5x + 7 + 2x$

3. $16 + 13p - 9p$

4. $y^2 + 13y - 8y$

5. $5(2h + 3) + 3h$

6. $12 + 18n + 7 - 14n$

Use the Distributive Property to write an equivalent expression.

7. $2(9 + 5k)$

8. $5(3m + 2)$

9. $6(g + h)$

10. $4d + 8$

11. $21p + 35q$

12. $18x + 9y$

Problem Solving REAL WORLD

13. The expression $15n + 12n + 100$ represents
the total cost in dollars for skis, boots, and a
lesson for n skiers. Simplify the expression
$15n + 12n + 100$. Then find the total cost for
8 skiers.

_____

14. Casey has n nickels. Megan has 4 times
as many nickels as Casey has. Write an
expression for the total number of nickels
Casey and Megan have. Then simplify the
expression.

_____

Lesson Check (CC.6.EE.3)

1. Tickets to a museum cost $8. The dinosaur exhibit costs $5 extra. The expression $8n + 5n$ represents the cost in dollars for n people to visit the museum and the exhibit. Which expression is equivalent to $8n + 5n$?

   (A) $13n$

   (B) $13n^2$

   (C) $40n$

   (D) $40n^2$

2. Which expression is equivalent to $3(2p - 3)$?

   (A) $5p - 3$

   (B) $5p - 9$

   (C) $6p - 3$

   (D) $6p - 9$

Spiral Review (CC.6.RP.3c, CC.6.RP.3d, CC.6.EE.2b, CC.6.EE.3)

3. A Mexican restaurant received 60 take-out orders. The manager found that 60% of the orders were for tacos and 25% of the orders were for burritos. How many orders were for other items? (Lesson 5.4)

   (A) 9

   (B) 15

   (C) 36

   (D) 51

4. The area of a rectangular field is 1,710 square feet. The length of the field is 45 feet. What is the width of the field? (Lesson 6.4)

   (A) 38 ft

   (B) 38 ft^2

   (C) 1,755 ft

   (D) 1,755 ft^2

5. Which of the following expressions has three terms? (Lesson 7.4)

   (A) $4x + 3$

   (B) $3y + 4x$

   (C) $2 + 4x + 7y$

   (D) $2 + 3x + 7y + 6z$

6. Boxes of cereal usually cost $4, but they are on sale for $1 off. A gallon of milk costs $3. The expression $4b - 1b + 3$ can be used to find the cost in dollars of buying b boxes of cereal and a gallon of milk. Which of the following shows this expression in simpler form? (Lesson 7.7)

   (A) $3b - 3$

   (B) $5b + 3$

   (C) $6b$

   (D) $3b + 3$

Identify Equivalent Expressions

COMMON CORE STANDARD CC.6.EE.4
Apply and extend previous understandings of
arithmetic to algebraic expressions.

Use properties of operations to determine whether
the expressions are equivalent.

1. $2s + 13 + 15s$ and
$17s + 13$

2. $5 \times 7h$ and $35h$

3. $10 + 8v - 3v$ and $18 - 3v$

_____equivalent_____

_____

_____

4. $(9w \times 0) - 12$ and $9w - 12$

5. $11(p + q)$ and
$11p + (7q + 4q)$

6. $6(4b + 3d)$ and $24b + 3d$

_____

_____

_____

7. $14m + 9 - 6m$ and $8m + 9$

8. $(y \times 1) + 2$ and $y + 2$

9. $4 + 5(6t + 1)$ and $9 + 30t$

_____

_____

_____

10. $9x + 0 + 10x$ and $19x + 1$

11. $12c - 3c$ and $3(4c - 1)$

12. $6a \times 4$ and $24a$

_____

_____

_____

Problem Solving  REAL WORLD

13. Rachel needs to write 3 book reports with
b pages and 3 science reports with s pages
during the school year. Write an algebraic
expression for the total number of pages
Rachel will need to write.

14. Rachel's friend Yassi has to write $3(b + s)$
pages for reports. Use properties of operations
to determine whether this expression is
equivalent to the expression for the number of
pages Rachel has to write.

_____

_____

Lesson Check (CC.6.EE.4)

1. Ian had 4 cases of comic books and 6 adventure books. Each case holds c comic books. He gave 1 case of comic books to his friend. Which expression gives the total number of books Ian has left?

   (A) $3c + 6$ (C) $4c + 5$

   (B) $3c - 6$ (D) $4c - 5$

2. At the beginning of spring, Xia made 5 flower planters with f flowers in each planter. At the beginning of summer, she made 8 flower planters with f flowers in each planter. Which expression gives the number of flowers Xia has in the planters?

   (A) 13   (C) $13f$

   (B) 40   (D) $40f$

Spiral Review (CC.6.RP.3c, CC.6.RP.3d, CC.6.EE.2c, CC.6.EE.3)

3. Keisha wants to read for 90 minutes. So far, she has read 30% of her goal. How much longer does she need to read? (Lesson 5.5)

   (A) 3 min

   (B) 27 min

   (C) 63 min

   (D) 87 min

4. Marvyn travels 105 miles on his scooter. He travels for 3 hours. How fast does he travel? (Lesson 6.5)

   (A) 35 miles per hour

   (B) 35 hours

   (C) 35 hours per mile

   (D) 35 miles

5. The expression $5(F - 32) \div 9$ gives the Celsius temperature for a Fahrenheit temperature of F degrees. The noon Fahrenheit temperature in Centerville was 86 degrees. What was the temperature in degrees Celsius? (Lesson 7.5)

   (A) 27 degrees Celsius

   (B) 30 degrees Celsius

   (C) 36 degrees Celsius

   (D) 44 degrees Celsius

6. At the library book sale, hardcover books sell for $4 and paperbacks sell for $2. The expression $4b + 2b$ represents the total cost for b hardcover books and b paperbacks. Which expression is **not** equivalent to $4b + 2b$? (Lesson 7.8)

   (A) $2(2b + b)$

   (B) $6b$

   (C) $3(2b)$

   (D) $6b^2$

COMMON CORE STANDARDS CC.6.EE.1, CC.6.EE.2a, CC.6.EE.2b, CC.6.EE.2c, CC.6.EE.3, CC.6.EE.4, CC.6.EE.6

Chapter 7 Extra Practice

Lessons 7.1 and 7.2

Find the value.

1. 4^3

2. 1^9

3. 10^4

4. 25^1

_____   _____   _____   _____

5. Tracie's website received $3 \times 3 \times 3 \times 3 \times 3 \times 3$ hits last month. Use an exponent to write the number of hits.

6. The distance from Earth to the moon is about 12^5 miles. Write 12^5 using repeated multiplication.

_____   _____

Evaluate the expression.

7. $3 + 4 \times 5^1$

8. $26 - 4^2 \div 2$

9. $(3^3 - 2^4) \times 5$

10. $20 - (5 - 2)^2 + 2 \times 3$

_____   _____   _____   _____

Lessons 7.3 and 7.4

11. Write an algebraic expression for the number of hours in m minutes.

12. Write a word expression for the algebraic expression $5y - 6$.

_____   _____

Lesson 7.5

Evaluate the expression for the given value of the variable.

13. $3p - 7$ for $p = 3$

14. $5 + (w - 5)^2$ for $w = 10$

15. $(x^2 - 2x) \div 4$ for $x = 6$

_____

_____

_____

Lesson 7.6

16. A lion runs 15 miles in 1 hour. Write an expression for the number of miles the lion can run in h hours.

17. Use your expression from Problem 16 to find the number of miles the lion could run in 0.25 hour.

_____

_____

Lesson 7.7

18. Mr. Johnson bought flowers to plant in flats in his yard. Each flat has 6 yellow flowers and 8 red flowers. The expression $6f + 8f$ represents the number of flowers that are in f flats. Simplify the expression by combining like terms.

_____

Lessons 7.8 and 7.9

Use properties of operations to determine whether the expressions are equivalent.

19. $7m + 10 + 9m$ and $16m + 10$

20. $2b \times 5$ and $7b$

21. $9 \times (4r - 6)$ and $36r - 54$

_____

_____

_____

22. $12 + 5(2 + y)$ and $5y + 22$

23. $15j + 11 - 6j$ and $9j + 11$

24. $8(3x + 1)$ and $24x + 1$

_____

_____

_____

School-Home Letter

Vocabulary

equation A statement that two mathematical expressions are equal.

inverse operations Operations that undo each other, such as addition and subtraction or multiplication and division.

solution of an equation A value of a variable that makes an equation true.

Dear Family,

Throughout the next few weeks, our math class will be learning about equations and inequalities. We will be learning how to write, model, and solve equations, and how to graph solutions to inequalities.

You can expect to see homework on writing and solving equations and inequalities.

Here is a sample of how your child was taught to solve a subtraction equation.

🔑 MODEL Solve Subtraction Equations

Solve the equation $m - 5 = 7$.

STEP 1

Write the equation.

$$m - 5 = 7$$

STEP 2

Use the Addition Property of Equality.

$$m - 5 + 5 = 7 + 5$$

STEP 3

Add.

$$m = 12$$

Tips

Checking Solutions

You can check the solution of an equation by substituting the value of the variable in the original equation. If the solution is correct, the two sides of the equation will be equal.

Activity

Pay attention to everyday situations that can be expressed as an equation. For example, "We bought 5 packages of pens at a discount store. We have a total of 40 pens. How many pens are in each package?" Write and solve an equation to answer the question.

Capítulo 8

Carta para la casa

Querida familia,

Durante las próximas semanas, en la clase de matemáticas aprenderemos sobre ecuaciones y desigualdades. También aprenderemos a escribir, modelar y resolver ecuaciones, y representar gráficamente las soluciones a las desigualdades.

Llevaré a la casa tareas para practicar el planteamiento y la solución de ecuaciones y desigualdades.

Este es un ejemplo de la manera como aprenderemos a resolver una ecuación de resta.

Vocabulario

ecuación · Una afirmación que señala que dos expresiones matemáticas son iguales.

operaciones inversas Operaciones que se cancelan entre ellas, como la suma y la resta, o la multiplicación y la división.

solución de una ecuación Un valor de una variable que hace verdadera una ecuación.

🔑 MODELO Resolver ecuaciones de resta

Resuelve la ecuación $m - 5 = 7$.

PASO 1

Escribe la ecuación.

$$m - 5 = 7$$

PASO 2

Usa la Propiedad de Suma de la Igualdad.

$$m - 5 + 5 = 7 + 5$$

PASO 3

Suma.

$$m = 12$$

Pistas

Comprobar soluciones

Puedes comprobar la solución de una ecuación substituyendo el valor de la variable en la ecuación original. Si la solución es correcta, los dos lados de la ecuación serán iguales.

Actividad

Preste atención a situaciones de la vida diaria que se puedan expresar como una ecuación. Por ejemplo: "Compramos 5 paquetes de bolígrafos en una tienda de descuento. Tenemos un total de 40 bolígrafos. ¿Cuántos bolígrafos hay en cada paquete?" Escriba y resuelva una ecuación para responder la pregunta.

Solutions of Equations

COMMON CORE STANDARD CC.6.EE.5
Reason about and solve one-variable equations and inequalities.

Determine whether the given value of the variable is a solution of the equation.

1. $x - 7 = 15$; $x = 8$

$$\underline{}\ 8\ \underline{} - 7 \overset{?}{=} 15$$

$$\underline{}\ 1\ \underline{} \neq 15$$

not a solution

2. $c + 11 = 20$; $c = 9$

3. $7n = 7$; $n = 0$

4. $\frac{1}{3}h = 6$; $h = 2$

5. $a - 1 = 70$; $a = 71$

6. $\frac{7}{8} + j = 1$; $j = \frac{1}{8}$

7. $16.1 + d = 22$; $d = 6.1$

8. $9 = \frac{3}{4}e$; $e = 12$

9. $15.5 - y = 7.9$; $y = 8.4$

Problem Solving REAL WORLD

10. Terrance needs to score 25 points to win a game. He has already scored 18 points. The equation $18 + p = 25$ gives the number of points p that Terrance still needs to score. Determine whether $p = 7$ or $p = 13$ is a solution of the equation, and tell what the solution means.

11. Madeline has used 50 sheets of a roll of paper towels, which is $\frac{5}{8}$ of the entire roll. The equation $\frac{5}{8}s = 50$ can be used to find the number of sheets s in a full roll. Determine whether $s = 32$ or $s = 80$ is a solution of the equation, and tell what the solution means.

Lesson Check (CC.6.EE.5)

1. Sheena received a gift card for $50. She has already used it to buy a lamp for $39.99. The equation $39.99 + x = 50$ can be used to find the amount x that is left on the gift card. Which is a solution of the equation?

   (A) $x = \$10.01$
   (B) $x = \$11.01$
   (C) $x = \$11.99$
   (D) $x = \$89.99$

2. When Peter had a fever, his temperature was 101.4°F. After taking some medicine, his temperature was 99.2°F. The equation $101.4 - d = 99.2$ gives the number of degrees d that Peter's temperature decreased. Which of the following is the solution of the equation?

   (A) $d = 1.2$
   (B) $d = 2.2$
   (C) $d = 3.2$
   (D) $d = 4.2$

Spiral Review (CC.6.RP.3c, CC.6.EE.1, CC.6.EE.4, CC.6.EE.6)

3. Melanie has saved $60 so far to buy a lawn mower. This is 20% of the price of the lawn mower. What is the full price of the lawn mower that she wants to buy? (Lesson 5.6)

   (A) $120
   (B) $300
   (C) $1,200
   (D) $3,000

4. A team of scientists is digging for fossils. The amount of soil in cubic feet that they remove is equal to 6^3. How many cubic feet of soil do the scientists remove? (Lesson 7.1)

   (A) 9 cubic feet
   (B) 18 cubic feet
   (C) 72 cubic feet
   (D) 216 cubic feet

5. Andrew made p picture frames. He sold 2 of them at a craft fair. Which expression could be used to find the number of picture frames Andrew has left? (Lesson 7.6)

   (A) $p - 2$
   (B) $2 - p$
   (C) $\frac{p}{2}$
   (D) $\frac{2}{p}$

6. Which expression is equivalent to $4 + 3(5 + x)$? (Lesson 7.9)

   (A) $7(5 + x)$
   (B) $3 + 4(5 + x)$
   (C) $4 + 15 + 3x$
   (D) $4 + 15 + x$

Write Equations

COMMON CORE STANDARD CC.6.EE.7
Reason about and solve one-variable equations and inequalities.

Write an equation for the word sentence.

1. 18 is 4.5 times a number.

$$18 = 4.5n$$

2. Eight more than the number of children is 24.

_____

3. The difference of a number and $\frac{2}{3}$ is $\frac{3}{8}$.

4. m minutes less than 80 minutes is 15 minutes.

5. A number divided by 0.5 is 29.

6. The product of the number of songs and $0.99 is $7.92.

Write a word sentence for the equation.

7. $x - 14 = 52$

8. $2.3m = 0.46$

9. $25 = k \div 5$

10. $4\frac{1}{3} + q = 5\frac{1}{6}$

Problem Solving REAL WORLD

11. An ostrich egg weighs 2.9 pounds. The difference between the weight of this egg and the weight of an emu egg is 1.6 pounds. Write an equation that could be used to find the weight w, in pounds, of the emu egg.

12. In one week, the number of bowls a potter made was 6 times the number of plates. He made 90 bowls during the week. Write an equation that could be used to find the number of plates p that the potter made.

Lesson Check (CC.6.EE.7)

1. Three friends are sharing the cost of a bucket of popcorn. The total cost of the popcorn is $5.70. Which equation could be used to find the amount a in dollars that each friend should pay?

(A) $a \div 3 = 5.70$

(B) $a \div 5.70 = 3$

(C) $3a = 5.70$

(D) $5.70a = 3$

2. Salimah had 42 photos on her phone. After she deleted some of them, she had 23 photos left. Which equation could be used to find the number of photos p that Salimah deleted?

(A) $p - 23 = 42$

(B) $p + 23 = 42$

(C) $p - 42 = 23$

(D) $p + 42 = 23$

Spiral Review (CC.6.RP.3d, CC.6.EE.1, CC.6.EE.3, CC.6.EE.5)

3. A rope is 72 feet long. What is the length of the rope in yards? (Lesson 6.1)

(A) 216 yards

(B) 69 yards

(C) 24 yards

(D) 6 yards

4. Julia evaluated the expression $3^3 + 20 \div 2^2$. What value did she get as her answer?

(Lesson 7.2)

(A) 11

(B) 14

(C) 29

(D) 32

5. The sides of a triangle have lengths s, $s + 4$, and $3s$. Which expression represents the perimeter of the triangle? (Lesson 7.7)

(A) $4s + 5$

(B) $5s + 4$

(C) $9s$

(D) $8s$

6. Which of the following equations has a solution of $p = 2\frac{1}{2}$? (Lesson 8.1)

(A) $p + 2\frac{1}{2} = 5$

(B) $p - 2\frac{1}{2} = 5$

(C) $2 + p = 2\frac{1}{2}$

(D) $4 - p = 2\frac{1}{2}$

Model and Solve Addition Equations

COMMON CORE STANDARD CC.6.EE.7
Reason about and solve one-variable equations and inequalities.

Model and solve the equation by using algebra tiles.

1. $x + 6 = 9$ **2.** $x + 5 = 6$ **3.** $9 = x + 1$

$$\underline{} \quad x = 3$$

4. $8 + x = 10$ **5.** $x + 7 = 11$ **6.** $4 = 2 + x$

Solve the equation by drawing a model.

7. $x + 4 = 7$ **8.** $x + 6 = 10$

Problem Solving REAL WORLD

9. The temperature at 10:00 was 10°F. This is 3°F warmer than the temperature at 8:00. Model and solve the equation $x + 3 = 10$ to find the temperature x in degrees Fahrenheit at 8:00.

10. Jaspar has 7 more checkers left than Karen does. Jaspar has 9 checkers left. Write and solve an addition equation to find out how many checkers Karen has left.

Lesson Check (CC.6.EE.7)

1. What is the solution of the equation that is modeled by the algebra tiles?

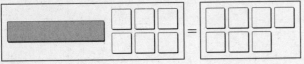

- Ⓐ $x = 1$
- Ⓑ $x = 6$
- Ⓒ $x = 7$
- Ⓓ $x = 13$

2. Alice has played soccer for 8 more years than Sanjay has. Alice has played for 12 years. The equation $y + 8 = 12$ can be used to find the number of years y Sanjay has played. How long has Sanjay played soccer?

- Ⓐ 4 years
- Ⓑ 6 years
- Ⓒ 16 years
- Ⓓ 20 years

Spiral Review (CC.6.RP.3d, CC.6.EE.2a, CC.6.EE.3, CC.6.EE.7)

3. A car's gas tank has a capacity of 16 gallons. What is the capacity of the tank in pints?

   (Lesson 6.2)

- Ⓐ 2 pints
- Ⓑ 4 pints
- Ⓒ 64 pints
- Ⓓ 128 pints

4. Craig scored p points in a game. Marla scored twice as many points as Craig but 5 fewer than Nelson scored. How many points did Nelson score? (Lesson 7.3)

- Ⓐ $2p + 5$
- Ⓑ $2p - 5$
- Ⓒ $\frac{1}{2}p + 5$
- Ⓓ $2(p + 5)$

5. Which expression is equivalent to $3x + 2(4y + x)$? (Lesson 7.8)

- Ⓐ $5x + 8y$
- Ⓑ $4x + 8y$
- Ⓒ $11x + 2y$
- Ⓓ $5x + 4y$

6. The Empire State Building in New York City is 443.2 meters tall. This is 119.2 meters taller than the Eiffel Tower in Paris. Which equation can be used to find the height h in meters of the Eiffel Tower? (Lesson 8.2)

- Ⓐ $h - 443.2 = 119.2$
- Ⓑ $h - 119.2 = 443.2$
- Ⓒ $443.2 + h = 119.2$
- Ⓓ $119.2 + h = 443.2$

Solve Addition and Subtraction Equations

COMMON CORE STANDARD CC.6.EE.7
Reason about and solve one-variable equations and inequalities.

Solve the equation, and check the solution.

1. $y - 14 = 23$

$y - 14 + 14 = 23 + 14$
$y = 37$

2. $x + 3 = 15$

3. $n + \dfrac{2}{5} = \dfrac{4}{5}$

4. $16 = m - 14$

5. $w - 13.7 = 22.8$

6. $s + 55 = 55$

7. $23 = x - 12$

8. $p - 14 = 14$

9. $m - 2\dfrac{3}{4} = 6\dfrac{1}{2}$

10. $t + 0.95 = 1.25$

11. $3\dfrac{1}{3} = b - \dfrac{2}{3}$

12. $48 = d + 23$

Problem Solving REAL WORLD

13. A recipe calls for $5\dfrac{1}{2}$ cups of flour. Lorenzo only has $3\dfrac{3}{4}$ cups of flour. Write and solve an equation to find the additional amount of flour Lorenzo needs to make the recipe.

14. Jan used 22.5 gallons of water in the shower. This amount is 7.5 gallons less than the amount she used for washing clothes. Write and solve an equation to find the amount of water Jan used to wash clothes.

Lesson Check (CC.6.EE.7)

1. The price tag on a shirt says $21.50. The final cost of the shirt, including sales tax, is $23.22. The equation $21.50 + t = 23.22$ can be used to find the amount of sales tax t in dollars. What is the sales tax?

- (A) $0.72
- (B) $1.72
- (C) $2.28
- (D) $44.72

2. The equation $\ell - 12.5 = 48.6$ can be used to find the original length ℓ in centimeters of a wire before it was cut. What was the original length of the wire?

- (A) 35.9 centimeters
- (B) 36.1 centimeters
- (C) 50.1 centimeters
- (D) 61.1 centimeters

Spiral Review (CC.6.RP.3d, CC.6.EE.2b, CC.6.EE.4, CC.6.EE.7)

3. Which rule can you use to convert a mass in centigrams to a mass in milligrams? (Lesson 6.3)

- (A) Multiply by 10.
- (B) Multiply by 100.
- (C) Divide by 10.
- (D) Divide by 100.

4. In the expression $4 + 3x + 5y$, what is the coefficient of x? (Lesson 7.4)

- (A) 3
- (B) 4
- (C) 5
- (D) 12

5. Which of the following expressions is equivalent to $10c$? (Lesson 7.9)

- (A) $5c + 5$
- (B) $10 + c$
- (C) $0(10c)$
- (D) $c + 9c$

6. Miranda bought a movie ticket and popcorn for a total of $10. The equation $7 + x = 10$ can be used to find the cost x in dollars of the popcorn. How much did the popcorn cost? (Lesson 8.3)

- (A) $3
- (B) $4
- (C) $7
- (D) $17

Model and Solve Multiplication Equations

COMMON CORE STANDARD CC.6.EE.7
Reason about and solve one-variable equations
and inequalities.

Model and solve the equation by using algebra tiles.

1. $2x = 8$ **2.** $5x = 10$ **3.** $21 = 3x$

_____ $x = 4$ _____   _____   _____

4. $4x = 20$ **5.** $6x = 6$ **6.** $4 = 2x$

_____   _____   _____

Solve the equation by drawing a model.

7. $6 = 3x$ **8.** $4x = 12$

_____   _____

Problem Solving REAL WORLD

9. A chef used 20 eggs to make 5 omelets.
Model and solve the equation $5x = 20$ to find
the number of eggs x in each omelet.

10. Last month, Julio played 3 times as many
video games as Scott did. Julio played
18 video games. Write and solve an
equation to find the number of video games
Scott played.

_____   _____

Lesson Check (CC.6.EE.7)

1. What is the solution of the equation that is modeled by the algebra tiles?

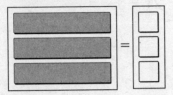

(A) $x = 0$ (C) $x = 3$

(B) $x = 1$ (D) $x = 6$

2. Carlos bought 5 tickets to a play for a total of $20. The equation $5c = 20$ can be used to find the cost c in dollars of each ticket. How much does each ticket cost?

(A) $4

(B) $5

(C) $10

(D) $15

Spiral Review (CC.6.RP.3d, CC.6.EE.2c, CC.6.EE.5, CC.6.EE.7)

3. A rectangle is 12 feet wide and 96 inches long. What is the area of the rectangle? (Lesson 6.4)

(A)   8 square feet

(B)   88 square feet

(C)   96 square feet

(D) 1,152 square feet

4. Evaluate the algebraic expression $24 - x \div y$ for $x = 8$ and $y = 2$. (Lesson 7.5)

(A) 4

(B) 8

(C) 16

(D) 20

5. Ana bought a 15.5-pound turkey at the grocery store this month. The equation $p - 15.5 = 2.5$ gives the weight p, in pounds, of the turkey she bought last month. Which of the following is a solution of the equation? (Lesson 8.1)

(A) $p = 3$

(B) $p = 13$

(C) $p = 18$

(D) $p = 30$

6. A pet store usually keeps 12 birds per cage, and there are 7 birds in the cage now. The equation $7 + x = 12$ can be used to find the remaining number of birds x that can be placed in the cage. What is the solution of the equation?

(A) $x = 4$

(B) $x = 5$

(C) $x = 19$

(D) $x = 20$

Solve Multiplication and Division Equations

COMMON CORE STANDARD CC.6.EE.7
Reason about and solve one-variable equations and inequalities.

Solve the equation, and check the solution.

1. $8p = 96$

$$\frac{8p}{8} = \frac{96}{8}$$

$$p = 12$$

2. $\frac{z}{16} = 8$

3. $3.5x = 14.7$

_____

4. $32 = 3.2c$

5. $\frac{2}{5}w = 40$

6. $\frac{a}{14} = 6.8$

_____

7. $1.6x = 1.6$

8. $23.8 = 3.5b$

9. $\frac{3}{5} = \frac{2}{3}t$

_____

10. $\frac{x}{7} = 0$

11. $4n = 9$

12. $\frac{3}{4}g = \frac{5}{8}$

_____

Problem Solving REAL WORLD

13. Anne runs 6 laps on a track. She runs a total of 1 mile, or 5,280 feet. Write and solve an equation to find the distance, in feet, that she runs in each lap.

14. DeShawn uses $\frac{3}{4}$ of a box of rice to cook dinner. The portion he uses weighs 12 ounces. Write and solve an equation to find the weight of the full box of rice.

_____

Lesson Check (CC.6.EE.7)

1. Estella buys 1.8 pounds of walnuts for a total of $5.04. She solves the equation $1.8p = 5.04$ to find the price p in dollars of one pound of walnuts. What does one pound of walnuts cost?

   (A) $0.36

   (B) $2.80

   (C) $3.24

   (D) $6.84

2. Gabriel wants to solve the equation $\frac{5}{8}m = 25$. Which step should he do to get m by itself on one side of the equation?

   (A) Multiply both sides by 25.

   (B) Divide both sides by 25.

   (C) Multiply both sides by $\frac{5}{8}$.

   (D) Divide both sides by $\frac{5}{8}$.

Spiral Review (CC.6.RP.3d, CC.6.EE.6, CC.6.EE.7)

3. At top speed, a coyote can run at a speed of 44 miles per hour. If a coyote could maintain its top speed, how far could it run in 15 minutes? (Lesson 6.5)

   (A) 2.93 miles

   (B) 11 miles

   (C) 176 miles

   (D) 660 miles

4. An online store sells DVDs for $10 each. The shipping charge for an entire order is $5.50. Frank orders d DVDs. Which expression represents the total cost for Frank's DVDs? (Lesson 7.6)

   (A) $d \times 10 + 5.50$

   (B) $d \times 5.50 + 10$

   (C) $d \times (10 + 5.50)$

   (D) $10 \times (d + 5.50)$

5. A ring costs $27 more than a pair of earrings. The ring costs $90. Which equation can be used to find the cost c in dollars of the earrings? (Lesson 8.2)

   (A) $27 = 90 + c$

   (B) $27 = c - 90$

   (C) $90 = 27 + c$

   (D) $90 = c - 27$

6. The equation $3s = 21$ can be used to find the number of students s in each van on a field trip. How many students are in each van? (Lesson 8.5)

   (A) 7 students

   (B) 8 students

   (C) 53 students

   (D) 63 students

Problem Solving • Equations with Fractions

COMMON CORE STANDARD CC.6.EE.7
Reason about and solve one-variable equations and inequalities.

Read each problem and solve.

1. Stu is 4 feet tall. This height represents $\frac{6}{7}$ of his brother's height. The equation $\frac{6}{7}h = 4$ can be used to find the height h, in feet, of Stu's brother. How tall is Stu's brother?

$$7 \times \frac{6}{7}h = 7 \times 4$$
$$6h = 28$$
$$\frac{6h}{6} = \frac{28}{6}$$
$$h = 4\frac{2}{3}$$

$4\frac{2}{3}$ **feet**

2. Bryce bought a bag of cashews. He served $\frac{7}{8}$ pound of cashews at a party. This amount represents $\frac{2}{3}$ of the entire bag. The equation $\frac{2}{3}n = \frac{7}{8}$ can be used to find the number of pounds n in a full bag. How many pounds of cashews were in the bag that Bryce bought?

_____

3. In Jaime's math class, 9 students chose soccer as their favorite sport. This amount represents $\frac{3}{8}$ of the entire class. The equation $\frac{3}{8}s = 9$ can be used to find the total number of students s in Jaime's class. How many students are in Jaime's math class?

_____

4. There are 15 blueberry muffins in a large basket. This represents $\frac{5}{9}$ of all the muffins that are in the basket. The equation $\frac{5}{9}m = 15$ can be used to find the total number of muffins m in the basket. How many muffins are in the basket?

_____

Lesson Check (CC.6.EE.7)

1. There are 32 people who voted for Petra for class president. This represents $\frac{1}{2}$ of the people who voted. How many people voted in the election?

Ⓐ 8

Ⓑ 16

Ⓒ 32

Ⓓ 64

2. Michele has spent $\frac{1}{2}$ hour on her homework so far. This amount of time represents $\frac{1}{5}$ of the total time she needs to spend doing homework. The equation $\frac{1}{5}h = \frac{1}{2}$ gives the total number of hours h it will take for Michele to complete her homework. How many hours will it take for Michele to do her homework?

Ⓐ $\frac{1}{10}$ hour

Ⓒ $\frac{2}{5}$ hour

Ⓑ $\frac{3}{10}$ hour

Ⓓ $2\frac{1}{2}$ hours

Spiral Review (CC.6.EE.1, CC.6.EE.3, CC.6.EE.7)

3. Which expression has the same value as $9 \times 9 \times 9 \times 9 \times 9$? (Lesson 7.1)

Ⓐ 5^9

Ⓑ 9×9

Ⓒ 9^5

Ⓓ 5×9

4. Which expression is equivalent to $5 + 3m + 2 + m$? (Lesson 7.7)

Ⓐ $8m + 3m$

Ⓑ $10m$

Ⓒ $7 + 3m$

Ⓓ $7 + 4m$

5. In a basketball game, Lena scored 8 more points than Ginger did. The equation $p + 8 = 15$ can be used to find the number of points p that Ginger scored. What is the solution of the equation? (Lesson 8.3)

Ⓐ $p = 7$

Ⓑ $p = 8$

Ⓒ $p = 17$

Ⓓ $p = 23$

6. While training for a sports event, Jeremy hiked 5.3 miles each day. The equation $5.3d = 42.4$ can be used to find the number of days d he hiked during training. How many days did Jeremy hike? (Lesson 8.6)

Ⓐ 8 days

Ⓑ 9 days

Ⓒ 22 days

Ⓓ 23 days

Name _____

Solutions of Inequalities

COMMON CORE STANDARD CC.6.EE.5

Reason about and solve one-variable equations and inequalities.

Determine whether the given value of the variable is a solution of the inequality.

1. $s \geq {}^-1; s = 1$

$$1 \overset{?}{\geq} {}^-1$$

solution

2. $p < 0; p = 4$

_____

3. $y \leq {}^-3; y = {}^-1$

_____

4. $u > -\frac{1}{2}; u = 0$

_____

5. $q \geq 0.6; q = 0.23$

_____

6. $b < 2\frac{3}{4}; b = \frac{2}{3}$

_____

7. $j \leq {}^-5.7; j = {}^-6$

_____

8. $a > {}^-8; a = {}^-7.5$

_____

9. $w \geq 4.5; w = 4.45$

_____

Give two solutions of the inequality.

10. $k < 2$

_____

11. $z \geq {}^-3$

_____

12. $f \leq {}^-5$

_____

Problem Solving REAL WORLD

13. The inequality $s \geq 92$ represents the score s that Jared must earn on his next test to get an A on his report card. Give two possible scores that Jared could earn to get the A.

14. The inequality $m \leq \$20$ represents the amount of money that Sheila is allowed to spend on a new hat. Give two possible money amounts that Sheila could spend on the hat.

_____

_____

Lesson Check (CC.6.EE.5)

1. Which of the following is NOT a solution of the inequality $g < {}^-1\frac{1}{2}$?

   Ⓐ $g = {}^-4$

   Ⓑ $g = {}^-7\frac{1}{2}$

   Ⓒ $g = 0$

   Ⓓ $g = {}^-2\frac{1}{2}$

2. The inequality $w \geq 3.2$ represents the weight of each pumpkin, in pounds, that is allowed to be picked to be sold. Which of the following give two weights of pumpkins that can be sold?

   Ⓐ 3.18 lb; 4 lb

   Ⓑ 3.2 lb; 3.3 lb

   Ⓒ 3.199 lb; 3.4 lb

   Ⓓ 2.987 lb; 3.2 lb

Spiral Review (CC.6.EE.1, CC.6.EE.3, CC.6.EE.7)

3. What is the value of $8 + (27 \div 9)^2$? (Lesson 7.2)

   Ⓐ 14

   Ⓑ 17

   Ⓒ 22

   Ⓓ 121

4. Rex bought x DVDs for $15 each and z CDs for $10 each. The expression $15x + 10z$ represents Rex's total cost. Which of the following is equivalent to Rex's total cost? (Lesson 7.8)

   Ⓐ $15 + x + 10z$

   Ⓑ $5(15x + 10z)$

   Ⓒ $5(3x + 2z)$

   Ⓓ $(15 + x) + (10 + z)$

5. Tina bought a T-shirt and sandals. The total cost was $41.50. The T-shirt cost $8.95. The equation $8.95 + c = 41.50$ can be used to find the cost c in dollars of the sandals. How much did the sandals cost? (Lesson 8.4)

   Ⓐ $32.55

   Ⓑ $33.45

   Ⓒ $49.25

   Ⓓ $50.45

6. Two-thirds of a number is equal to 20. What is the number? (Lesson 8.7)

   Ⓐ 30

   Ⓑ 20

   Ⓒ $13\frac{1}{3}$

   Ⓓ $\frac{20}{3}$

Write Inequalities

COMMON CORE STANDARD CC.6.EE.8
Reason about and solve one-variable equations and inequalities.

Write an inequality for the word sentence. Tell what type of numbers the variable in the inequality can represent.

1. The width w is greater than 4 centimeters.

   The inequality symbol for "is greater than" is $>$.

   $w > 4$, where w is the width in centimeters. w is

   a positive number.

2. The score s in a basketball game is greater than or equal to 10 points.

   _____

   _____

3. The mass m is less than 5 kilograms.

   _____

   _____

4. The height h is greater than 2.5 meters.

   _____

   _____

5. The temperature t is less than or equal to $^-3°$.

   _____

   _____

Write a word sentence for the inequality.

6. $k < {}^-7$

   _____

7. $z \geq 14$

   _____

8. $m \leq 2\frac{3}{5}$

   _____

9. $f > 0.24$

   _____

Problem Solving REAL WORLD

10. Tabby's mom says that she must read for at least 30 minutes each night. If m represents the number of minutes reading, what inequality can represent this situation?

    _____

11. Phillip has a $25 gift card to his favorite restaurant. He wants to use the gift card to buy lunch. If c represents the cost of his lunch, what inequality can describe all of the possible amounts of money, in dollars, that Phillip can spend on lunch?

    _____

Lesson Check (CC.6.EE.8)

1. At the end of the first round in a quiz show, Jeremy has at most ⁻20 points. Which of the following inequalities means "at most ⁻20"?

   Ⓐ $x < {}^{-}20$

   Ⓑ $x \leq {}^{-}20$

   Ⓒ $x > {}^{-}20$

   Ⓓ $x \geq {}^{-}20$

2. Which of the following describes the solutions of $y \geq 7.9$?

   Ⓐ no more than 7.9

   Ⓑ at most 7.9

   Ⓒ at least 7.9

   Ⓓ more than 7.9

Spiral Review (CC.6.EE.2a, CC.6.EE.4, CC.6.EE.5, CC.6.EE.7)

3. Let y represent Jaron's age in years. If Dawn were 5 years older, she would be Jaron's age. Which expression represents Dawn's age? **(Lesson 7.3)**

   Ⓐ $5y$

   Ⓑ $y \div 5$

   Ⓒ $y - 5$

   Ⓓ $y + 5$

4. Which expression is equivalent to $7 \times 3g$?
   (Lesson 7.9)

   Ⓐ $10g$

   Ⓑ $21g$

   Ⓒ 10

   Ⓓ 21

5. Which of the following is a solution of the equation $8 = 8f$? **(Lesson 8.5)**

   Ⓐ $f = 64$

   Ⓑ $f = 8$

   Ⓒ $f = 0$

   Ⓓ $f = 1$

6. Which of the following shows two solutions of the inequality $k \leq {}^{-}2$? **(Lesson 8.8)**

   Ⓐ $k = 0, k = {}^{-}2$

   Ⓑ $k = {}^{-}2, k = {}^{-}4$

   Ⓒ $k = {}^{-}2.9, k = {}^{-}1\frac{1}{2}$

   Ⓓ $k = {}^{-}3, k = 0$

Graph Inequalities

COMMON CORE STANDARD CC.6.EE.8
Reason about and solve one-variable equations
and inequalities.

Graph the inequality.

1. $h \geq 3$

Draw a filled-in circle at ___3___ to show that 3
is a solution. Shade to the __right__ of __3__ to
show that values greater than 3 are solutions.

2. $x < -\dfrac{4}{5}$

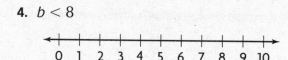

3. $y > {}^-2$

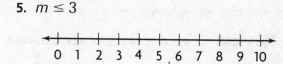

4. $b < 8$

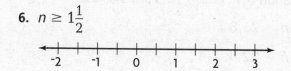

5. $m \leq 3$

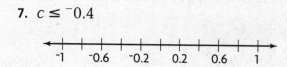

6. $n \geq 1\dfrac{1}{2}$

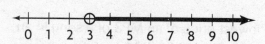

7. $c \leq {}^-0.4$

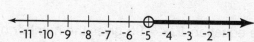

Write the inequality represented by the graph.

8.

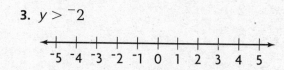

_____

9.

_____

Problem Solving REAL WORLD

10. The inequality $x \leq 2$ represents the
elevation x of a certain object found
at a dig site. Graph the solutions of
the inequality on the number line.

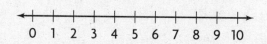

11. The inequality $x \geq 144$ represents the possible
scores x needed to pass a certain test.
Graph the solutions of the inequality on the
number line.

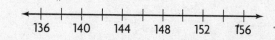

Lesson Check (CC.6.EE.8)

1. Which inequality is shown in the graph?

(A) $x < {}^-2$

(B) $x > {}^-2$

(C) $x \le {}^-2$

(D) $x \ge {}^-2$

2. Which of the following describes the graph of $g < 0.6$?

(A) Empty circle at 0.6 with shading to the left

(B) Empty circle at 0.6 with shading to the right

(C) Filled-in circle at 0.6 with shading to the left

(D) Filled-in circle at 0.6 with shading to the right

Spiral Review (CC.6.EE.2b, CC.6.EE.5, CC.6.EE.7, CC.6.EE.8)

3. Which expression shows the product of 5 and the difference of 12 and 9? **(Lesson 7.4)**

(A) $5 - 12 - 9$

(B) $5 \times 12 \times 9$

(C) $5 \times (12 - 9)$

(D) $(5 - 12) \times 9$

4. Which of the following is a solution of the equation $8.7 + n = 15.1$? **(Lesson 8.1)**

(A) $n = 23.8$

(B) $n = 22.8$

(C) $n = 7.4$

(D) $n = 6.4$

5. The equation $12x = 96$ gives the number of 12-centimeter pieces that can be cut from a 96-centimeter ribbon. What is the solution of the equation? **(Lesson 8.6)**

(A) $x = \frac{1}{8}$

(B) $x = 8$

(C) $x = 84$

(D) $x = 1,152$

6. The lowest price of an MP3 of a song in an online store is $0.99. Which of the following inequalities represents the price p of any MP3 in the store? **(Lesson 8.9)**

(A) $p < 0.99$

(B) $p \le 0.99$

(C) $p > 0.99$

(D) $p \ge 0.99$

COMMON CORE STANDARDS CC.6.EE.5, CC.6.EE.7, CC.6.EE.8

Chapter 8 Extra Practice

Lesson 8.1

Determine whether the given value of the variable is a solution of the equation.

1. $5 - a = 5; a = 0$

2. $\frac{3}{4}d = 6; d = 8$

3. $0.8 + k = 10; k = 0.2$

Lesson 8.2

Write an equation for the word sentence.

4. 7 less than the number of pencils is 15.

5. 12 times the number of tennis balls is 48.

Lessons 8.3 - 8.6

Model and solve the equation by using algebra tiles.

6. $8 = 8x$

7. $x + 5 = 9$

8. $8 = 1 + x$

Solve the equation, and check the solution.

9. $c + 14 = 35$

10. $n - 5.1 = 8.8$

11. $1\frac{1}{2} = v + \frac{3}{4}$

12. $16 = m - 7$

13. $12x = 72$

14. $\frac{b}{3} = 18$

15. $13 = 5.2y$

16. $\frac{1}{4} = \frac{2}{3}s$

Lesson 8.7

17. In Rachel's reading class, 8 students chose mystery as their favorite type of book. This amount represents $\frac{2}{5}$ of the entire class. The equation $\frac{2}{5}s = 8$ scan be used to find the total number of students s in Rachel's class. How many students are in Rachel's reading class?

18. There are 9 raisin bagels in a bin. This amount represents $\frac{3}{8}$ of all the bagels in the bin. The equation $\frac{3}{8}b = 9$ can be used to find the total number of bagels b in the bin. How many bagels are in the bin?

Lesson 8.8

Determine whether the given value of the variable is a solution of the inequality.

19. $c > 2.5$; $c = 3$

20. $y \leq {}^-7$; $y = {}^-4$

21. $n \geq \frac{-1}{2}$; $n = 0$

Lesson 8.9

Write an inequality for the word sentence.

22. The weight w is at least 4 pounds.

23. The temperature t is less than 0 degrees.

Lesson 8.10

Graph the inequality.

24. $x \geq 5$

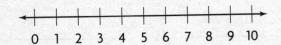

25. $m < 2$

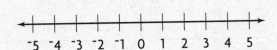

26. $p > {}^-3$

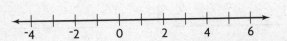

27. $h \leq {}^-1\frac{1}{2}$

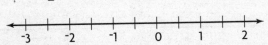

Chapter 9 — School-Home Letter

Vocabulary

dependent variable A variable whose value depends on the value of another quantity.

independent variable A variable whose value determines the value of another quantity.

linear equation An equation that, when graphed, forms a straight line.

Dear Family,

Throughout the next few weeks, our math class will be learning about linear equations. We will learn how to write equations and graph equations.

You can expect to see homework with real-world problems that involve tables, coordinate planes, and ordered pairs.

Here is a sample of how your child was taught to write an equation, given a table of values.

🔑 MODEL Write an Equation

Write an equation for the relationship shown in the table.

STEP 1

Think: "What is being done to each x to get y?" The y-values are less than the corresponding x-values. The equation might involve subtraction or division.

x	7	9	11	13
y	1	3	5	7

STEP 2

For the first pair of values, $y = x \div 7$. Is this true for the other pairs? $9 \div 7 \neq 3$ No, $y = x \div 7$ does not work for all pairs of values.

STEP 3

Try subtraction. For the first pair of values, $y = x - 6$. Is this true for the other pairs? $9 - 6 = 3$ $11 - 6 = 5$ $13 - 6 = 7$ Yes.

So, the equation $y = x - 6$ represents the relationship.

Tips

Writing Equations

When writing an equation to represent a relationship, be sure that the equation works for *all* pairs of values.

Activity

Look around your home for ideas of linear relationships (for example, 8 granola bars in 1 box). Then make a table of values. Tell what x and y represent. Write an equation and graph the relationship.

Carta para la casa

Querida familia,

Durante las próximas semanas, en la clase de matemáticas aprenderemos sobre ecuaciones lineales. También aprenderemos cómo escribir y graficar ecuaciones.

Llevaré a casa tareas con problemas del mundo real que incluyan tablas, planos cartesianos y pares ordenados.

Este es un ejemplo de la manera cómo aprenderemos a escribir una ecuación, dada una tabla de valores.

MODELO Escribir una ecuación

Escribe una ecuación para la relación que se muestra en la tabla.

PASO 1

Piensa: "¿Qué se hace en cada x para obtener y?" Los valores y son menores que sus correspondientes valores x. La ecuación podría incluir resta o división.

x	7	9	11	13
y	1	3	5	7

PASO 2

Para el primer par de valores, $y = x \div 7$. ¿Es esto verdadero para los otros pares? $9 \div 7 \neq 3$ No, $y = x \div 7$ no funciona para los otros pares de valores.

PASO 3

Intenta restar. Para el primer par de valores, $y = x - 6$. ¿Es esto verdadero para los otros pares? $9 - 6 = 3$
$11 - 6 = 5$ $13 - 6 = 7$ ¡Sí!
Por tanto, la ecuación $y = x - 6$ representa la relación.

Pistas

Escribir ecuaciones

Al escribir una ecuación para representar una relación, asegúrate de que la ecuación funcione para *todos* los pares de valores.

Actividad

En casa, echen un vistazo para encontrar ideas que representen relaciones lineales (por ejemplo, 8 barras de granola en 1 caja). Luego, hagan una tabla de valores. Explique qué representan x y y. Escriban una ecuación y representen gráficamente la relación.

Independent and Dependent Variables

COMMON CORE STANDARD CC.6.EE.9
Represent and analyze quantitative relationships between dependent and independent variables.

Lesson 9.1

Identify the independent and dependent variables. Then write an equation to represent the relationship between them.

1. Sandra has a coupon to save $3 off her next purchase at a restaurant. The cost of her meal c will be the price of the food p that she orders, minus $3.

The __cost of her meal__ depends on the __price of her food__.

dependent variable: __c__

independent variable: __p__

equation: __c__ = __$p - 3$__

2. An online clothing store charges $6 for shipping, no matter the price of the items. The total cost c in dollars is the price of the items ordered p plus $6 for shipping.

dependent variable: _____

independent variable: _____

equation: _____ = _____

3. Melinda is making necklaces. She uses 12 beads for each necklace. The total number of beads b depends on the number of necklaces n.

dependent variable: _____

independent variable: _____

equation: _____ = _____

4. Tanner is 2 years younger than his brother. Tanner's age t in years is 2 less than his brother's age b.

dependent variable: _____

independent variable: _____

equation: _____ = _____

5. Byron is playing a game. He earns 10 points for each question he answers correctly. His total score s equals the number of correct answers a times 10.

dependent variable: _____

independent variable: _____

equation: _____ = _____

Problem Solving  REAL WORLD

6. Maria earns $45 for every lawn that she mows. Her earnings e in dollars depend on the number of lawns n that she mows. Write an equation that represents this situation.

7. Martin sells cars. He earns $100 per day, plus any commission on his sales. His daily salary s in dollars depends on the amount of commission c. Write an equation to represent his daily salary.

_____

_____

Lesson Check (CC.6.EE.9)

1. There are 12 boys in a math class. The total number of students s depends on the number of girls in the class g. Which equation represents this situation?

   (A) $g = 12s$

   (B) $s = 12g$

   (C) $g = 12 + s$

   (D) $s = 12 + g$

2. A store received a shipment of soup cans. The clerk put an equal number of cans on each of 4 shelves. Which equation represents the relationship between the total number of cans t and the number of cans on each shelf n?

   (A) $n = t \div 4$

   (B) $n = t - 4$

   (C) $n = 4t$

   (D) $n = t + 4$

Spiral Review (CC.6.EE.2c, CC.6.EE.7, CC.6.EE.8)

3. The expression $9C \div 5 + 32$ gives the Fahrenheit temperature for a Celsius temperature of C degrees. Gwen had a Celsius temperature of 35 degrees. What was her temperature in degrees Fahrenheit? (Lesson 7.5)

   (A) 92 degrees

   (B) 95 degrees

   (C) 98 degrees

   (D) 104 degrees

4. Which equation represents the sentence below? (Lesson 8.2)

   The difference of a number n and 1.8 is 2.

   (A) $\frac{n}{1.8} = 2$

   (B) $n - 1.8 = 2$

   (C) $2 - 1.8 = n$

   (D) $1.8n = 2$

5. Drew drank 4 cups of orange juice. This is $\frac{2}{5}$ of the total amount of juice that was in the container. Solve $\frac{2}{5}x = 4$ for x. How much juice was in the container? (Lesson 8.7)

   (A) 0.8 cup

   (B) 1.6 cups

   (C) 10 cups

   (D) 20 cups

6. Which of the following shows all of the solutions to $x \leq {}^-4.5$? (Lesson 8.10)

   (A)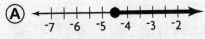

   (B)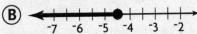

   (C)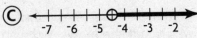

   (D)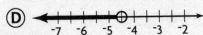

Name _____

Equations and Tables

COMMON CORE STANDARD CC.6.EE.9

Represent and analyze quantitative relationships between dependent and independent variables.

Use the equation to complete the table.

1. $y = 6x$

Input	Output
x	y
2	**12**
5	**30**
8	**48**

2. $y = x - 7$

Input	Output
x	y
10	
15	
20	

3. $y = 3x + 4$

Input	Output
x	y
3	
4	
5	

Write an equation for the relationship shown in the table. Then find the unknown value in the table.

4.

x	2	3	4	5
y	16	?	32	40

5.

x	18	20	22	24
y	9	10	?	12

_____

6.

x	8	10	12	14
y	13	15	17	?

7.

x	14	17	20	23
y	5	?	11	14

_____

Problem Solving  REAL WORLD

8. Tickets to a play cost $11 each. There is also a service charge of $4 per order. Write an equation for the relationship that gives the total cost y in dollars for an order of x tickets.

9. Write an equation for the relationship shown in the table. Then use the equation to find the estimated number of shrimp in a 5-pound bag.

Weight of bag (pounds), x	1	2	3	4
Estimated number of shrimp, y	24	48	72	96

_____

Lesson Check (CC.6.EE.9)

1. Which equation represents the relationship shown in the table?

x	8	10	12	14
y	4	6	8	10

Ⓐ $y = 2x$

Ⓑ $y = \frac{x}{2}$

Ⓒ $y = x - 4$

Ⓓ $y = x + 4$

2. There is a one-time fee of $27 to join a gym. The monthly cost of using the gym is $18. What is the equation for the relationship that gives the total cost y in dollars of joining the gym and using it for x months?

Ⓐ $y = 18x + 27$

Ⓑ $y = 18x - 27$

Ⓒ $y = 27x + 18$

Ⓓ $y = 27x - 18$

Spiral Review (CC.6.EE.5, CC.6.EE.6, CC.6.EE.7, CC.6.EE.9)

3. Mindy wants to buy several books that each cost $10. She has a coupon for $6 off her total cost. Which expression represents her total cost for b books? (Lesson 7.6)

Ⓐ $6b - 10$

Ⓑ $6b + 10$

Ⓒ $10b - 6$

Ⓓ $10b + 6$

4. When a coupon of $1.25 off is used, the cost of a taco meal is $4.85. The equation $p - 1.25 = 4.85$ can be used to find the regular price p in dollars of a taco meal. How much does a regular taco meal cost? (Lesson 8.4)

Ⓐ $3.60

Ⓑ $3.70

Ⓒ $6.00

Ⓓ $6.10

5. Which of the following is NOT a solution of the inequality $n < {}^-7$? (Lesson 8.8)

Ⓐ $n = {}^-7$

Ⓑ $n = {}^-7.2$

Ⓒ $n = {}^-7\frac{1}{2}$

Ⓓ $n = {}^-7.9$

6. Marcus sold brownies at a bake sale. He sold d dollars worth of brownies. He spent $5.50 on materials, so his total profit p can be found by subtracting $5.50 from his earnings. Which equation represents this situation? (Lesson 9.1)

Ⓐ $p = d + 5.50$

Ⓑ $p = d - 5.50$

Ⓒ $p = 5.50d$

Ⓓ $p = d \div 5.50$

Problem Solving • Analyze Relationships

COMMON CORE STANDARD CC.6.EE.9
Represent and analyze quantitative relationships
between dependent and independent variables.

The table shows the number of cups of yogurt needed to make different amounts of a fruit smoothie. Use the table for 1–3.

Batches, b	3	4	5	6
Cups of Yogurt, c	9	12	15	18

1. Write an equation to represent the relationship.

   The number of cups needed is ___3___ multiplied by the number of batches,

   so __c__ = __3__ × __b__.

   _____

2. How much yogurt is needed for 9 batches of smoothie?

   _____

3. Jerry used 33 cups of yogurt to make smoothies.
   How many batches did he make?

The table shows the relationship between Winn's age and his sister's age. Use the table for 4–6.

Winn's age, w	8	9	10	11
Winn's sister's age, s	12	13	14	15

4. Write an equation to represent the relationship.   s = _____

   _____

5. When Winn is 14 years old, how old will his sister be?   _____

   _____

6. When Winn's sister is 23 years old, how old will Winn be?   _____

Lesson Check (CC.6.EE.9)

1. The table shows the total cost c in dollars of n gift baskets. What will be the cost of 9 gift baskets?

n	3	4	5	6
c	$36	$48	$60	$72

- (A) $21
- (B) $84
- (C) $108
- (D) $118

2. The table shows the number of minutes m that Tara has practiced after d days. If Tara has practiced for 70 minutes, how many days has she practiced?

d	1	3	5	7
m	35	105	175	245

- (A) 2 days
- (B) 4 days
- (C) 6 days
- (D) 8 days

Spiral Review (CC.6.EE.3, CC.6.EE.7, CC.6.EE.8, CC.6.EE.9)

3. Soccer shirts cost $15 each, and soccer shorts cost $18 each. The expression $15n + 18n$ represents the total cost in dollars of n uniforms. Simplify the expression by combining like terms. **(Lesson 7.7)**

- (A) 33
- (B) $33n$
- (C) $15 + 18n$
- (D) $15n + 18$

4. Which equation has the greatest solution? **(Lesson 8.6)**

- (A) $\frac{x}{3} = 15$
- (B) $3x = 15$
- (C) $\frac{1}{5}x = 3$
- (D) $15x = 3$

5. The lowest price of an MP3 of a song in an online store is $0.99. Which of the following inequalities represents the price p of any MP3 in the store? **(Lesson 8.9)**

- (A) $p < 0.99$
- (B) $p \le 0.99$
- (C) $p > 0.99$
- (D) $p \ge 0.99$

6. Which of the following equations represents the relationship in the table? **(Lesson 9.2)**

x	8	10	12	14
y	4	5	6	7

- (A) $y = x - 4$
- (B) $x = y - 4$
- (C) $y = \frac{x}{2}$
- (D) $x = \frac{y}{2}$

Name _____

Graph Relationships

COMMON CORE STANDARD CC.6.EE.9
Represent and analyze quantitative relationships between dependent and independent variables.

Graph the relationship represented by the table.

1.

x	1	2	3	4	5
y	25	50	75	100	125

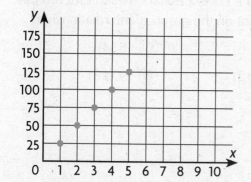

2.

x	10	20	30	40	50
y	350	300	250	200	150

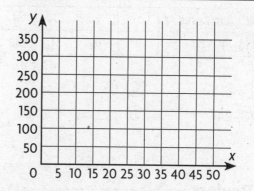

Graph the relationship represented by the table to find the unknown value of y.

3.

x	3	4	5	6	7
y	8	7		5	4

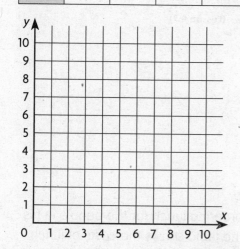

4.

x	1	3	5	7	9
y	1		3	4	5

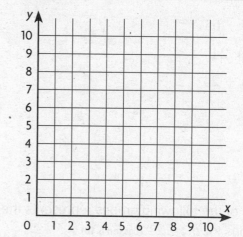

Problem Solving REAL WORLD

5. Graph the relationship represented by the table.

DVDs Purchased	1	2	3	4
Cost ($)	15	30	45	60

6. Use the graph to find the cost of purchasing 5 DVDs.

Cost of DVDs

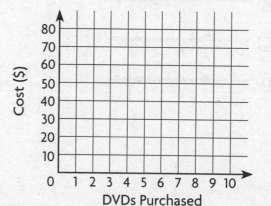

_____

Lesson Check (CC.6.EE.9)

1. Mei wants to graph the relationship represented by the table. Which ordered pair is a point on the graph of the relationship?

T-shirts purchased, x	1	2	3	4
Cost ($), y	8	16	24	32

Ⓐ (1, 2)
Ⓑ (3, 24)
Ⓒ (8, 16)
Ⓓ (32, 4)

2. An online bookstore charges $2 to ship any book. Cole graphs the relationship that gives the total cost y in dollars to buy and ship a book that costs x dollars. Which ordered pair is a point on the graph of the relationship?

Ⓐ (4, 6)
Ⓑ (5, 2)
Ⓒ (6, 4)
Ⓓ (9, 18)

Spiral Review (CC.6.EE.3, CC.6.EE.7, CC.6.EE.8, CC.6.EE.9)

3. Which of the following expressions is equivalent to $6(g + 4)$? (Lesson 7.8)

Ⓐ $6g + 4$
Ⓑ $6g + 64$
Ⓒ $g + 24$
Ⓓ $6g + 24$

4. There are 6 girls in a music class. This represents $\frac{3}{7}$ of the entire class. Solve $\frac{3}{7}s = 6$ for s to find the number of students in the class. (Lesson 8.7)

Ⓐ 6
Ⓑ 14
Ⓒ 18
Ⓓ 21

5. Which of the following graphs represents the solutions for $n > {}^-2$? (Lesson 8.10)

Ⓐ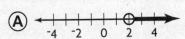
Ⓑ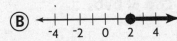
Ⓒ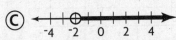
Ⓓ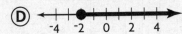

6. Sam is ordering lunch for the people in his office. The table shows the costs of lunch based on the number of people. How much will lunch cost for 35 people? (Lesson 9.3)

Number of people, n	5	10	15	20
Cost ($), c	40	80	120	160

Ⓐ $25
Ⓑ $160
Ⓒ $200
Ⓓ $280

Equations and Graphs

COMMON CORE STANDARD CC.6.EE.9

Represent and analyze quantitative relationships between dependent and independent variables.

Graph the linear equation.

1. $y = x - 3$

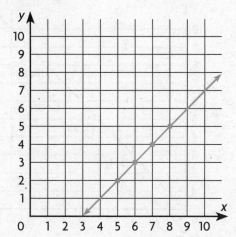

x	y
5	2
6	3
7	4
8	5

2. $y = x \div 3$

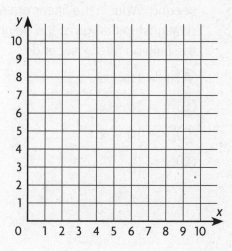

Write a linear equation for the relationship shown by the graph.

3.

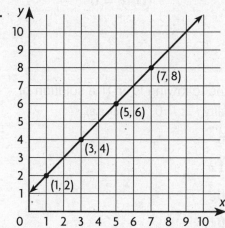

4.

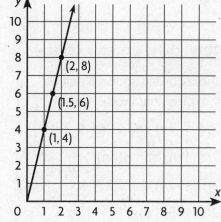

Problem Solving REAL WORLD

5. Dee is driving at an average speed of 50 miles per hour. Write a linear equation for the relationship that gives the distance y in miles that Dee drives in x hours.

_____

6. Graph the relationship from Exercise 5.

Dee's Distance

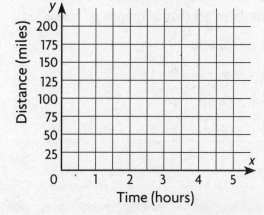

Lesson Check (CC.6.EE.9)

1. A balloon rises at a rate of 10 feet per second. What is the linear equation for the relationship that gives the height y in feet of the balloon after x seconds?

   (A) $y = 10x$

   (B) $y = 10 + x$

   (C) $y = 10 - x$

   (D) $y = \frac{x}{10}$

2. What linear equation is shown by the graph?

   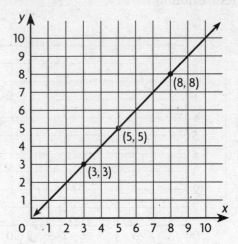

   (A) $y = 3x$ (C) $y = x + 8$

   (B) $y = x$ (D) $y = 0$

Spiral Review (CC.6.EE.4, CC.6.EE.5, CC.6.EE.9)

3. Which of the following shows a pair of equivalent expressions? (Lesson 7.9)

   (A) $9 + 3(4 + 7n)$ and $12(4 + 7n)$

   (B) $4 + 2(5 + n)$ and $6(5n)$

   (C) $3 + 2(9 + 2n)$ and $21 + 4n$

   (D) $6 + 2(3 + 8n)$ and $6 + 16n$

4. Which of the following is NOT a solution of the inequality $j \geq 0.6$? (Lesson 8.8)

   (A) $j = 0.6$

   (B) $j = 0.12$

   (C) $j = 0.8$

   (D) $j = 0.61$

5. Red grapes cost $2.49 per pound. Which of the following equations shows the relationship between the cost c and the number of pounds of grapes p? (Lesson 9.1)

   (A) $c = 2.49p$

   (B) $c = p \div 2.49$

   (C) $c = 2.49 + p$

   (D) $c = p - 2.49$

6. It costs $8 per hour to rent a bike. Niko graphs this relationship using x for number of hours and y for total cost. Which ordered pair is a point on the graph of the relationship? (Lesson 9.4)

   (A) $(4, 8)$

   (B) $(6, 14)$

   (C) $(24, 3)$

   (D) $(5, 40)$

Chapter 9 Extra Practice

Lesson 9.1

Identify the dependent and independent variables. Then write an equation to represent the relationship between them.

1. Kevin will make some money babysitting today. He owes his brother $10. The amount of money he will have left m is equal to his babysitting earnings e decreased by 10.

   dependent variable: _____

   independent variable: _____

   equation: _____

2. A teacher grades 4 essays each hour. The total number of essays she can grade e is equal to 4 multiplied by the number of hours h she spends grading.

   dependent variable: _____

   independent variable: _____

   equation: _____

Lesson 9.2

Use the equation to complete the table.

3. $y = x - 1$

Input	Output
x	y
6	
8	
10	

4. $y = \frac{x}{3} + 2$

Input	Output
x	y
3	
9	
15	

Write an equation for the relationship shown in the table. Then find the unknown value.

5.

x	3	5	7	9
y	0	2	?	6

6.

x	8	12	16	20
y	2	?	4	5

_____

_____

Lesson 9.3

A day care center is ordering chairs. The table shows the
total cost based on the number of chairs ordered.

Cost of Chairs for Day Care Center				
Number of Chairs, *n*	3	4	5	6
Cost ($), *c*	54	72	90	108

7. Find a pattern and write an
   equation.

   c = _____

8. How much will it cost the
   center to order 9 chairs?

   _____

9. If the center spends $180
   on chairs, how many chairs
   does the center purchase?

   _____

Lesson 9.4

Graph the relationship shown by the table to find the unknown value of *y*.

10.

x	2	3	4	5	6
y	5	6		8	9

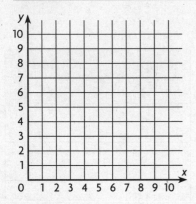

11.

x	1	2	3	4	5
y	1	3	5		9

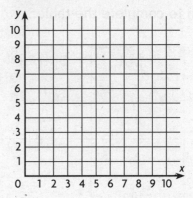

Lesson 9.5

12. Graph the linear equation.
    $y = 4x - 3$

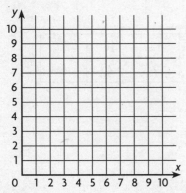

13. Write the linear equation for the relationship
    shown by the graph.

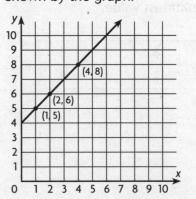

(4, 8)
(2, 6)
(1, 5)

_____

School-Home Letter

© Houghton Mifflin Harcourt Publishing Company

Dear Family,

Throughout the next few weeks, our math class will be learning about area of parallelograms, triangles, trapezoids, regular polygons, and composite figures. We will also be learning how the area of a figure changes when the figure's dimensions change.

You can expect to see homework in which students use formulas to find the area of a variety of figures.

Here is a sample of how your child was taught to find the area of a trapezoid.

Vocabulary

area The number of square units needed to cover a figure.

parallelogram A quadrilateral whose opposite sides are parallel and congruent.

regular polygon A polygon in which all sides are congruent and all angles are congruent.

trapezoid A quadrilateral with exactly one pair of parallel sides.

🔒 MODEL Solve Area Problems

Find the area of the trapezoid.

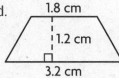

1.8 cm
1.2 cm
3.2 cm

STEP 1

Write the formula.

$A = \frac{1}{2}(b_1 + b_2)h$

STEP 2

Substitute 1.8 for b_1, 3.2 for b_2, and 1.2 for h.

$A = \frac{1}{2} \times (1.8 + 3.2) \times 1.2$

STEP 3

Add inside the parentheses. Then multiply.

$A = \frac{1}{2} \times 5 \times 1.2$

$A = 3$

So, the area is 3 cm^2.

Tips

Changing Dimensions

When you multiply all dimensions of a figure by a number, the area is multiplied by the square of that number.

Activity

Using a ruler, work together to construct a triangle that has an area of 8 square inches. There are many possible triangles. Sketch a triangle, and then use the area formula to check. If the area is not equal to 8 square inches, adjust the height and base as needed.

Carta
para la casa

Querida familia,

Durante las próximas semanas, en la clase de matemáticas aprenderemos sobre el área de paralelogramos, triángulos, trapecios, polígonos regulares y figuras compuestas. También aprenderemos a cómo cambia el área de una figura cuando cambian sus dimensiones.

Llevaré a la casa tareas en las que usaré fórmulas para hallar el área de distintas figuras.

Este es un ejemplo de la manera como aprenderemos a hallar el área de un trapecio.

🔒 MODELO   Resolver problemas de área

Halla el área del trapecio.

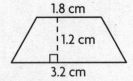

Pistas

Cambiar dimensiones

Cuando multiplicas todas dimensiones de una figura por un número, el área se multiplica por el cuadrado de ese número.

PASO 1

Escribe la fórmula.

$A = \frac{1}{2}(b_1 + b_2)h$

PASO 2

Reemplaza la b_1 con 1.8, la b_2 con 3.2 y la h con 1.2.

$A = \frac{1}{2} \times (1.8 + 3.2) \times 1.2$

PASO 3

Suma los paréntesis. Luego multiplica.

$A = \frac{1}{2} \times 5 \times 1.2$

$A = 3$

Por tanto, el área es 3 cm².

Actividad

Usando una regla, trabajen juntos para construir un triángulo que tenga un área de 8 pulgadas cuadradas. Hay muchos triángulos posibles. Dibujen un triángulo, luego apliquen la fórmula para encontrar el área, para verificar. Si el área no es igual a 8 pulgadas cuadradas, ajusten la altura y la base según sea necesario.

Name _____

Area of Parallelograms

COMMON CORE STANDARD CC.6.G.1
Solve real-world and mathematical problems involving area, surface area, and volume.

Find the area of the figure.

1.

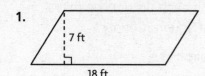
7 ft
18 ft

$A = bh$
$A = \textbf{18} \times \textbf{7}$
$A = \textbf{126 ft}^2$

2.

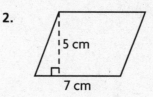
5 cm
7 cm

_____ cm^2

Find the unknown measurement for the figure.

3. square

$A =$ _____

$s = 9$ yd

4. parallelogram

$A = 247$ in.^{2}

$b = 19$ in.

$h =$ _____

5. parallelogram

$A = 9.18$ m^2

$b = 2.7$ m

$h =$ _____

6. parallelogram

$A = 8\frac{3}{4}$ yd^2

$b = 3\frac{1}{2}$ yd

$h =$ _____

7. parallelogram

$A = 0.2$ in.^{2}

$b =$ _____

$h = 0.4$ in.

8. parallelogram

$A =$ _____

$b = 4\frac{3}{10}$ m

$h = 2\frac{1}{10}$ m

9. square

$A =$ _____

$s = 35$ cm

10. parallelogram

$A = 6.3$ mm^2

$b =$ _____

$h = 0.9$ mm

Problem Solving

11. Ronna has a sticker in the shape of a parallelogram. The sticker has a base of 6.5 cm and a height of 10.1 cm. What is the area of the sticker?

12. A parallelogram-shaped tile has an area of 48 in.^{2}. The base of the tile measures 12 in. What is the measure of its height?

_____

_____

Lesson Check (CC.6.G.1, CC.6.EE.2c)

1. Cougar Park is shaped like a parallelogram and has an area of $\frac{1}{16}$ square mile. Its base is $\frac{3}{8}$ mile. What is its height?

   (A) $\frac{1}{6}$ mile

   (B) $\frac{4}{9}$ mile

   (C) $2\frac{1}{4}$ miles

   (D) 6 miles

2. Square County is a square-shaped county divided into 16 equal-sized square districts. If the side length of each district is 4 miles, what is the area of Square County?

   (A) 16 square miles

   (B) 64 square miles

   (C) 256 square miles

   (D) 324 square miles

Spiral Review (CC.6.EE.5, CC.6.EE.8, CC.6.EE.9)

3. Which of the following makes the inequality true? **(Lesson 8.1)**

   $$y < {}^-4$$

   (A) $y = 3$

   (B) $y = 0$

   (C) $y = {}^-2$

   (D) $y = {}^-6$

4. On a winter's day, 9°F is the highest temperature recorded. Which inequality represents the temperature, t, in degrees Fahrenheit, at any time on this day? **(Lesson 8.9)**

   (A) $t < 9$

   (B) $t \leq 9$

   (C) $t > 9$

   (D) $t \geq 9$

5. In 2 seconds, an elevator travels 40 feet. In 3 seconds, the elevator travels 60 feet. In 4 seconds, the elevator travels 80 feet. Which is an equation that gives the relationship between the number of seconds x and the distance y the elevator travels? **(Lesson 9.2)**

   (A) $y = x \div 20$

   (B) $y = x + 18$

   (C) $y = 40x$

   (D) $y = 20x$

6. The linear equation $y = 4x$ represents the number of bracelets y that Jolene can make in x hours. Which ordered pair lies on the graph of the equation? **(Lesson 9.5)**

   (A) $(0, 4)$

   (B) $(2, 6)$

   (C) $(4, 16)$

   (D) $(6, 20)$

Explore Area of Triangles

COMMON CORE STANDARD CC.6.G.1
Solve real-world and mathematical problems involving area, surface area, and volume.

Find the area of each triangle.

1.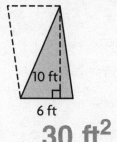
10 ft
6 ft

30 ft²

2.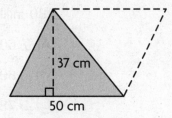
37 cm
50 cm

_____

3.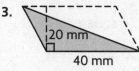
20 mm
40 mm

_____

4.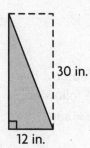
30 in.
12 in.

_____

5.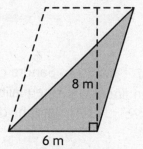
8 m
6 m

_____

6.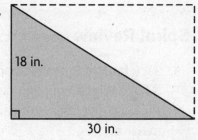
18 in.
30 in.

_____

7.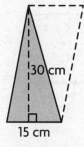
30 cm
15 cm

_____

8.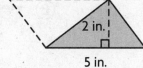
2 in.
5 in.

_____

9.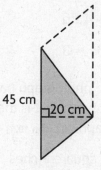
45 cm
20 cm

_____

Problem Solving REAL WORLD

10. Fabian is decorating a triangular pennant for a football game. The pennant has a base of 10 inches and a height of 24 inches. What is the total area of the pennant?

_____

11. Ryan is buying a triangular tract of land. The triangle has a base of 100 yards and a height of 300 yards. What is the area of the tract of land?

_____

Lesson Check (CC.6.G.1)

1. What is the area of a triangle with a height of 14 feet and a base of 10 feet?

   (A) 24 square feet

   (B) 35 square feet

   (C) 70 square feet

   (D) 140 square feet

2. What is the area of a triangle with a height of 40 millimeters and a base of 380 millimeters?

   (A) 7,600 square millimeters

   (B) 3,800 square millimeters

   (C) 780 square millimeters

   (D) 380 square millimeters

Spiral Review (CC.6.EE.7, CC.6.EE.8, CC.6.G.1)

3. Jack bought 3 protein bars for a total of $4.26. Which equation could be used to find the cost c in dollars of each protein bar? (Lesson 8.2)

   (A) $\frac{c}{3} = 4.26$

   (B) $\frac{c}{4.26} = 3$

   (C) $3c = 4.26$

   (D) $4.26c = 3$

4. Sandra correctly sketched a graph for the inequality $y \leq {}^-7$. Which of the following graphs did Sandra sketch? (Lesson 8.10)

   (A)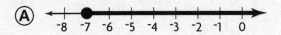

   (B)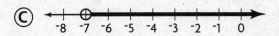

   (C)

   (D)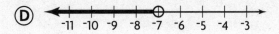

5. A square photograph has a perimeter of 20 inches. What is the area of the photograph? (Lesson 10.1)

   (A) 16 square inches

   (B) 25 square inches

   (C) 100 square inches

   (D) 400 square inches

Name _____

Area of Triangles

COMMON CORE STANDARD CC.6.G.1
Solve real-world and mathematical problems
involving area, surface area, and volume.

Find the area.

1.

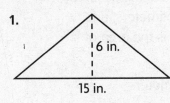

6 in.

15 in.

$A = \frac{1}{2}bh$

$A = \frac{1}{2} \times 15 \times 6$

$A = 45$

Area = 45 in.^{2}

2.

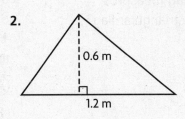

0.6 m

1.2 m

_____

3.

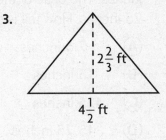

$2\frac{2}{3}$ ft

$4\frac{1}{2}$ ft

_____

Find the unknown measurement for the triangle.

4. $A = 0.225$ mi^2

   $b = 0.6$ mi

   $h =$

_____

5. $A = 4.86$ yd^2

   $b =$

   $h = 1.8$ yd

_____

6. $A = 63$ m^2

   $b =$

   $h = 12$ m

_____

7. $A = 2.5$ km^2

   $b = 5$ km

   $h =$

_____

Problem Solving REAL WORLD

8. Bayla draws a triangle with a base of 15 cm
   and a height of 8.5 cm. If she colors the space
   inside the triangle, what area does she color?

_____

9. Alicia is making a triangular sign for the school
   play. The area of the sign is 558 in.^{2}. The base
   of the triangle is 36 in. What is the height of
   the triangle?

_____

Lesson Check (CC.6.G.1, CC.6.EE.2c)

1. A triangular flag has an area of 187.5 square inches. The base of the flag measures 25 inches. How tall is the triangular flag?

   (A)   7.5 inches

   (B)   15 inches

   (C)   425 inches

   (D) 2,345.75 inches

2. A piece of stained glass in the shape of a right triangle has sides measuring 8 centimeters, 15 centimeters, and 17 centimeters. What is the area of the piece?

   (A)   60 square centimeters

   (B)   68 square centimeters

   (C) 120 square centimeters

   (D) 127.5 square centimeters

Spiral Review (CC.6.EE.7, CC.6.EE.9, CC.6.G.1)

3. Tina bought a T-shirt and sandals. The total cost was $41.50. The T-shirt cost $8.95. The equation $8.95 + c = 41.50$ can be used to find the cost c in dollars of the sandals. How much did the sandals cost? (Lesson 8.4)

   (A) $32.55   (C) $49.25

   (B) $33.45   (D) $50.45

4. There are 37 paper clips in a box. Carmen places more paper clips in the box. Which equation models the total number of paper clips p in the box after Carmen places n more paper clips in the box? (Lesson 9.1)

   (A) $n = 37 - p$ (C) $p = 37 - n$

   (B) $n = 37 + p$ (D) $p = 37 + n$

5. Which ordered pair is on the graph of the equation represented by the table? (Lesson 9.4)

People in group, x	1	2	3	4
Total cost of ordering lunch special ($), y	6	12	18	24

   (A) (1, 2)

   (B) (5, 30)

   (C) (6, 1)

   (D) (7, 12)

6. Maleek draws a line to cut the parallelogram in half. If he colors one half of the parallelogram, what area does he color? (Lesson 10.2)

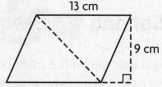

   (A) 44 square centimeters

   (B) 58.5 square centimeters

   (C) 117 square centimeters

   (D) 234 square centimeters

Explore Area of Trapezoids

COMMON CORE STANDARD CC.6.G.1
Solve real-world and mathematical problems involving area, surface area, and volume.

1. Trace and cut out two copies of the trapezoid. Arrange the trapezoids to form a parallelogram. Find the areas of the parallelogram and the trapezoids using square units.

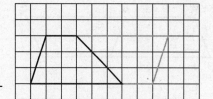

parallelogram: 24 square units; trapezoids: 12 square units

Find the area of the trapezoid.

2.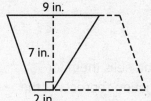
9 in.
7 in.
2 in.

_____ in.²

3.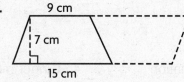
9 cm
7 cm
15 cm

_____ cm²

4.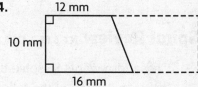
12 mm
10 mm
16 mm

_____ mm²

5.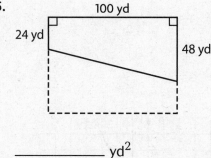
100 yd
24 yd
48 yd

_____ yd²

6.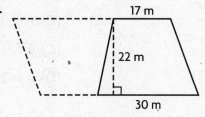
17 m
22 m
30 m

_____ m²

7.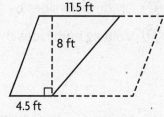
11.5 ft
8 ft
4.5 ft

_____ ft²

Problem Solving REAL WORLD

8. A cake is made out of two identical trapezoids. Each trapezoid has a height of 11 inches and bases of 9 inches and 14 inches. What is the area of one of the trapezoid pieces?

_____

9. A sticker is in the shape of a trapezoid. The height is 3 centimeters, and the bases are 2.5 centimeters and 5.5 centimeters. What is the area of the sticker?

_____

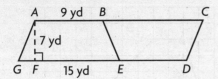

Lesson Check (CC.6.G.1)

1. What is the area of figure *ABEG*?

   ```
        A    9 yd   B          C
       ┌─────────────┐─────────┐
       │ 7 yd                  │
       └──┐_____  │
       G  F   15 yd    E        D
   ```

   (A) 84 square yards

   (B) 168 square yards

   (C) 472.5 square yards

   (D) 945 square yards

2. Maggie colors a figure in the shape of a trapezoid. The trapezoid is 6 inches tall. The bases are 4.5 inches and 8 inches. What is the area of the figure that Maggie colored?

   (A) 37.5 square inches

   (B) 75 square inches

   (C) 108 square inches

   (D) 216 square inches

Spiral Review (CC.6.EE.7, CC.6.EE.9)

3. Cassandra wants to solve the equation $30 = \frac{2}{5}p$. Which of the following should she do to isolate the variable? (Lesson 8.6)

   (A) Divide both sides by 30.

   (B) Multiply both sides by 30.

   (C) Divide both sides by $\frac{2}{5}$.

   (D) Multiply both sides by $\frac{2}{5}$.

4. Ginger makes pies and sells them for $14 each. Which equation represents the situation, if y represents the money that Ginger earns and x represents the number of pies sold? (Lesson 9.2)

   (A) $x = 14y$

   (B) $x = \frac{14}{y}$

   (C) $y = 14x$

   (D) $y = 14 + x$

5. What is the equation for the graph shown at right? (Lesson 9.5)

   (A) $y = 2x$

   (B) $y = \frac{1}{2}x$

   (C) $y = 4x$

   (D) $y = \frac{1}{4}x$

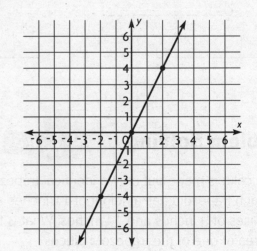

Name _____

Area of Trapezoids

COMMON CORE STANDARD CC.6.G.1
Solve real-world and mathematical problems
involving area, surface area, and volume.

Find the area of the trapezoid.

1. $A = \frac{1}{2}(b_1 + b_2)h$

$A = \frac{1}{2} + (\underline{11} + \underline{17}) \times 18$

$A = \frac{1}{2} \times \underline{28} \times 18$

$A = \underline{252}$ cm²

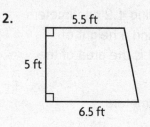

11 cm
18 cm
17 cm

2.

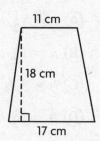

5.5 ft
5 ft
6.5 ft

$A =$ _____

3.

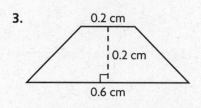

0.2 cm
0.2 cm
0.6 cm

$A =$ _____

4.

10 in.
$2\frac{1}{2}$ in.
5 in.

$A =$ _____

Find the height of the trapezoid.

5.

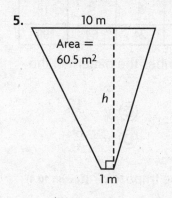

10 m
Area = 60.5 m²
h
1 m

$h =$ _____

6.

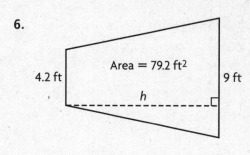

4.2 ft
Area = 79.2 ft²
h
9 ft

$h =$ _____

Problem Solving REAL WORLD

7. Sonia makes a wooden frame around a square
picture. The frame is made of 4 congruent
trapezoids. The shorter base is 9 in., the
longer base is 12 in., and the height is 1.5 in.
What is the area of the picture frame?

_____

8. Bryan cuts a piece of cardboard in the shape
of a trapezoid. The area of the cutout is
43.5 square centimeters. If the bases are
6 centimeters and 8.5 centimeters long, what
is the height of the trapezoid?

_____

Lesson Check (CC.6.G.1, CC.6.EE.2c)

1. Gold bars have cross sections that are trapezoids. A cross section of a certain gold bar has bases measuring 4.2 centimeters and 6.8 centimeters and a height of 3.6 centimeters. What is the area of the cross section?

   (A) 19.8 square centimeters

   (B) 21.84 square centimeters

   (C) 26.52 square centimeters

   (D) 39.6 square centimeters

2. Which of the following dimensions form a trapezoid with an area of $4\frac{1}{8}$ square units?

   (A) $h = 1\frac{1}{2}, b_1 = 6, b_2 = 3\frac{1}{2}$

   (B) $h = 1\frac{1}{2}, b_1 = 2, b_2 = 3\frac{1}{2}$

   (C) $h = 3, b_1 = 2, b_2 = 3\frac{1}{2}$

   (D) $h = 1\frac{1}{2}, b_1 = 2, b_2 = 7$

Spiral Review (CC.6.EE.7, CC.6.EE.9, CC.6.G.1)

3. Which of the following addition equations has the solution $c = \frac{2}{5}$? (Lesson 8.7)

   (A) $\frac{1}{2} + c = \frac{9}{10}$

   (B) $\frac{1}{5} + c = \frac{1}{5}$

   (C) $\frac{1}{2} + c = \frac{5}{7}$

   (D) $\frac{2}{3} + c = \frac{4}{5}$

4. The table shows the total cost y for x pounds of cashews.

   Cost of Cashews

Number of Pounds, x	2	4	9	15
Cost ($), y	12	24	54	90

   Which equation describes the pattern in the table? (Lesson 9.3)

   (A) $y = 6 + x$ (C) $y = \frac{12}{x}$

   (B) $y = 6x$ (D) $y = \frac{6}{x}$

5. An artist sells her work for $2 per square inch. What is the cost of a piece of art in the shape of a parallelogram with a base of 8 inches and a height of 6 inches?

   (Lesson 10.1)

   (A) $48

   (B) $96

   (C) $144

   (D) $192

6. What is the area of the trapezoid? (Lesson 10.4)

   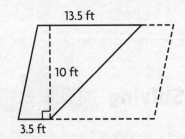

   (A) 41.125 square feet

   (B) 42.5 square feet

   (C) 85 square feet

   (D) 170 square feet

Area of Regular Polygons

COMMON CORE STANDARD CC.6.G.1
Solve real-world and mathematical problems
involving area, surface area, and volume.

Find the area of the regular polygon.

1.

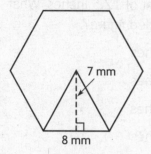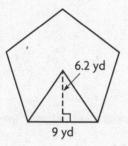

7 mm

8 mm

number of congruent triangles inside the figure: ____6____

area of each triangle: $\frac{1}{2} \times$ ___8___ $\times$ ___7___ = ___28___ mm²

area of hexagon: ___168 mm²___

2.

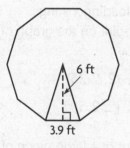

6.2 yd

9 yd

_____

3.

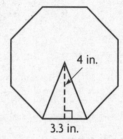

4 in.

3.3 in.

_____

4.

6 ft

3.9 ft

_____

5.

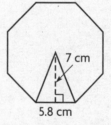

7 cm

5.8 cm

_____

Problem Solving REAL WORLD

6. Stu is making a stained glass window in the
shape of a regular pentagon. The pentagon
can be divided into congruent triangles, each
with a base of 8.7 inches and a height of
6 inches. What is the area of the window?

_____

7. A dinner platter is in the shape of a regular
decagon. The platter has an area of
161 square inches and a side length of
4.6 inches. What is the area of each triangle?
What is the height of each triangle?

_____

Lesson Check (CC.6.G.1, CC.6.EE.2c)

1. What is the area of the regular hexagon?

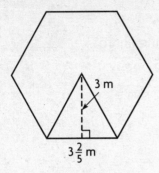

3 m

$3\frac{2}{5}$ m

Ⓐ $5\frac{1}{10}$ square meters

Ⓑ $30\frac{3}{5}$ square meters

Ⓒ $56\frac{2}{5}$ square meters

Ⓓ $61\frac{1}{5}$ square meters

2. A regular 7-sided figure is divided into 7 congruent triangles, each with a base of 12 inches and a height of 12.5 inches. What is the area of the 7-sided figure?

Ⓐ 1,050 square inches

Ⓑ 525 square inches

Ⓒ 150 square inches

Ⓓ 75 square inches

Spiral Review (CC.6.EE.5, CC.6.EE.9, CC.6.G.1)

3. Which of the following inequalities does NOT contain the solution $b = 4$? (Lesson 8.8)

Ⓐ $2 + b \geq 2$

Ⓑ $3b \leq 14$

Ⓒ $8 - b \leq 15$

Ⓓ $b - 3 \geq 5$

4. Each song that Tara downloads costs $1.25. She graphs the relationship that gives the cost y in dollars of downloading x songs. Which ordered pair is a point on the graph of the relationship? (Lesson 9.4)

Ⓐ (1.25, 1)   Ⓒ (2, 2.25)

Ⓑ (1.25, 1.25)   Ⓓ (2, 2.5)

5. What is the area of triangle ABC? (Lesson 10.2)

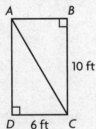

A   B

10 ft

D   6 ft   C

Ⓐ 15 square feet

Ⓑ 16 square feet

Ⓒ 30 square feet

Ⓓ 32 square feet

6. Marcia cut a trapezoid out of a large piece of felt. The trapezoid has a height of 9 cm and bases of 6 cm and 11 cm. What is the area of Marcia's felt trapezoid? (Lesson 10.5)

Ⓐ 75 square centimeters

Ⓑ 76.5 square centimeters

Ⓒ 153 square centimeters

Ⓓ 297 square centimeters

Composite Figures

COMMON CORE STANDARD CC.6.G.1
Solve real-world and mathematical problems
involving area, surface area, and volume.

Find the area of the figure.

1.

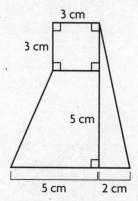

area of square $A = s \times s$

$= \underline{\quad 3 \quad} \times \underline{\quad 3 \quad} = \underline{\quad 9 \quad}$ cm^2

area of triangle $A = \frac{1}{2}bh$

$= \frac{1}{2} \times \underline{\quad 2 \quad} \times \underline{\quad 8 \quad} = \underline{\quad 8 \quad}$ cm^2

area of trapezoid $A = \frac{1}{2}(b_1 + b_2)h$

$= \frac{1}{2} \times (\underline{\quad 5 \quad} + \underline{\quad 3 \quad}) \times \underline{\quad 5 \quad} = \underline{\quad 20 \quad}$ cm^2

area of composite figure $A = \underline{\quad 9 \quad}$ cm$^2 + \underline{\quad 8 \quad}$ cm$^2 + \underline{\quad 20 \quad}$ cm^2

$= \underline{\quad 37 \quad}$ cm^2

2.

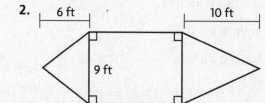

_____

3.

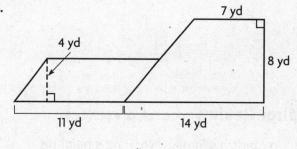

_____

Problem Solving REAL WORLD

4. Janelle is making a poster. She cuts a triangle
out of poster board. What is the area of the
poster board that she has left?

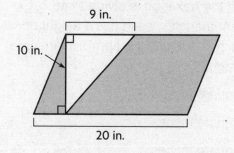

_____

5. Michael wants to place grass on the sides
of his lap pool. Find the area of the shaded
regions that he wants to cover with grass.

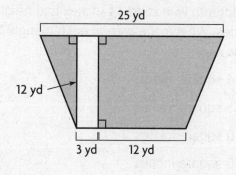

_____

Lesson Check (CC.6.G.1, CC.6.EE.2c)

1. What is the area of the composite figure?

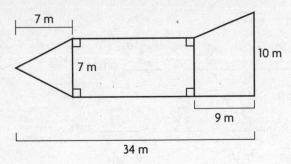

(A) 164 square meters

(B) 171 square meters

(C) 227 square meters

(D) 339 square meters

2. What is the area of the shaded region?

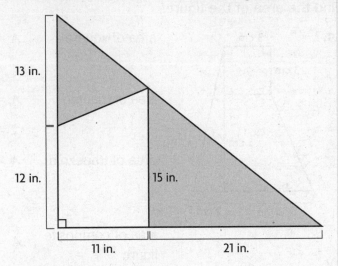

(A) 200 square inches

(B) 251.5 square inches

(C) 400 square inches

(D) 652 square inches

Spiral Review (CC.6.EE.8, CC.6.EE.9, CC.6.G.1)

3. In Maritza's family, everyone's height is greater than 60 inches. Which inequality represents the height h, in inches, of any member of Maritza's family? **(Lesson 8.9)**

(A) $h < 60$ (C) $h > 60$

(B) $h \le 60$ (D) $h \ge 60$

4. The linear equation $y = 2x$ represents the cost y for x pounds of apples. Which ordered pair lies on the graph of the equation?
(Lesson 9.5)

(A) $(0, 1)$ (C) $(4, 2)$

(B) $(2, 4)$ (D) $(6, 8)$

5. Two congruent triangles fit together to form a parallelogram with base 14 inches and height 10 inches. What is the area of each triangle?
(Lesson 10.3)

(A) 24 square inches

(B) 35 square inches

(C) 70 square inches

(D) 140 square inches

6. A regular hexagon has sides measuring 7 inches. If the hexagon is divided into 6 congruent triangles, each has a height of about 6 inches. What is the approximate area of the hexagon? **(Lesson 10.6)**

(A) 252 square inches

(B) 168 square inches

(C) 126 square inches

(D) 42 square inches

Problem Solving • Changing Dimensions

COMMON CORE STANDARD CC.6.G.1
Solve real-world and mathematical problems
involving area, surface area, and volume.

Read each problem and solve.

1. The dimensions of a 5-in. by 3-in. rectangle are multiplied by 6.
   How is the area affected?

   new dimensions: $l = 6 \times 5 = 30$ in.
   $w = 6 \times 3 = 18$ in.

   original area: $A = 5 \times 3 = 15$ in.^{2}

   new area: $A = 30 \times 18 = 540$ in.^{2}

   $\dfrac{\text{new area}}{\text{original area}} = \dfrac{540}{15} = 36$

   The area was multiplied by ___36___.

2. The dimensions of a 7-cm by 2-cm rectangle are
   multiplied by 3. How is the area affected?

   multiplied by _____

3. The dimensions of a 3-ft by 6-ft rectangle are
   multiplied by $\frac{1}{3}$. How is the area affected?

   multiplied by _____

4. The dimensions of a triangle with base 10 in. and
   height 4.8 in. are multiplied by 4. How is the area affected?

   multiplied by _____

5. The dimensions of a 1-yd by 9-yd rectangle are
   multiplied by 5. How is the area affected?

   multiplied by _____

6. The dimensions of a 4-in. square are multiplied
   by 3. How is the area affected?

   multiplied by _____

7. The dimensions of a triangle with base 1.5 m and
   height 6 m are multiplied by 2. How is the area affected?

   multiplied by _____

8. The dimensions of a triangle are multiplied by $\frac{1}{4}$. The
   area of the smaller triangle can be found by multiplying
   the area of the original triangle by what number?

   _____

Lesson Check (CC.6.G.1)

1. The dimensions of Rectangle A are 6 times the dimensions of Rectangle B. How do the areas of the rectangles compare?

   (A) Area of Rectangle A = 6 × Area of Rectangle B

   (B) Area of Rectangle A = 12 × Area of Rectangle B

   (C) Area of Rectangle A = 24 × Area of Rectangle B

   (D) Area of Rectangle A = 36 × Area of Rectangle B

2. A model of a triangular piece of jewelry has an area that is $\frac{1}{4}$ the area of the jewelry. How do the dimensions of the triangles compare?

   (A) Model dimensions = $\frac{1}{2}$ jewelry dimensions

   (B) Model dimensions = $\frac{1}{4}$ jewelry dimensions

   (C) Model dimensions = $\frac{1}{8}$ jewelry dimensions

   (D) Model dimensions = $\frac{1}{16}$ jewelry dimensions

Spiral Review (CC.6.EE.8, CC.6.G.1)

3. Trent graphed $y > 3$ on a number line. Which of the following could be Trent's graph? (Lesson 8.10)

   (A)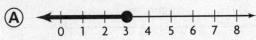

   (B)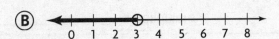

   (C)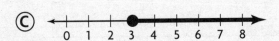

   (D)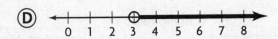

4. The parallelogram below is made from two congruent trapezoids. What is the area of the shaded trapezoid? (Lesson 10.4)

   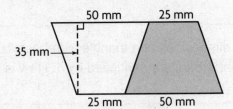

   (A) 2,625 square millimeters

   (B) 1,750 square millimeters

   (C) 1,312.5 square millimeters

   (D) 1,250.5 square millimeters

5. A rectangle has a length of 24 inches and a width of 36 inches. A square with side length 5 inches is cut from the middle and removed. What is the area of the figure that remains? (Lesson 10.7)

   (A) 360 square inches

   (B) 432 square inches

   (C) 839 square inches

   (D) 864 square inches

Figures on the Coordinate Plane

COMMON CORE STANDARD CC.6.G.3
Solve real-world and mathematical problems involving area, surface area, and volume.

1. The vertices of triangle *DEF* are $D(^-2, 3)$, $E(3, ^-2)$, and $F(^-2, ^-2)$. Graph the triangle, and find the length of side $\overline{DF}$.

   Vertical distance of *D* from 0: $|3| =$ __**3**__ units

   Vertical distance of *F* from 0: $|^-2| =$ __**2**__ units

   The points are in different quadrants, so add to find the distance from *D* to *F*: __**3**__ + __**2**__ = __**5**__ units.

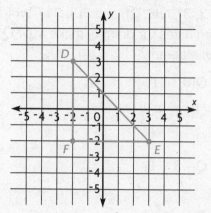

Graph the figure and find the length of side $\overline{BC}$.

2. $A(1, 4)$, $B(1, ^-2)$, $C(^-3, ^-2)$, $D(^-3, 3)$

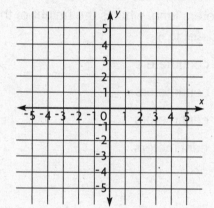

Length of $\overline{BC} =$ _____ units

3. $A(^-1, 4)$, $B(5, 4)$, $C(5, 1)$, $D(^-1, 1)$

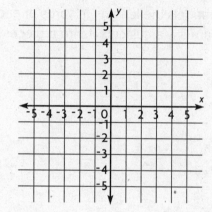

Length of $\overline{BC} =$ _____ units

Problem Solving REAL WORLD

4. On a map, a city block is a square with three of its vertices at $(^-4, 1)$, $(1, 1)$, and $(1, ^-4)$. What are the coordinates of the remaining vertex?

5. A carpenter is making a shelf in the shape of a parallelogram. She begins by drawing parallelogram *RSTU* on a coordinate plane with vertices $R(1, 0)$, $S(^-3, 0)$, and $T(^-2, 3)$. What are the coordinates of vertex *U*?

_____

_____

Lesson Check (CC.6.G.3)

1. The coordinates of points *M*, *N*, and *P* are *M*(⁻2, 3), *N*(4, 3), and *P*(5, ⁻1). Which coordinates for point *Q* make *MNPQ* a parallelogram?

   Ⓐ *Q*(0, ⁻1)

   Ⓑ *Q*(⁻1, 0)

   Ⓒ *Q*(⁻1, ⁻1)

   Ⓓ *Q*(⁻3, ⁻1)

2. Dirk draws quadrilateral *RSTU* with vertices *R*(⁻1, 2), *S*(4, 2), *T*(5, ⁻1), and *U*(⁻2, ⁻1). Which is the best way to classify the quadrilateral?

   Ⓐ parallelogram

   Ⓑ rectangle

   Ⓒ square

   Ⓓ trapezoid

Spiral Review (CC.6.EE.9, CC.6.G.1)

3. Marcus needs to cut a 5-yard length of yarn into equal pieces for his art project. Which equation models the length *l* in yards of each piece of yarn if Marcus cuts it into *p* pieces? **(Lesson 9.1)**

   Ⓐ $l = 5p$

   Ⓑ $l = 5 \div p$

   Ⓒ $p = 5 + l$

   Ⓓ $p = 5 - l$

4. The area of a triangular flag is 330 square centimeters. If the base of the triangle is 30 centimeters long, what is the height of the triangle? **(Lesson 10.3)**

   Ⓐ 4,950 centimeters

   Ⓑ 720 centimeters

   Ⓒ 22 centimeters

   Ⓓ 11 centimeters

5. A trapezoid is $6\frac{1}{2}$ feet tall. Its bases are 9.2 feet and 8 feet long. What is the area of the trapezoid? **(Lesson 10.5)**

   Ⓐ 23.7 square feet

   Ⓑ 55.9 square feet

   Ⓒ 239.2 square feet

   Ⓓ 478.4 square feet

6. The dimensions of the rectangle below will be multiplied by 3. How will the area be affected? **(Lesson 10.8)**

   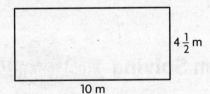

   $4\frac{1}{2}$ m

   10 m

   Ⓐ The area will be multiplied by 3.

   Ⓑ The area will be multiplied by 9.

   Ⓒ The area will be divided by 3.

   Ⓓ The area will be divided by 9.

Chapter 10 Extra Practice

Lessons 10.1 - 10.5

Find the area of the shaded figure.

1.

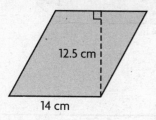

12.5 cm

14 cm

_____

2.

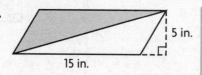

5 in.

15 in.

_____

3.

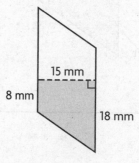

15 mm

8 mm

18 mm

_____

4.

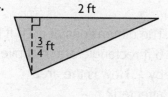

2 ft

$\frac{3}{4}$ ft

_____

5.

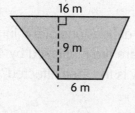

16 m

9 m

6 m

_____

6.

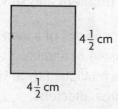

$4\frac{1}{2}$ cm

$4\frac{1}{2}$ cm

_____

Find the unknown measurement for the figure.

7. parallelogram

$A = 28.2 \text{ ft}^2$

$b = 6 \text{ ft}$

$h = $ _____

8. triangle

$A = 160 \text{ mi}^2$

$b = $ _____

$h = 16 \text{ mi}$

9.

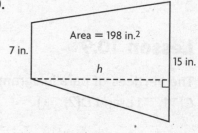

Area = 198 in.²

7 in.

h

15 in.

$h = $ _____

Lesson 10.6

Find the area of the regular polygon.

10.

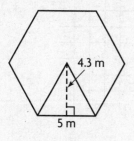

4.3 m

5 m

_____

11.

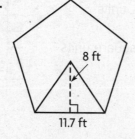

8 ft

11.7 ft

_____

12.

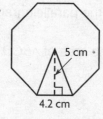

5 cm

4.2 cm

_____

Lesson 10.7

Find the area of the shaded region.

13.

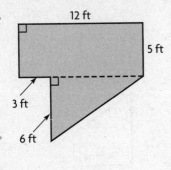

12 ft
5 ft
3 ft
6 ft

14.

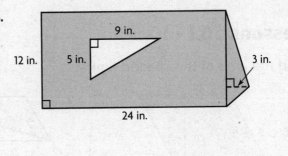

9 in.
12 in.
5 in.
3 in.
24 in.

Lesson 10.8

Read each problem and solve.

15. The dimensions of a triangle with base 4 m and height 5 m are multiplied by 3. How is the area affected?

multiplied by _____

16. The dimensions of a 5 in. square are multiplied by 4. How is the area affected?

multiplied by _____

17. The dimensions of a 10 ft by 6 ft rectangle are multiplied by $\frac{1}{3}$. How is the area affected?

multiplied by _____

Lesson 10.9

The vertices of parallelogram *ABCD* are $A(^-2, \,^-4)$, $B(^-5, \,^-4)$, $C(^-1, \,^-1)$, and $D(2, \,^-1)$.

18. Graph the parallelogram.

19. What is the length of side $\overline{BA}$? _____ units

20. If $\overline{BA}$ is the base of parallelogram *ABCD*, what is the height of the parallelogram? _____ units

21. What is the area of *ABCD*? _____ square units

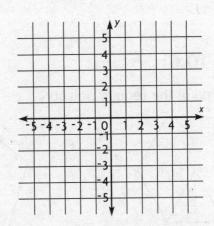

Dear Family,

Throughout the next few weeks, our math class will be learning about surface area and volume. We will also be exploring nets of solid figures.

You can expect to see homework that provides practice in calculating the volume of prisms.

Here is a sample of how your child was taught to find the volume of a prism.

Vocabulary

net An arrangement of two-dimensional figures that can be folded to form a three-dimensional figure.

surface area The total area of all the faces and surfaces of a solid figure.

volume The number of cubic units needed to fill a given space.

🔑 MODEL Solve Volume Problems

Find the volume of the prism.

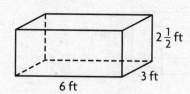

$2\frac{1}{2}$ ft

3 ft

6 ft

STEP 1

Write the formula.

$V = l \times w \times h$

STEP 2

Substitute 6 for l, 3 for w, and $2\frac{1}{2}$ for h.

$V = 6 \times 3 \times 2\frac{1}{2}$

STEP 3

Change mixed numbers to improper fractions. Then multiply.

$V = 6 \times 3 \times \frac{5}{2}$

$V = 45$

So, the volume is 45 ft³.

Tips

Choosing Units

The surface area of a solid figure is always expressed in square units, such as square meters (m²) or square inches (in.²). The volume of a solid figure is always expressed in cubic units, such as cubic meters (m³) or cubic inches (in.³).

Activity

Cut open an empty cereal box and lay it flat to create a net for the box. Measure the length and width of each rectangle in the net, find the area of each rectangle, and add these areas to find the surface area of the box. You can then tape the box back together and calculate its volume.

Carta para la casa

Vocabulario

modelo plano Una presentación de figuras bidimensionales que puede doblarse para formar una figura tridimensional.

área total El área de todas las caras y superficies de un cuerpo geométrico.

volumen El número de unidades cúbicas necesario para llenar un espacio dado.

Querida familia,

Durante las próximas semanas, en la clase de matemáticas aprenderemos sobre área y volumen. También aprenderemos sobre modelos planos de figuras geométricas.

Llevaré a la casa tareas para practicar el cálculo del volumen de prismas.

Este es un ejemplo de la manera como aprenderemos a hallar el volumen de un prisma.

🔑 MODELO — Resolver problemas de volumen

Halla el volumen del prisma.

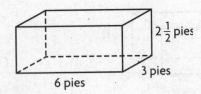

$2\frac{1}{2}$ pies

3 pies

6 pies

PASO 1

Escribe la fórmula.

$V = l \times w \times h$

PASO 2

Reemplaza *l* con 6, *w* con 3, y *h* con $2\frac{1}{2}$.

$V = 6 \times 3 \times 2\frac{1}{2}$

PASO 3

Convierte los números mixtos en fracciones impropias. Luego multiplica.

$V = 6 \times 3 \times \frac{5}{2}$

$V = 45$

Por tanto, el volumen es 45 pies^3.

Pistas

Elegir unidades

El área total de un cuerpo geométrico siempre se expresa en unidades cuadradas, como metros cuadrados (m^2) o pulgadas cuadradas (pulgs.^{2}). El volumen de un cuerpo geométrico siempre se expresa en unidades cúbicas, como metros cúbicos (m^3) o pulgadas cúbicas (pulgs.^{3}).

Actividad

Abra una caja vacía de cereal y extiéndala sobre una mesa, para crear un modelo plano para la caja. Mida la longitud y la anchura de cada rectángulo del modelo plano, halle el área de cada rectángulo y sume estas áreas para hallar el área total de la caja. Después, vuelva a armar la caja usando cinta adhesiva y calcule su volumen.

Three-Dimensional Figures and Nets

COMMON CORE STANDARD CC.6.G.4
Solve real-world and mathematical problems
involving area, surface area, and volume.

Identify and draw a net for the solid figure.

1. 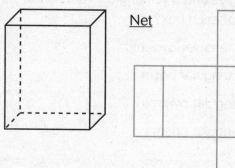 Net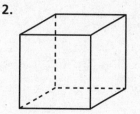

figure: rectangular prism

2. Net

figure: _____

3. Net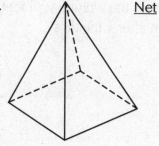

figure: _____

4. Net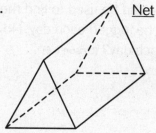

figure: _____

Problem Solving **REAL WORLD**

5. Hobie's Candies are sold in triangular-pyramid-shaped boxes. How many triangles are needed to make one box?

_____

6. Nina used plastic rectangles to make 6 rectangular prisms. How many rectangles did she use?

_____

Lesson Check (CC.6.G.4)

1. How many vertices does a square pyramid have?

   (A) 5

   (B) 6

   (C) 10

   (D) 12

2. Each box of Fred's Fudge is constructed from 2 triangles and 3 rectangles. What is the shape of each box?

   (A) rectangular pyramid

   (B) rectangular prism

   (C) triangular pyramid

   (D) triangular prism

Spiral Review (CC.6.EE.7, CC.6.EE.9, CC.6.G.1, CC.6.G.3)

3. Bryan jogged the same distance each day for 7 days. He ran a total of 22.4 miles. The equation $7d = 22.4$ can be used to find the distance d in miles he jogged each day. How far did Bryan jog each day? (Lesson 8.6)

   (A) 3.2 miles

   (B) 4.9 miles

   (C) 8.4 miles

   (D) 15.4 miles

4. A hot-air balloon is at an altitude of 240 feet. The balloon descends 30 feet per minute. Which is equation gives the altitude y, in feet, of the hot-air balloon after x minutes? (Lesson 9.2)

   (A) $y = 240x + 30$

   (B) $y = 240x - 30$

   (C) $y = 240 + 30x$

   (D) $y = 240 - 30x$

5. A regular heptagon has sides measuring 26 mm and is divided into 7 congruent triangles. Each triangle has a height of 27 mm. What is the area of the heptagon? (Lesson 10.6)

   (A) 702 mm^2

   (B) 1,404 mm^2

   (C) 2,457 mm^2

   (D) 2,650 mm^2

6. Alexis draws quadrilateral STUV with vertices $S(1, 3)$, $T(2, 2)$, $U(2, ^-3)$, and $V(1, ^-2)$. Which is the best way to classify the quadrilateral? (Lesson 10.9)

   (A) parallelogram

   (B) rectangle

   (C) square

   (D) trapezoid

Explore Surface Area Using Nets

COMMON CORE STANDARD CC.6.G.4
Solve real-world and mathematical problems involving area, surface area, and volume.

Use the net to find the surface area of the rectangular prism.

1.
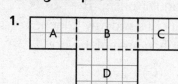

A: 6 squares
B: 8 squares
C: 6 squares
D: 12 squares
E: 8 squares
F: 12 squares

52 square units

2.
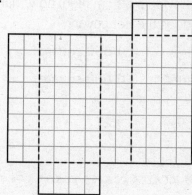

Find the surface area of the rectangular prism.

3.
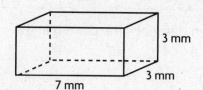
3 mm
3 mm
7 mm

_____

4.
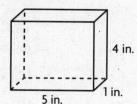
4 in.
5 in.
1 in.

_____

5.
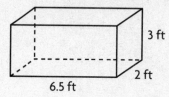
3 ft
2 ft
6.5 ft

_____

Problem Solving  REAL WORLD

6. Jeremiah is covering a cereal box with fabric for a school project. If the box is 6 inches long by 2 inches wide by 14 inches high, how much surface area does Jeremiah have to cover?

7. Tia is making a case for her calculator. It is a rectangular prism that will be 3.5 inches long by 1 inch wide by 10 inches high. How much material (surface area) will she need to make the case?

_____

_____

Lesson Check (CC.6.G.4)

1. Gabriela drew a net of a rectangular prism on centimeter grid paper. If the prism is 7 cm long by 10 cm wide by 8 cm high, how many grid squares does the net cover?

   (A) 206 squares   (C) 560 squares

   (B) 412 squares   (D) 600 squares

2. Ben bought a cell phone that came in a box shaped like a rectangular prism. The box is 5 inches long by 3 inches wide by 2 inches high. What is the surface area of the box?

   (A) 30 in.^{2} (C) 62 in.^{2}

   (B) 31 in.^{2} (D) 80 in.^{2}

Spiral Review (CC.6.EE.5, CC.6.EE.9, CC.6.G.1, CC.6.G.4)

3. Katrin wrote the inequality $x < 533$. Which of the following is NOT a solution of the inequality? (Lesson 8.8)

   (A) $x = 531$

   (B) $x = 529$

   (C) $x = 535$

   (D) $x = 527$

4. The table shows the number of mixed CDs y that Jason makes in x hours.

Mixed CDs				
Hours, x	2	3	5	10
CDs, y	10	15	25	50

   Which equation describes the pattern in the table? (Lesson 9.3)

   (A) $y = x + 8$

   (B) $y = 5x$

   (C) $y = \frac{x}{5}$

   (D) $y = x - 40$

5. A square measuring 9 inches by 9 inches is cut from a corner of a square measuring 15 inches by 15 inches. What is the area of the L-shaped figure that is formed? (Lesson 10.7)

   (A) 36 square inches

   (B) 42 square inches

   (C) 60 square inches

   (D) 144 square inches

6. Boxes of Clancy's Energy Bars are rectangular prisms. How many lateral faces does each box have? (Lesson 11.1)

   (A) 1

   (B) 2

   (C) 4

   (D) 6

Name _____

Surface Area of Prisms

COMMON CORE STANDARD CC.6.G.4
Solve real-world and mathematical problems
involving area, surface area, and volume.

Use a net to find the surface area.

1.

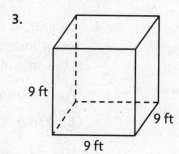

2 cm
6 cm   5 cm

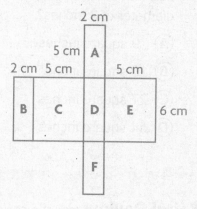

2 cm
5 cm A
2 cm 5 cm   5 cm
B   C   D   E   6 cm
F

Area of A and F = 2 × (5 × 2) = 20 cm^2
Area of B and D = 2 × (6 × 2) = 24 cm^2
Area of C and E = 2 × (6 × 5) = 60 cm^2
S.A.= 20 cm^2 + 24 cm^2 + 60 cm^2 = 104 cm^2

2.

6 in.
3.5 in.   4 in.

3.

9 ft
9 ft
9 ft

4.

8 cm   6 cm   12 cm
10 cm

_____   _____   _____

Problem Solving 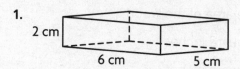 REAL WORLD

5. A shoe box measures 15 in. by 7 in. by $4\frac{1}{2}$ in.
What is the surface area of the box?

6. Vivian is working with a styrofoam cube for
art class. The length of one side is 5 inches.
How much surface area does Vivian have to
work with?

_____   _____

Lesson Check (CC.6.G.4)

1. Which could be the surface area of a cubic box that contains a baseball that has a diameter of 3 inches?

  (A) 9 square inches

  (B) 18 square inches

  (C) 27 square inches

  (D) 54 square inches

2. A piece of wood used for construction is 2 inches by 4 inches by 24 inches. What is the surface area of the wood?

  (A) 152 square inches

  (B) 192 square inches

  (C) 304 square inches

  (D) 384 square inches

Spiral Review (CC.6.EE.9, CC.6.G.1, CC.6.G.4)

3. Detergent costs $4 per box. Kendra graphs the equation that gives the cost *y* of buying *x* boxes of detergent. Which ordered pair is on Kendra's graph? (Lesson 9.4)

  (A) (12, 3)

  (B) (2, 6)

  (C) (4, 1)

  (D) (5, 20)

4. A trapezoid with bases that measure 8 inches and 11 inches has a height of 3 inches. What is the area of the trapezoid? (Lesson 10.5)

  (A) 9.5 square inches

  (B) 28.5 square inches

  (C) 44 square inches

  (D) 57 square inches

5. City Park is a right triangle with a base of 40 yd and a height of 25 yd. On a map, the park has a base of 40 in. and a height of 25 in. How do the areas of the park and the map of the park compare? (Lesson 10.8)

  (A) Area of park = 6 × Area on map

  (B) Area of park = 18 × Area on map

  (C) Area of park = 36 × Area on map

  (D) Area of park = 1,296 × Area on map

6. What is the surface area of the prism shown by the net? (Lesson 11.2)

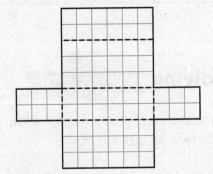

  (A) 12 square units

  (B) 36 square units

  (C) 72 square units

  (D) 80 square units

Name _____

Surface Area of Pyramids

COMMON CORE STANDARD CC.6.G.4
Solve real-world and mathematical problems involving area, surface area, and volume.

Use a net to find the surface area of the square pyramid.

1.

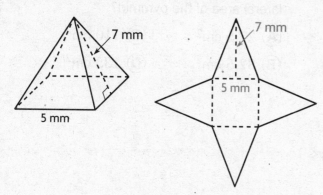

Base: $A = 5^2 = 25$ mm^2

Face: $A = \dfrac{1}{2}(5)(7)$

$\qquad = 17.5$ mm^2

S.A. $= 25 + 4 \times 17.5$

$\qquad = 25 + 70$

$\qquad = 95$ mm^2

2.

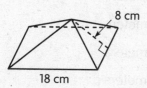

8 cm

18 cm

3.

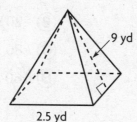

9 yd

2.5 yd

4.

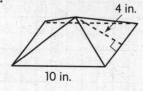

4 in.

10 in.

_____

Problem Solving REAL WORLD

5. Cho is building a sandcastle in the shape of a triangular pyramid. The area of the base is 7 square feet. Each side of the base has a length of 4 feet and the height of each face is 2 feet. What is the surface area of the pyramid?

6. The top of a skyscraper is shaped like a square pyramid. Each side of the base has a length of 60 meters and the height of each triangle is 20 meters. What is the lateral area of the pyramid?

_____

Lesson Check (CC.6.G.4)

1. A square pyramid has a base with a side length of 12 in. Each face has a height of 7 in. What is the surface area of the pyramid?

   (A) 480 in.²

   (B) 312 in.²

   (C) 186 in.²

   (D) 144 in.²

2. The faces of a triangular pyramid have a base of 5 cm and a height of 11 cm. What is the lateral area of the pyramid?

   (A) 27.5 cm²

   (B) 82.5 cm²

   (C) 110 cm²

   (D) 135 cm²

Spiral Review (CC.6.EE.9, CC.6.G.1, CC.6.G.3, CC.6.G.4)

3. What is the linear equation represented by the graph? **(Lesson 9.5)**

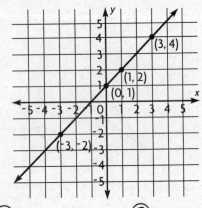

   (A) $y = x + 1$

   (B) $y = x - 1$

   (C) $y = x$

   (D) $y = 1 - x$

4. A regular octagon has sides measuring about 4 cm. If the octagon is divided into 8 congruent triangles, each has a height of 5 cm. What is the area of the octagon?

   (Lesson 10.6)

   (A) 10 square centimeters

   (B) 20 square centimeters

   (C) 80 square centimeters

   (D) 160 square centimeters

5. Carly draws quadrilateral JKLM with vertices $J(^-3, 3)$, $K(3, 3)$, $L(2, ^-1)$, and $M(^-2, ^-1)$. Which is the best way to classify the quadrilateral? **(Lesson 10.9)**

   (A) parallelogram

   (B) rectangle

   (C) square

   (D) trapezoid

6. A rectangular prism has the dimensions 8 feet by 3 feet by 5 feet. What is the surface area of the prism? **(Lesson 11.3)**

   (A) 158 square feet

   (B) 120 square feet

   (C) 79 square feet

   (D) 16 square feet

Fractions and Volume

COMMON CORE STANDARD CC.6.G.2
Solve real-world and mathematical problems involving area, surface area, and volume.

Find the volume of the rectangular prism.

1.

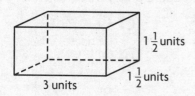

3 units
$1\frac{1}{2}$ units
$1\frac{1}{2}$ units

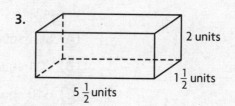

Number of cubes with side length $\frac{1}{2}$ unit: 54

$54 \div 8 = 6$ with a remainder of 6

$54 \div 8 = 6 + \frac{6}{8} = 6\frac{3}{4}$

Volume = $6\frac{3}{4}$ cubic units

2.

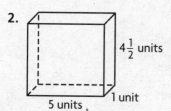

5 units
$4\frac{1}{2}$ units
1 unit

_____

3.

$5\frac{1}{2}$ units
2 units
$1\frac{1}{2}$ units

_____

4.

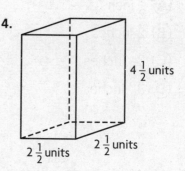

$4\frac{1}{2}$ units
$2\frac{1}{2}$ units
$2\frac{1}{2}$ units

_____

Problem Solving REAL WORLD

5. Miguel is pouring liquid into a container that is $4\frac{1}{2}$ inches long by $3\frac{1}{2}$ inches wide by 2 inches high. How many cubic inches of liquid will fit in the container?

_____

6. A shipping crate is shaped like a rectangular prism. It is $5\frac{1}{2}$ feet long by 3 feet wide by 3 feet high. What is the volume of the crate?

_____

Lesson Check (CC.6.G.2)

1. A rectangular prism is 4 units by $2\frac{1}{2}$ units by $1\frac{1}{2}$ units. How many cubes with a side length of $\frac{1}{2}$ unit will completely fill the prism?

   (A) 15
   (C) 64
   (B) 60
   (D) 120

2. A rectangular prism is filled with 196 cubes with $\frac{1}{2}$-unit side lengths. What is the volume of the prism in cubic units?

   (A) $24\frac{1}{2}$
   (C) 49
   (B) $28\frac{3}{4}$
   (D) 98

Spiral Review (CC.6.G.1, CC.6.G.4)

3. A parallelogram-shaped piece of stained glass has a base measuring $2\frac{1}{2}$ inches and a height of $1\frac{1}{4}$ inches. What is the area of the piece of stained glass? **(Lesson 10.1)**

   (A) $\frac{1}{2}$ inch
   (B) 2 inches
   (C) $3\frac{1}{8}$ inches
   (D) $3\frac{3}{4}$ inches

4. A flag for the sports club is a rectangle measuring 20 inches by 32 inches. Within the rectangle is a yellow square with a side length of 6 inches. What is the area of the flag that is not part of the yellow square? **(Lesson 10.7)**

   (A) 364 square inches
   (B) 604 square inches
   (C) 640 square inches
   (D) 676 square inches

5. What is the surface area of the rectangular prism shown by the net? **(Lesson 11.2)**

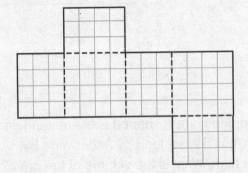

   (A) 6 square units
   (C) 40 square units
   (B) 16 square units
   (D) 80 square units

6. What is the surface area of the square pyramid? **(Lesson 11.4)**

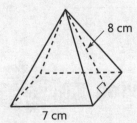

8 cm

7 cm

   (A) 77 square centimeters
   (B) 161 square centimeters
   (C) 176 square centimeters
   (D) 273 square centimeters

© Houghton Mifflin Harcourt Publishing Company

Name _____

Volume of Rectangular Prisms

COMMON CORE STANDARD CC.6.G.2

Solve real-world and mathematical problems involving area, surface area, and volume.

Find the volume.

1. $9\frac{1}{4}$ m, $3\frac{1}{4}$ m, 5 m

$$V = lwh$$
$$V = 5 \times 3\frac{1}{4} \times 9\frac{1}{4}$$
$$V = 150\frac{5}{16} \text{ m}^3$$

2. 2 in., $2\frac{1}{2}$ in., $5\frac{1}{2}$ in.

_____

3. $4\frac{1}{2}$ mm, $4\frac{1}{2}$ mm, $4\frac{1}{2}$ mm

_____

4. 6 ft, $2\frac{1}{2}$ ft, $7\frac{1}{2}$ ft

_____

5. $4\frac{1}{2}$ m, 8 m²

_____

6. $2\frac{1}{4}$ ft, 6 ft, $2\frac{1}{4}$ ft

_____

7. 14 m, $7\frac{1}{4}$ m, $9\frac{1}{2}$ m

_____

8. $\frac{1}{3}$ in., $\frac{1}{3}$ in., $\frac{1}{3}$ in.

_____

9. $3\frac{1}{2}$ cm, 48 cm²

_____

Problem Solving 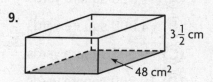 REAL WORLD

10. A cereal box is a rectangular prism that is 8 inches long and $2\frac{1}{2}$ inches wide. The volume of the box is 200 in.³. What is the height of the box?

_____

11. A stack of paper is $8\frac{1}{2}$ in. long by 11 in. wide by 4 in. high. What is the volume of the stack of paper?

_____

Lesson Check (CC.6.G.2)

1. A kitchen sink is a rectangular prism with a length of $19\frac{7}{8}$ inches, a width of $14\frac{3}{4}$ inches, and height of 10 inches. Which of these is the best estimate of the sink's volume?

   (A)   300 cubic inches

   (B)   1,500 cubic inches

   (C)   3,000 cubic inches

   (D)   15,000 cubic inches

2. A storage container is a rectangular prism that is 65 centimeters long and 40 centimeters wide. The volume of the container is 62,400 cubic centimeters. What is the height of the container?

   (A)   12 centimeters

   (B)   24 centimeters

   (C)   48 centimeters

   (D)   78 centimeters

Spiral Review (CC.6.G.1, CC.6.G.2, CC.6.G.4)

3. Carrie started at the southeast corner of Franklin Park, walked north 240 yards, turned and walked west 80 yards, and then turned and walked diagonally back to where she started. What is the area of the triangle enclosed by the path she walked? (Lesson 10.3)

   (A)   320 square yards

   (B)   4,800 square yards

   (C)   9,600 square yards

   (D)   19,200 square yards

4. The dimensions of a rectangular garage are 100 times the dimensions of a floor plan of the garage. The area of the floor plan is 8 square inches. What is the area of the garage? (Lesson 10.8)

   (A)   400 square inches

   (B)   800 square inches

   (C)   6,400 square inches

   (D)   80,000 square inches

5. Shiloh wants to create a paper-mâché box shaped like a rectangular prism. If the box will be 4 inches by 5 inches by 8 inches, how much paper does she need to cover the box? (Lesson 11.3)

   (A)   184 square inches

   (B)   160 square inches

   (C)   92 square inches

   (D)   34 square inches

6. A box is filled with 220 cubes with a side length of $\frac{1}{2}$ unit. What is the volume of the box in cubic units? (Lesson 11.5)

   (A) $27\frac{1}{2}$ cubic units

   (B) $54\frac{1}{2}$ cubic units

   (C)   110 cubic units

   (D)   440 cubic units

Name _____

Problem Solving • Geometric Measurements

COMMON CORE STANDARD CC.6.G.4
Solve real-world and mathematical problems
involving area, surface area, and volume.

Read each problem and solve.

1. The outside of an aquarium tank is 50 cm long, 50 cm
   wide, and 30 cm high. It is open at the top. The glass
   used to make the tank is 1 cm thick. How much water
   can the tank hold?

   $l = 50 - 2 = 48$, $w = 50 - 2 = 48$,
   $h = 30 - 1 = 29$
   $V = l \times w \times h$
   $\quad = 48 \times 48 \times 29$
   $\quad = 66{,}816$ $\underline{66{,}816 \text{ cm}^3}$

2. Arnie keeps his pet snake in an open-topped glass cage.
   The outside of the cage is 73 cm long, 60 cm wide, and
   38 cm high. The glass used to make the cage is 0.5 cm
   thick. What is the inside volume of the cage?

   _____

3. A gift box measures 14 in. by 12 in. by 6 in. How much
   wrapping paper is needed to exactly cover the box?

   _____

4. A display number cube measures 20 in. on a side. The
   sides are numbered 1–6. The odd-numbered sides are
   covered in blue fabric and the even-numbered sides are
   covered in red fabric. How much red fabric was used?

   _____

5. The caps on the tops of staircase posts are shaped like
   square pyramids. The side length of the base of each cap
   is 4 inches. The height of the face of each cap is 5 inches.
   What is the surface area of the caps for two posts?

   _____

6. A water irrigation tank is shaped like a cube and has a
   side length of $2\frac{1}{2}$ feet. How many cubic feet of water are
   needed to completely fill the tank?

   _____

Lesson Check (CC.6.G.4)

1. Maria wants to know how much wax she will need to fill a candle mold shaped like a rectangular prism. Which measure should she find?

   (A) the perimeter of the mold

   (B) the area of the mold

   (C) the surface area of the mold

   (D) the volume of the mold

2. The outside of a closed glass display case measures 22 inches by 15 inches by 12 inches. The glass is $\frac{1}{2}$ inch thick. How much air is contained in the case?

   (A) 2,600 cubic inches

   (B) 3,234 cubic inches

   (C) 3,585.125 cubic inches

   (D) 3,960 cubic inches

Spiral Review (CC.6.G.1, CC.6.G.2, CC.6.G.3, CC.6.G.4)

3. A trapezoid with bases that measure 5 centimeters and 7 centimeters has a height of 4.5 centimeters. What is the area of the trapezoid? (Lesson 10.5)

   (A) 27 square centimeters

   (B) 42.75 square centimeters

   (C) 54 square centimeters

   (D) 157.5 square centimeters

4. Sierra has plotted two vertices of a rectangle at (3, 2) and (8, 2). What is the length of the side of the rectangle? (Lesson 10.9)

   (A) 3 units

   (B) 5 units

   (C) 8 units

   (D) 11 units

5. What is the surface area of the square pyramid? (Lesson 11.4)

   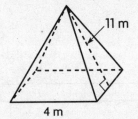

   11 m

   4 m

   (A) 38 square meters

   (B) 104 square meters

   (C) 192 square meters

   (D) 209 square meters

6. A shipping company has a rule that all packages must be rectangular prisms with a volume of no more than 9 cubic feet. Which of the following are the dimensions of a package that meets the company's requirements? (Lesson 11.6)

   (A) $l = 2$ feet, $w = 2$ feet, $h = 3$ feet

   (B) $l = 2$ feet, $w = 1.5$ feet, $h = 3.5$ feet

   (C) $l = 3$ feet, $w = 1$ feet, $h = 3.1$ feet

   (D) $l = 3$ feet, $w = 1.5$ feet, $h = 2$ feet

Chapter 11 Extra Practice

Lesson 11.1

Identify and draw a net for the solid figure.

1.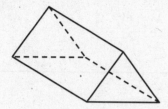

_____

2.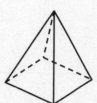

_____

3.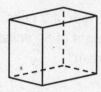

_____

4.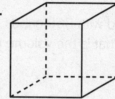

_____

Lesson 11.2

Use the net to find the surface area of the rectangular prism.

5.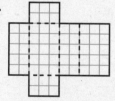

_____

6.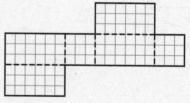

_____

Lesson 11.3

Use the net to find the surface area of the prism.

7.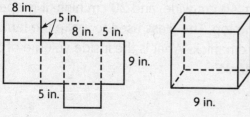

_____

8.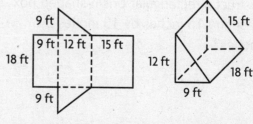

_____

Lesson 11.4

Find the surface area of the square pyramid.

9.

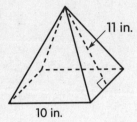

11 in.

10 in.

_____

10.

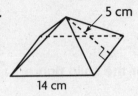

5 cm

14 cm

_____

Lesson 11.5

Solve.

11. A rectangular prism is filled with 360 cubes with $\frac{1}{2}$-unit side lengths. What is the volume of the prism in cubic units?

_____

12. A rectangular prism has a length of 2 units, a width of $1\frac{1}{2}$ units, and a height of $3\frac{1}{2}$ units. What is the volume of the prism?

_____

Lesson 11.6

Find the volume.

13.

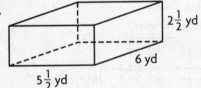

$2\frac{1}{2}$ yd

6 yd

$5\frac{1}{2}$ yd

_____

14.

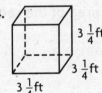

$3\frac{1}{4}$ ft

$3\frac{1}{4}$ ft

$3\frac{1}{4}$ ft

_____

Lesson 11.7

Solve.

15. How much cardboard would you need to construct a rectangular prism-shaped box measuring 15 inches by 13 inches by 7 inches?

_____

16. The outside of an aquarium tank is 50 cm long, 40 cm wide, and 20 cm high. It is open at the top. The glass used to make the tank is 1 cm thick. What is the inside volume of the tank?

_____

© Houghton Mifflin Harcourt Publishing Company

Vocabulary

dot plot A number line with dots that show the frequency of the values in a data set.

frequency table A table that shows the number of times each value or group of values in a data set occur.

histogram A type of bar graph that shows the frequencies of data in equal intervals.

Dear Family,

Throughout the next few weeks, our math class will be learning how to collect, organize, and analyze data. We will also be learning how to find measures of center.

You can expect to see homework that requires students to create and interpret a variety of graphs.

Here is a sample of how your child was taught to make a histogram.

🔑 MODEL Make a Histogram

Make a histogram for the ages of people at a restaurant.

32, 44, 22, 16, 35, 28, 37, 41, 37, 20, 31, 18, 20, 49, 56, 8

Tips

Making a Histogram

The intervals in a histogram must be the same size.

STEP 1

Make a frequency table using intervals of 10.

STEP 2

Set up the intervals on the horizontal axis and choose a scale for the vertical axis.

STEP 3

Graph the number of people in each interval.

STEP 4

Give the graph a title and label the axes.

Interval	0–9	10–19	20–29	30–39	40–49	50–59
Frequency	1	2	4	5	3	1

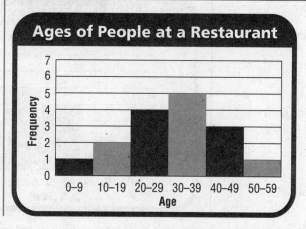

Ages of People at a Restaurant

Activity

Keep track of a piece of household data for one week, such as the number of cans or bottles recycled each day. Work together to choose an appropriate graph to display the data.

Carta para la casa

© Houghton Mifflin Harcourt Publishing Company

Vocabulario

diagrama de puntos Una recta numérica con puntos que muestran la frecuencia de los valores en un conjunto de datos.

tabla de frecuencia Una tabla que muestra el número de veces que ocurre cada valor o grupo de valores en un conjunto de datos.

histograma Un tipo de gráfica de barras que muestra las frecuencias de los datos a intervalos iguales.

Querida familia,

Durante las próximas semanas, en la clase de matemáticas aprenderemos a recolectar, organizar y analizar datos. También aprenderemos a hallar los valores centrales.

Llevaré a la casa tareas para practicar la creación e interpretación de distintos tipos de gráficas.

Este es un ejemplo de la manera como aprenderemos a hacer un histograma.

🔑 MODELO Hacer un histograma

Haz un histograma para las edades de los clientes de un restaurante.

32, 44, 22, 16, 35, 28, 37, 41, 37, 20, 31, 18, 20, 49, 56, 8

Pistas

Haz un histograma

Los intervalos de un histograma tienen que ser de igual tamaño.

PASO 1

Haz una tabla de frecuencias usando intervalos de 10.

Intervalo	0–9	10–19	20–29	30–39	40–49	50–59
Frecuencia	1	2	4	5	3	1

PASO 2

Forma los intervalos en el eje horizontal y elige una escala para el eje vertical.

PASO 3

Representa el número de personas en cada intervalo en la gráfica.

PASO 4

Ponle un título a la gráfica y rotula los ejes.

Actividad

Lleve la cuenta de datos de su hogar de una semana, como el número de botellas recicladas cada día, por una semana. Trabajen juntos para elegir la gráfica apropiada para mostrar esos datos.

Name _____

Recognize Statistical Questions

COMMON CORE STANDARD CC.6.SP.1
Develop understanding of statistical variability.

Identify the statistical question. Explain your reasoning.

1. **A.** How many touchdowns did the quarterback throw during the last game of the season?

   B. How many touchdowns did the quarterback throw each game of the season?

   B; the number of touchdowns in each game can vary.

2. **A.** What was the score in the first frame of a bowling game?

   B. What are the scores in 10 frames of a bowling game?

   _____

   _____

   _____

   _____

3. **A.** How many hours of television did you watch each day this week?

   B. How many hours of television did you watch on Saturday?

   _____

   _____

   _____

   _____

Write a statistical question you could ask in the situation.

4. A teacher recorded the test scores of her students.

   _____

   _____

5. A car salesman knows how many of each model of a car was sold in a month.

   _____

   _____

Problem Solving

6. The city tracked the amount of waste that was recycled from 2000 to 2007. Write a statistical question about the situation.

   _____

   _____

   _____

7. The daily low temperature is recorded for a week. Write a statistical question about the situation.

   _____

   _____

   _____

Lesson Check (CC.6.SP.1)

1. Which question is a statistical question?

   Ⓐ When is your birthday?

   Ⓑ What is the distance across the Golden Gate Bridge?

   Ⓒ How many free throws did Terry make in each game for the season?

   Ⓓ Do you have any siblings?

2. Which question is a statistical question?

   Ⓐ How tall is the Eiffel Tower?

   Ⓑ What was the lowest amount of precipitation in one month last year?

   Ⓒ What is the speed limit?

   Ⓓ How far is the post office from the bank?

Spiral Review (CC.6.G.1, CC.6.G.2, CC.6.G.4)

3. A regular decagon has side lengths of 4 centimeters long. If the decagon is divided into 10 congruent triangles, each has an approximate height of 6.2 centimeters. What is the approximate area of the decagon? (Lesson 10.6)

   Ⓐ   12.4 square centimeters

   Ⓑ   24.8 square centimeters

   Ⓒ 124 square centimeters

   Ⓓ 248 square centimeters

4. Mikki uses the net shown to make a solid figure. (Lesson 11.1)

   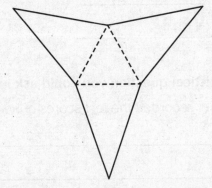

   What solid figure does Mikki make?

   Ⓐ square prism   Ⓒ triangular pyramid

   Ⓑ square pyramid   Ⓓ triangular prism

5. A prism is filled with 30 cubes with $\frac{1}{2}$-unit side lengths. What is the volume of the prism in cubic units? (Lesson 11.5)

   Ⓐ 60 cubic units

   Ⓑ 15 cubic units

   Ⓒ $3\frac{3}{4}$ cubic units

   Ⓓ $3\frac{1}{6}$ cubic units

6. A tank in the shape of a rectangular prism has a length of 22 inches, a width of 12 inches, and a height of 15 inches. If the tank is filled halfway with water, how much water is in the tank? (Lesson 11.7)

   Ⓐ   774 cubic inches

   Ⓑ 1,548 cubic inches

   Ⓒ 1,980 cubic inches

   Ⓓ 3,960 cubic inches

Name _____

Describe Data Collection

COMMON CORE STANDARDS CC.6.SP.5a, CC.6.SP.5b

Summarize and describe distributions.

Describe the data set by listing the attribute measured, the unit of measure, the likely means of measurement, and the number of observations.

1. Daily temperature

Daily High Temperature (°F)				
78	83	72	65	70
76	75	71	80	75
73	74	81	79	69
81	78	76	80	82
70	77	74	71	73

Attribute: daily temperature;

unit of measure: degrees

Fahrenheit; means of

measurement: thermometer;

number of observations: 25

2. Plant heights

Height of Plants (inches)				
10.3	9.7	6.4	8.1	11.2
5.7	11.7	7.5	9.6	6.9

3. Cereal in boxes

Amount of Cereal in Boxes (cups)							
8	7	8.5	5	5	5	6.5	6
8	8.5	7	7	9	8	8	9

4. Dog weights

Weight of Dogs (pounds)							
22	17	34	23	19	18	20	20

Problem Solving 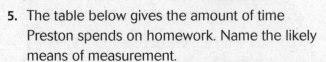 REAL WORLD

5. The table below gives the amount of time Preston spends on homework. Name the likely means of measurement.

Amount of Time Spent on Homework (hours)							
5	3	1	2	4	1	3	2

6. The table below shows the speed of cars on a highway. Name the unit of measure.

Speeds of Cars (miles per hour)							
71	55	53	65	68	61	59	62
70	69	57	50	56	66	67	63

Lesson Check (CC.6.SP.5a, CC.6.SP.5b)

1. What is the attribute of the data set shown in the table?

Mass of Produce (grams)				
2.4	1.7	3.2	1.1	2.6
3.3	1.3	2.6	2.7	3.1

(A) grams   (C) mass of produce

(B) scale   (D) ruler

2. What is the number of observations of the data set shown below?

Swim Times (min)		
1.02	1.12	1.09
1.01	1.08	1.03

(A) 4   (C) 8

(B) 6   (D) 10

Spiral Review (CC.6.G.1, CC.6.G.2, CC.6.G.4, CC.6.SP.1)

3. What is the area of the figure shown below?
(Lesson 10.7)

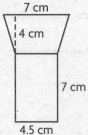

7 cm

4 cm

7 cm

4.5 cm

(A) 77.5 square centimeters

(B) 54.5 square centimeters

(C) 59.5 square centimeters

(D) 45.5 square centimeters

4. Each base of a triangular prism has an area of 43 square centimeters. Each lateral face has an area of 25 square centimeters. What is the surface area of the prism? **(Lesson 11.3)**

(A) 68 square centimeters

(B) 75 square centimeters

(C) 118 square centimeters

(D) 161 square centimeters

5. How much sand can this container hold?
(Lesson 11.6)

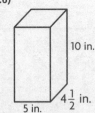

10 in.

$4\frac{1}{2}$ in.

5 in.

(A) 235 cubic inches

(B) 225 cubic inches

(C) 100 cubic inches

(D) 39 cubic inches

6. Which of the following is NOT a statistical question? **(Lesson 12.1)**

(A) What are the weights of the puppies in the pet store?

(B) What are the ages of the puppies in the pet store?

(C) How much does Rover weigh today?

(D) How long are the puppies' tails in the pet store?

Name _____

Dot Plots and Frequency Tables

COMMON CORE STANDARD CC.6.SP.4

Summarize and describe distributions.

For 1–4, use the chart.

1. The chart shows the number of pages of a novel that Julia reads each day. Complete the dot plot using the data in the table.

Pages Read				
12	14	12	18	20
15	15	19	12	15
14	11	13	18	15
15	17	12	11	15

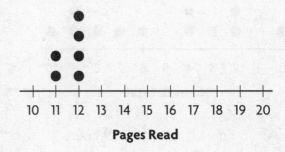

Pages Read

2. What number of pages does Julia read most often? Explain.

_____

_____

3. Make a frequency table in the space below. Use the intervals 10–13, 14–17, and 18–21.

4. Make a relative frequency table in the space below.

Problem Solving

5. The frequency table shows the ages of the actors in a youth theater group. What percent of the actors are 10 to 12 years old?

Actors in a Youth Theater Group	
Age	Frequency
7–9	8
10–12	22
13–15	10

_____

Lesson Check (CC.6.SP.4)

1. The dot plot shows the number of hours Mai babysat each week. How many hours is Mai most likely to babysit?

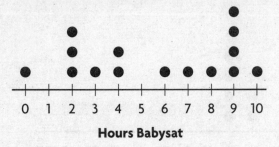

Hours Babysat

(A) 5 hours   (C) 9 hours

(B) 6 hours   (D) 10 hours

2. The frequency table shows the ratings that a movie received from online reviewers. What percent of the reviewers gave the movie a 4-star rating?

Movie Ratings	
Rating	Frequency
1 star	2
2 stars	5
3 stars	7
4 stars	6

(A) 3%   (C) 30%

(B) 20%   (D) 60%

Spiral Review (CC.6.G.1, CC.6.G.2, CC.6.G.4, CC.6.SP.5b)

3. The dimensions of a rectangular playground are 50 times the dimensions of a scale drawing of the playground. The area of the scale drawing is 6 square feet. What is the area of the actual playground? **(Lesson 10.8)**

(A)   56 square feet

(B)   300 square feet

(C)   15,000 square feet

(D) 150,000 square feet

4. A square pyramid has a base side length of 8 feet. The height of each lateral face is 12 feet. What is the surface area of the pyramid? **(Lesson 11.4)**

(A) 112 square feet

(B) 208 square feet

(C) 256 square feet

(D) 448 square feet

5. A gift box is in the shape of a rectangular prism. The box has a length of 24 centimeters, a width of 10 centimeters, and a height of 13 centimeters. What is the volume of the box? **(Lesson 11.7)**

(A) 3,120 cubic centimeters

(B) 1,560 cubic centimeters

(C) 1,364 cubic centimeters

(D)   682 cubic centimeters

6. For a science experiment, Juanita records the height of a plant every day in centimeters. What is the attribute measured in her experiment? **(Lesson 12.2)**

(A) height

(B) mass

(C) centimeters

(D) days

Name _____

Histograms

COMMON CORE STANDARD CC.6.SP.4

Summarize and describe distributions.

For 1–4 use the data at right.

1. Complete the histogram for the data.

2. What do the numbers on the *y*-axis represent?

   _____

3. How many students scored from 60 to 69?

   _____

4. Use your histogram to find the number of students who got a score of 80 or greater. Explain.

   _____

   _____

   _____

Scores on a Math Test									
85	87	69	90	82	75	74	76	84	87
99	65	75	76	83	87	91	83	92	69

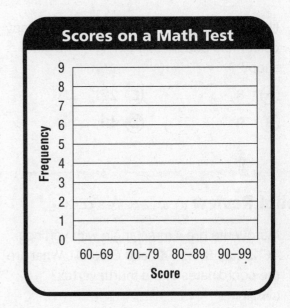

Scores on a Math Test

Problem Solving REAL WORLD

For 5–6, use the histogram.

5. For which two age groups are there the same number of customers?

   _____

6. How many customers are in the restaurant? How do you know?

   _____

   _____

   _____

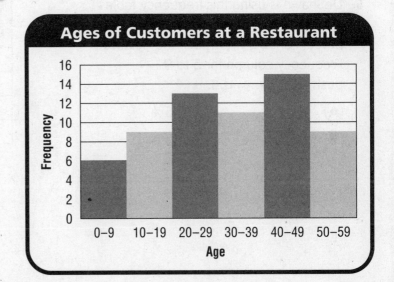

Ages of Customers at a Restaurant

Lesson Check (CC.6.SP.4)

1. The histogram shows the amount, to the nearest dollar, that customers spent at a museum gift shop. How many customers spent less than $20?

   Ⓐ 6   Ⓒ 13

   Ⓑ 8   Ⓓ 14

Amount Spent at Museum Gift Shop

2. Use the histogram in Problem 1. How many customers bought something at the gift shop?

   Ⓐ 8   Ⓒ 27

   Ⓑ 9   Ⓓ 49

Spiral Review (CC.6.G.2, CC.6.G.3, CC.6.SP.4)

3. Marguerite drew a rectangle with vertices $A(^-2, ^-1)$, $B(^-2, ^-4)$, and $C(1, ^-4)$. What are the coordinates of the fourth vertex? **(Lesson 10.9)**

   Ⓐ $(1, ^-1)$ Ⓒ $(2, ^-1)$

   Ⓑ $(^-1, 1)$ Ⓓ $(2, ^-4)$

4. A rectangular swimming pool can hold 1,408 cubic feet of water. The pool is 22 feet long and has a depth of 4 feet. What is the width of the pool? **(Lesson 11.6)**

   Ⓐ 16 feet   Ⓒ 88 feet

   Ⓑ 64 feet   Ⓓ 352 feet

5. DeShawn is using this frequency table to make a relative frequency table. What percent should he write in the Relative Frequency column for 5 to 9 push-ups? **(Lesson 12.3)**

   Ⓐ 7%   Ⓒ 65%

   Ⓑ 35%   Ⓓ 70%

DeShawn's Daily Push-Ups	
Number of Push-Ups	Frequency
0–4	3
5–9	7
10–14	8
15–19	2

Name _____

Mean as Fair Share and Balance Point

COMMON CORE STANDARD CC.6.SP.5c

Summarize and describe distributions.

Use counters to find the mean of the data set.

1. Six students count the number of buttons on their shirts.
   The students have 0, 4, 5, 2, 3, and 4 buttons.

   Make ___**6**___ stacks of counters with heights 0, 4, 5, 2, 3, and 4.

   Rearrange the counters so that all ___**6**___ stacks have the same height.

   After rearranging, every stack has ___**3**___ counters.

   So, the mean of the data set is ___**3**___.

2. Four students completed 1, 2, 2, and 3 chin-ups. _____

Make a dot plot for the data set and use it to check whether the given value is a balance point for the data set.

3. Sandy's friends ate 0, 2, 3, 4, 6, 6, and 7 pretzels.
   Sandy says the mean of the data is 4. Is Sandy correct?

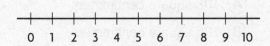

   0 1 2 3 4 5 6 7 8 9 10

The total distance from 4 for

values less than 4 is _____.
The total distance from 4
for values greater than 4 is

_____. The mean of 4

_____ a balance point.

So, Sandy _____ correct.

Problem Solving REAL WORLD

4. Three baskets contain 8, 8, and 11 soaps.
   Can the soaps be rearranged so that there
   is an equal whole number of soaps in each
   basket? Explain why or why not.

   _____

   _____

   _____

   _____

5. Five pages contain 6, 6, 9, 10, and 11 stickers.
   Can the stickers be rearranged so that there
   is an equal whole number of stickers on each
   page? Explain why or why not.

   _____

   _____

   _____

   _____

Lesson Check (CC.6.SP.5c)

1. What is the mean of 9, 12, and 15 stamps?

   Ⓐ 6 stamps

   Ⓑ 9 stamps

   Ⓒ 12 stamps

   Ⓓ 15 stamps

2. Four friends spent $9, $11, $11, and $17 on dinner. If they split the bill equally, how much does each person owe?

   Ⓐ $6

   Ⓑ $11

   Ⓒ $12

   Ⓓ $17

Spiral Review (CC.6.G.4, CC.6.SP.5b)

3. Which of the following could be the net of a cube? (Lesson 11.1)

   Ⓐ 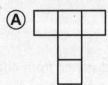   Ⓒ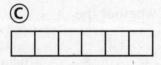

   Ⓑ 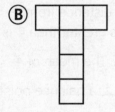   Ⓓ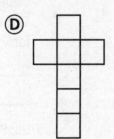

4. Sarah paints the box below. She paints the whole box except for the front face. What area of the box does she paint? (Lesson 11.7)

   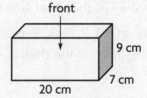

   Ⓐ 406 square centimeters

   Ⓑ 486 square centimeters

   Ⓒ 586 square centimeters

   Ⓓ 766 square centimeters

5. Chloe collected data and then displayed her results in the table to the right. What is the unit of measure of the data? (Lesson 12.2)

   Ⓐ Monday–Friday

   Ⓑ °F

   Ⓒ Noon

   Ⓓ 80°F

Temperature at Noon	
Monday	80°F
Tuesday	84°F
Wednesday	78°F
Thursday	90°F
Friday	80°F

Name _____

Measures of Center

COMMON CORE STANDARD CC.6.SP.5c
Summarize and describe distributions.

Use the table for 1–4.

1. What is the mean of the data?

$$\frac{10 + 8 + 11 + 12 + 6}{5} = \frac{47}{5} = 9.4$$

___9.4 points___

Number of Points Blaine Scored in Five Basketball Games	
Game	Points Scored
1	10
2	8
3	11
4	12
5	6

2. What is the median of the data?

_____

3. What is the mode(s) of the data?

_____

4. Suppose Blaine played a sixth game and scored 10 points during the game. Find the new mean, median, and mode.

_____

_____

Problem Solving REAL WORLD

5. An auto manufacturer wants their line of cars to have a median gas mileage of 25 miles per gallon or higher. The gas mileage for their five models are 23, 25, 26, 29, and 19. Do their cars meet their goal? Explain.

_____

_____

_____

_____

6. A sporting goods store is featuring several new bicycles, priced at $300, $250, $325, $780, and $350. They advertise that the average price of their bicycles is under $400. Is their ad correct? Explain.

_____

_____

_____

_____

Lesson Check (CC.6.SP.5c)

1. The prices for a video game at 5 different stores are $39.99, $44.99, $29.99, $35.99, and $31.99. What is the mode(s) of the data?

- Ⓐ $31.99
- Ⓑ $44.99 and $29.99
- Ⓒ $36.59
- Ⓓ There is no mode.

2. Manuel is keeping track of how long he practices the saxophone each day. The table gives his practice times for the past five days. What is the mean of his practice times?

Manuel's Practice Time	
Day	**Minutes Practiced**
Monday	25
Tuesday	45
Wednesday	30
Thursday	65
Friday	30

- Ⓐ 25 minutes
- Ⓒ 39 minutes
- Ⓑ 30 minutes
- Ⓓ 40 minutes

Spiral Review (CC.6.G.4, CC.6.SP.4, CC.6.SP.5c)

3. What is the surface area of the triangular prism shown below? (Lesson 11.3)

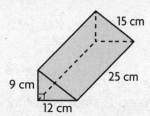

- Ⓐ 1,008 cm²
- Ⓒ 783 cm²
- Ⓑ 954 cm²
- Ⓓ 708 cm²

5. Six people eat breakfast together at a restaurant. The costs of their orders are $4, $5, $9, $8, $6, and $10. If they want to split the check evenly, how much should each person pay? (Lesson 12.5)

- Ⓐ $6
- Ⓒ $8
- Ⓑ $7
- Ⓓ $9

4. Kate records the number of miles that she bikes each day. She displayed the number of daily miles in the dot plot below. Each dot represents the number of miles she biked in one day. How many days did she bike 4–7 miles? (Lesson 12.3)

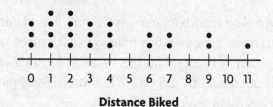

Distance Biked

- Ⓐ 4
- Ⓒ 6
- Ⓑ 5
- Ⓓ 7

Effects of Outliers

COMMON CORE STANDARD CC.6.SP.5d
Summarize and describe distributions.

1. Identify the outlier in the data set of students in each class. Then describe the effect the outlier has on the mean and median.

Students in Each Class				
30	22	26	21	24
28	23	26	28	12

<u>12; Possible answer: The outlier decreases the mean from about 25.3</u>

<u>to 24. The outlier decreases the median from 26 to 25.</u>

2. Identify the outlier in the data set of pledge amounts. Then describe the effect the outlier has on the mean and median.

Pledge Amounts			
$100	$10	$15	$20
$17	$24	$32	$36

_____

_____

3. In a set of points that Milton scored in basketball games, there is an outlier. Before one game, Milton injured his knee. Do you think the outlier is greater or less than the rest of the numbers of points? Explain.

_____

_____

Problem Solving REAL WORLD

4. Duke's science quiz scores are 99, 91, 60, 94, and 95. Describe the effect of the outlier on the mean and median.

_____

_____

_____

5. The number of people who attended an art conference for five days was 42, 27, 35, 39, and 96. Describe the effect of the outlier on the mean and median.

_____

_____

_____

Lesson Check (CC.6.SP.5d)

1. Which set of data contains an outlier?

   (A) 2, 4, 5, 3, 1

   (B) 77, 18, 23, 29

   (C) 89, 75, 83, 71, 78

   (D) 41, 46, 44, 51, 47

2. The number of counties in several states is 64, 15, 42, 55, 41, 60, and 52. How does the outlier change the median?

   (A) It decreases the median by 1.5.

   (B) It increases the median by 1.5.

   (C) It decreases the median by 2.5.

   (D) It increases the median by 2.5.

Spiral Review (CC.6.G.4, CC.6.SP.4, CC.6.SP.5b, CC.6.SP.5c)

3. Hector covers each face of the pyramid below with construction paper. The area of the base of the pyramid is 28 square feet. What area will he cover with paper?
   (Lesson 11.4)

   (A) 84 square inches

   (B) 140 square inches

   (C) 196 square inches

   (D) 364 square inches

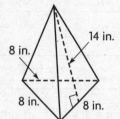

4. Mr. Stevenson measured the heights of several students and recorded his findings in the chart below. How many observations did he complete? (Lesson 12.2)

Heights of Students (cm)						
160	138	148	155	159	154	155
140	135	144	142	162	170	171

   (A) 14

   (B) 36

   (C) 160

   (D) 171

5. Kendra is making a histogram for the data in the chart. She uses the intervals 0–4, 5–9, 10–14, and 15–19. What should be the height of the longest bar in her histogram?
   (Lesson 12.4)

Lengths of Lizards (cm)				
8	3	12	12	15
19	4	16	9	5
5	10	14	15	8

   (A) 4   (C) 15

   (B) 5   (D) 19

6. Sharon has 6 photo files on her computer. The numbers below are the sizes of the files in kilobytes. What is the median number of kilobytes for the files? (Lesson 12.6)

   69.7, 38.5, 106.3, 109.8, 75.6, 89.4

   (A) 75.6

   (B) 81.6

   (C) 82.5

   (D) 89.4

Name _____

Problem Solving • Data Displays

COMMON CORE STANDARD CC.6.SP.4
Summarize and describe data distributions.

Read each problem and solve.

1. Josie collected data on the number of siblings
   her classmates have. Make a data display and
   determine the percent of Josie's classmates that
   have more than 2 siblings.

   5, 1, 2, 1, 2, 4, 3, 2, 2, 6

   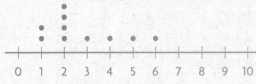

   40%

2. The following data show the number of field goals
   a kicker attempted each game. Make a data display
   and tell which number of field goals is the mode.

   4, 6, 2, 1, 3, 1, 2, 1, 5, 2, 2, 3

3. The math exam scores for a class are shown below.
   Make a data display. What percent of the scores are
   90 and greater?

   91, 68, 83, 75, 81, 99, 97, 80, 85, 70, 89, 92, 77, 95,
   100, 64, 88, 96, 76, 88

4. The heights of students in a class are shown below
   in inches. Make a data display. What percent of the
   students are taller than 62 inches?

   63, 57, 60, 64, 59, 62, 65, 58, 63, 65, 58, 61, 63, 64

5. The ages of employees are shown below. Which
   age is the mode?

   21, 18, 17, 19, 18, 23, 18, 16, 22, 18, 21, 18

Lesson Check (CC.6.SP.4)

1. The number of student absences is shown below. What is the mode of the absences?

   2, 1, 3, 2, 1, 1, 3, 2, 2, 10, 4, 5, 1, 5, 1

   (A) 1

   (B) 2

   (C) 3

   (D) 5

2. Kelly is making a histogram of the number of pets her classmates own. The number of pets range from 0 to 7. Which of the following could she use for intervals in her histogram?

   (A) 0–1, 2–3, 4–5, 6–7

   (B) 0–2, 2–3, 4–5, 6–7

   (C) 0–3, 4–5, 6–7

   (D) 0–1, 2–4, 5–7

Spiral Review (CC.6.G.2, CC.6.SP.4, CC.6.SP.5c, CC.6.SP.5d)

3. The area of the base of the rectangular prism shown below is 45 square millimeters. The height is $5\frac{1}{2}$ millimeters. What is the volume of the prism? (Lesson 11.6)

   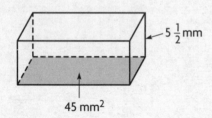

   5 $\frac{1}{2}$ mm

   45 mm²

   (A) $247\frac{1}{2}$ mm²   (C) $166\frac{3}{8}$ mm²

   (B) $225\frac{1}{2}$ mm²   (D) $50\frac{1}{2}$ mm²

4. The frequency table shows the number of runs scored by the Cougars in 20 of their baseball games. In what percent of the games did they score 5 or fewer runs? (Lesson 12.3)

Runs Scored by the Cougars	
Number of Runs	Frequency
0–2	14
3–5	3
6–8	2
9–11	1

   (A) 17%   (C) 70%

   (B) 34%   (D) 85%

5. There are 5 plates of bagels. The numbers of bagels on the plates are 8, 10, 9, 10, and 8. Shane rearranges the bagels so that each plate has the same amount. How many bagels are now on each plate? (Lesson 12.5)

   (A) 8   (C) 10

   (B) 9   (D) 11

6. By how much does the median of the data set 12, 9, 9, 11, 14, 28 change if the outlier is removed? (Lesson 12.5)

   (A) It decreases by 28.

   (B) It decreases by 3.

   (C) It increases by 9.

   (D) It decreases by 0.5.

Name _____

Chapter 12 Extra Practice

Lesson 12.1 (CC.6.SP.1)

1. Write a statistical question you could ask in the situation.

A baker recorded the number of bagels sold each day for a month.

_____

Lesson 12.2 (CC.6.SP.5a, CC.6.SP.5b)

2. Describe the data set by listing the attribute measured, the unit of measure, the likely means of measurement, and the number of observations.

attribute: _____

unit of measure: _____

likely means of measurement: _____

number of observations: _____

Mass of Strawberries (grams)				
12	20	15.5	17	18
9.5	15	21	24	17

Lessons 12.3 and 12.4 (CC.6.SP.4)

Kimiko is the owner of an online shoe store. In order to improve her advertising, she collects data on the ages of 25 of her customers. Her data is shown in the chart.

Ages of Customers				
22	37	59	45	44
18	20	25	46	52
22	31	38	31	22
50	18	24	29	46
51	19	35	36	45

3. Complete the relative frequency table below.

Ages of Customers		
Age	Frequency	Relative Frequency
10–19		
20–29		
30–39		
40–49		
50–59		

4. Complete the histogram for the data.

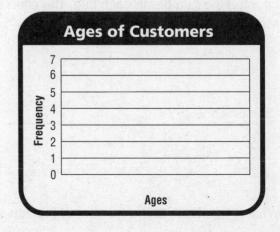

Lessons 12.5 – 12.7 (CC.6.SP.5c, CC.6.SP.5d)

5. Three plates had 4, 8, and 9 muffins. The muffins are rearranged so that each plate contains the same number of muffins. How many muffins are on each plate? _____

Solve.

6. Carla finds the mass in kilograms of several rocks in her school's geology lab. The masses are 4.5, 3.8, 4.8, 3.8, 4.2, and 4.1. Find the mean, median, and mode of Carla's data.

Mean: _____   Median: _____

Mode: _____

7. Suppose a 0.7-kg rock is added to the geology lab in Problem 6. Find the new mean and median. Describe the effect that the outlier has on the mean and median.

Mean: _____   Median: _____

_____

_____

_____

8. Gavin records the times in minutes of several DVDs in his collection. The times are 125, 98, 150, 134, 203, 180, and 90. Find the mean, median, and mode of Gavin's data.

Mean: _____   Median: _____

Mode: _____

9. Suppose a 28-minute DVD is added to Gavin's collection in Problem 8. Find the new mean and median. Describe the effect that the outlier has on the mean and median.

Mean: _____   Median: _____

_____

_____

_____

Lesson 12.8 (CC.6.SP.4)

Draw a dot plot of the data. Then use the plot to find the value that appears with the greatest frequency.

10. Megan opened several bags of pretzels and counted the number in each bag. The chart shows Megan's data. Complete the dot plot.

Number of Pretzels										
12	11	9	8	13	12	10	9	11	8	13
11	10	9	7	12	11	9	10	12	13	12
14	15	12	11	8	7	9	13	12	15	10

11. What is the mode of the number of pretzels in a bag? _____

School-Home Letter

Vocabulary

box plot A type of graph that shows how data are distributed by using the median, quartiles, least value, and greatest value.

interquartile range The difference between the upper quartile and the lower quartile of a data set.

lower quartile The median of the lower half of a data set.

upper quartile The median of the upper half of a data set.

Dear Family,

Throughout the next few weeks, our math class will be learning about variability and patterns in data. We will also be summarizing data by finding measures of center and variability.

You can expect to see homework with real-world problems that involve box plots.

Here is a sample of how your child was taught to make a box plot.

🔑 MODEL Make a Box Plot

Make a box plot for the numbers of tickets won at a fair:

10, 5, 0, 4, 8, 7, 10, 3

Tips

Finding Quartiles

The median is the mean of the two middle numbers, 5 and 7. Since the median is not part of the data set, draw a line to separate the data in half. To find the lower quartile, find the median of the first four numbers. To find the upper quartile, find the median of the last four numbers.

STEP 1

Write the numbers in order from least to greatest.

0 3 4 5 7 8 10 10

STEP 2

Find the least value, lower quartile, median, upper quartile, and greatest value.

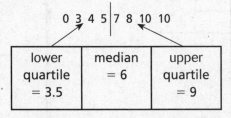

lower quartile = 3.5	median = 6	upper quartile = 9

STEP 3

Plot the five points. The middle three values form the box. Draw lines to extend to the two outside points.

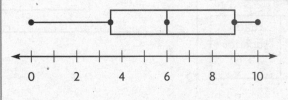

Activity

Determine the number of shoes each person in the family has. Ask relatives and friends until you have 10 data values. Make a list of the numbers from least to greatest. Make a box plot for the 10 data values.

Capítulo 13

Carta para la casa

Vocabulario

diagrama de caja Una gráfica que muestra cómo se distribuyen los datos usando la mediana, cuartiles, el valor menor y el valor mayor.

rango intercuartílico La diferencia entre el cuartil superior y el cuartil inferior en un conjunto de datos.

cuartil inferior La mediana de la mitad inferior de un conjunto de datos.

cuartil superior La mediana de la mitad superior de un conjunto de datos.

Querida familia,

Durante las próximas semanas, en la clase de matemáticas aprenderemos sobre la variabilidad y los patrones en los datos. También resumiremos datos hallando las medidas del centro y la variabilidad.

Llevaré a la casa tareas con problemas de la vida real que usan diagramas de caja.

Este es un ejemplo de la manera como aprendimos a hacer un diagrama de caja.

🔑 MODELO   Hacer un diagrama de caja

Haz un diagrama de caja del número de boletos ganados en una feria:

10, 5, 0, 4, 8, 7, 10, 3

Pistas

Para hallar cuartiles

La mediana es el promedio de los dos números centrales, 5 y 7. Como la mediana no es parte del conjunto de datos, traza una recta que separe los datos en dos mitades. Para hallar el cuartil inferior, busca la mediana de los primeros cuatro números. Para hallar el cuartil superior, busca la mediana de los últimos cuatro números.

PASO 1

Escribe los números en orden de menor a mayor.

0 3 4 5 7 8 10 10

PASO 2

Halla el valor menor, cuartil inferior, mediana, cuartil superior y valor mayor.

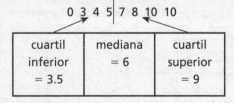

cuartil inferior = 3.5	mediana = 6	cuartil superior = 9

PASO 3

Traza los cinco puntos. Los tres del medio forman la caja. Traza rectas para prolongar los dos puntos exteriores.

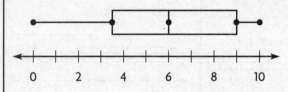

Actividad

Determine cuántos pares de zapatos tiene cada miembro de la familia. Pregunte a sus parientes y amigos hasta que tenga 10 datos. Hagan una lista de los números de menor a mayor. Hagan un diagrama de caja para los 10 datos.

© Houghton Mifflin Harcourt Publishing Company

Name _____

Patterns in Data

COMMON CORE STANDARD CC.6.SP.5c
Summarize and describe distributions.

For 1–3, use the dot plot.

1. The dot plot shows the number of omelets ordered at Paul's Restaurant each day. Does the dot plot contain any gaps?

   Yes; from 12 to 13, and at 17
   _____

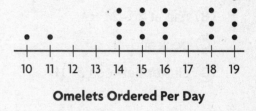

Omelets Ordered Per Day

2. Identify any clusters in the data.

   _____

   _____

3. Summarize the information in the dot plot.

   _____

   _____

   _____

   _____

For 4–5, use the histogram.

4. The histogram shows the number of people that visited a local shop each day in January. How many peaks does the histogram have?

   _____

5. Describe how the data values change across the intervals.

   _____

   _____

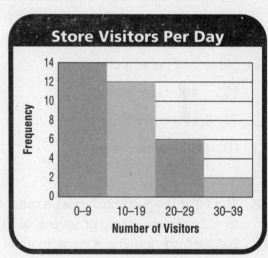

Store Visitors Per Day

Problem Solving REAL WORLD

6. Look at the dot plot at the right. Does the graph have line symmetry? Explain.

   _____

   _____

   _____

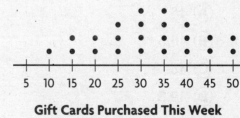

Gift Cards Purchased This Week

Lesson Check (CC.6.SP.5c)

1. Which does NOT describe the histogram?

   (A) peak at 10–14

   (B) gap at 20–24

   (C) peak at 5–9

   (D) cluster between 5–19

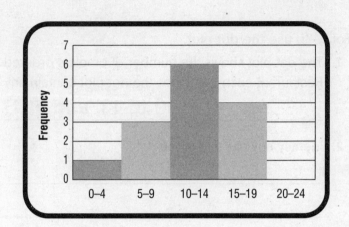

2. Meg makes a dot plot for the data 9, 9, 4, 5, 5, 3, 4, 5, 3, 8, 8, 6. Where does a gap occur?

   (A) 4

   (B) 5

   (C) 7

   (D) 8

Spiral Review (CC.6.G.2, CC.6.SP.4, CC.6.SP.5c)

3. A rectangular fish tank is 20 inches long, 12 inches wide, and 20 inches tall. If the tank is filled halfway with water, how much water is in the tank? (Lesson 11.7)

   (A) 240 cubic inches

   (B) 400 cubic inches

   (C) 2,400 cubic inches

   (D) 4,800 cubic inches

4. Look at the histogram below. How many students scored an 81 or higher on the math test? (Lesson 12.4)

   (A) 6 students

   (B) 7 students

   (C) 12 students

   (D) 14 students

5. The Little League coach uses a radar gun to measure the speed of several of Kyle's baseball pitches. The speeds, in miles per hour, are given below. What is the median of Kyle's pitch speeds? (Lesson 12.6)

   48, 39, 45, 51, 53

   (A) 45

   (B) 46.5

   (C) 48

   (D) 49.5

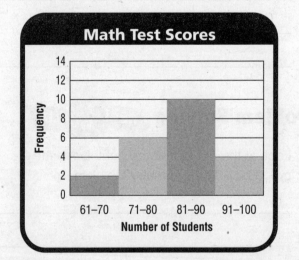

Name _____

Box Plots

COMMON CORE STANDARD CC.6.SP.4

Summarize and describe distributions.

Find the median, lower quartile, and upper quartile of the data.

1. the amounts of juice in 12 glasses, in fluid ounces:

    11, 8, 4, 9, 12, 14, 9, 16, 15, 11, 10, 7

    Order the data from least to greatest: 4, 7, 8, 9, 9, 10, 11, 11, 12, 14, 15, 16

    median: **10.5**   lower quartile: **8.5**   upper quartile: **13**

2. the lengths of 10 pencils, in centimeters:

    18, 15, 4, 9, 14, 17, 16, 6, 8, 10

    median: _____   lower quartile: _____   upper quartile: _____

3. Make a box plot to display the data set in Exercise 2.

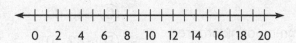

Lengths of Pencils (centimeters)

4. The numbers of students on several teams are 9, 4, 5, 10, 11, 9, 8, and 6.
   Make a box plot for the data.

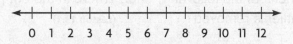

Number of Students on a Team

Problem Solving REAL WORLD

5. The amounts spent at a gift shop today are $19, $30, $28, $22, $20, $26, and $26. What is the median? What is the lower quartile?

6. The weights of six puppies in ounces are 8, 5, 7, 5, 6, and 9. What is the upper quartile of the data?

_____   _____

Lesson Check (CC.6.SP.4)

1. The values in a data set are 15, 7, 11, 12, 6, 3, 10, and 6. Where would you draw the box in a box plot for the data?

   (A) from 3 to 11.5

   (B) from 3 to 15

   (C) from 8.5 to 15

   (D) from 6 to 11.5

2. Which data set has a lower quartile of 18?

   (A) 17, 24, 25, 19, 11, 6, 10

   (B) 18, 22, 16, 15, 14, 9, 9

   (C) 22, 26, 17, 11, 14, 22, 18

   (D) 22, 27, 14, 21, 22, 26, 18

Spiral Review (CC.6.SP.1, CC.6.SP.5c, CC.6.SP.5d)

3. Which of the following is NOT a statistical question? (Lesson 12.1)

   (A) What is the average number of school lunches bought per day?

   (B) How many lunches did Mark buy this week?

   (C) What is the most common drink ordered with a school lunch?

   (D) On what day of the week does the cafeteria sell the most lunches?

4. The prices of several chairs are $89, $76, $81, $91, $88, and $70. What is the mean of the chair prices? (Lesson 12.6)

   (A) $99.00

   (B) $91.00

   (C) $83.00

   (D) $82.50

5. By how much does the mean of the following data set change if the outlier is removed? (Lesson 12.7)

   13, 19, 16, 40, 12

   (A) It decreases by 5.

   (B) It decreases by 40.

   (C) It increases by 5.

   (D) It increases by 40.

6. Where in the dot plot does a cluster occur? (Lesson 13.1)

   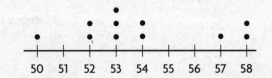

   (A) 50 to 58

   (B) 52 to 54

   (C) 55 to 56

   (D) 55 to 58

Mean Absolute Deviation

Use counters and a dot plot to find the mean absolute deviation of the data.

1. the number of hours Maggie spent practicing soccer for 4 different weeks:

   9, 6, 6, 7

   mean = 7 hours

   $$\frac{2 + 1 + 1 + 0}{4} = \frac{4}{4} = 1$$

   mean absolute deviation = _____**1 hour**_____

2. the heights of 7 people in inches:

   60, 64, 58, 60, 70, 71, 65

   mean = 64 inches

   mean absolute deviation = _____

Use the dot plot to find the mean absolute deviation of the data.

3. mean = 10

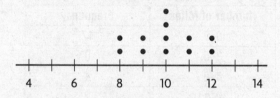

   Ages of Students in Dance Class

   mean absolute deviation = _____

4. mean = 8

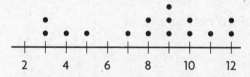

   Weekly Hours Spent Doing Homework

   mean absolute deviation = _____

Problem Solving REAL WORLD

5. In science class, Troy found the mass, in grams, of 6 samples to be 10, 12, 7, 8, 5, and 6. What is the mean absolute deviation?

6. Five recorded temperatures are 71°F, 64°F, 72°F, 81°F, and 67°F. What is the mean absolute deviation?

_____

_____

Lesson Check (CC.6.SP.5c)

1. Six test grades are 86, 88, 92, 90, 82, and 84. The mean of the data is 87. What is the mean absolute deviation?

    (A) 2

    (B) 3

    (C) 6

    (D) 18

2. Eight heights in inches are 42, 36, 44, 46, 48, 42, 48, and 46. The mean of the data is 44. What is the mean absolute deviation?

    (A) 5 inches

    (B) 4 inches

    (C) 3 inches

    (D) 2 inches

Spiral Review (CC.6.G.2, CC.6.SP.4)

3. What is the volume of a rectangular prism with dimensions 4 meters, $1\frac{1}{2}$ meters, and 5 meters? (Lesson 11.6)

    (A) 10 cubic meters

    (B) 20 cubic meters

    (C) 30 cubic meters

    (D) 40 cubic meters

4. Carrie is making a frequency table showing the number of miles she walked each day during the 30 days of September. What value should she write in the Frequency column for 9 to 11 miles? (Lesson 12.3)

Carrie's Daily Walks	
Number of Miles	Frequency
0–2	17
3–5	8
6–8	4
9–11	?

    (A) 1   (C) 10

    (B) 3   (D) 29

5. The following data shows the number of laps each student completed. What number of laps is the mode? (Lesson 12.8)

    9, 6, 7, 8, 5, 1, 8, 10

    (A) 6

    (B) 7

    (C) 8

    (D) 9

6. What is the upper quartile of the following data? (Lesson 13.2)

    43, 48, 55, 50, 58, 49, 38, 42, 50

    (A) 42.5

    (B) 49

    (C) 52.5

    (D) 58

Measures of Variability

COMMON CORE STANDARD CC.6.SP.5c
Summarize and describe distributions.

1. Find the range and interquartile range of the data in the box plot.

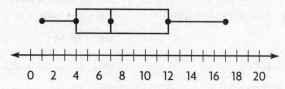

0 2 4 6 8 10 12 14 16 18 20

Miles Walked

For the range, find the difference between the greatest and least values.

$\underline{17} - \underline{1} = \underline{16}$

range: _____ **16 miles** _____

For the interquartile range, find the difference between the upper and lower quartiles.

$\underline{12} - \underline{4} = \underline{8}$

interquartile range: _____ **8 miles** _____

Use the box plot for 2 and 3.

2. What is the range of the data?

_____

3. What is the interquartile range of the data?

_____

50   60   70   80   90   100

Quiz Scores

Find the mean absolute deviation for the set.

4. heights in centimeters of several flowers:

14, 7, 6, 5, 13

mean absolute deviation: _____

5. ages of several children:

5, 7, 4, 6, 3, 5, 3, 7

mean absolute deviation: _____

Problem Solving REAL WORLD

6. The following data set gives the amount of time, in minutes, it took five people to cook a recipe. What is the mean absolute deviation for the data?

33, 38, 31, 36, 37

_____

7. The prices of six food processors are $63, $59, $72, $68, $61, and $67. What is the mean absolute deviation for the data?

_____

Lesson Check (CC.6.SP.5c)

1. Daily high temperatures recorded in a certain city are 65°F, 66°F, 70°F, 58°F, and 61°F. What is the mean absolute deviation for the data?

   Ⓐ 2.67°F   Ⓒ 12°F

   Ⓑ 3.6°F   Ⓓ 16°F

2. Eight different cereals have 120, 160, 135, 144, 153, 122, 118, and 134 calories per serving. What is the interquartile range for the data?

   Ⓐ 27.5 calories   Ⓒ 134.5 calories

   Ⓑ 42.0 calories   Ⓓ 148.5 calories

Spiral Review (CC.6.SP.4, CC.6.SP.5c)

3. Look at the histogram. How many days did the restaurant sell more than 59 pizzas?
   (Lesson 12.4)

   Ⓐ 4   Ⓒ 15

   Ⓑ 8   Ⓓ 20

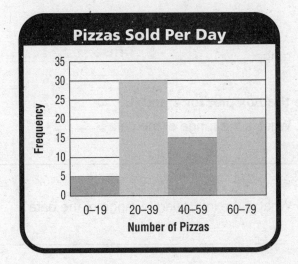

4. Look at the histogram. Where does a peak in the data occur? (Lesson 13.1)

   Ⓐ 0–19 pizzas

   Ⓑ 20–39 pizzas

   Ⓒ 40–59 pizzas

   Ⓓ 60–79 pizzas

5. Which data set has a mode of 14?
   (Lesson 12.6)

   Ⓐ 12, 14, 15

   Ⓑ 13, 15, 10, 18

   Ⓒ 14, 0, 0

   Ⓓ 14, 14, 18, 20

6. The data set below lists the ages of people on a soccer team. The mean of the data is 23. What is the mean absolute deviation?
   (Lesson 13.3)

   24, 22, 19, 19, 23, 23, 26, 27, 24

   Ⓐ 2   Ⓒ 21

   Ⓑ 8   Ⓓ 23

Choose Appropriate Measures
of Center and Variability

COMMON CORE STANDARD CC.6.SP.5d
Summarize and describe distributions.

1. The distances, in miles, that 6 people travel to get to work are 14, 12, 2, 16, 16, and 18. Decide which measure(s) of center best describes the data set. Explain your reasoning.

   The _____ is less than 4 of the data points, and the _____ describes only 2 of the data points. So, the _____ best describes the data.

   mean = ___13 miles___

   median = ___15 miles___

   mode = ___16 miles___

2. The numbers of pets that several children have are 2, 1, 2, 3, 4, 3, 10, 0, 1, and 0. Make a box plot of the data and find the range and interquartile range. Decide which measure better describes the data set and explain your reasoning.

   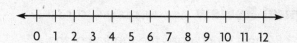

   0 1 2 3 4 5 6 7 8 9 10 11 12

   range = _____

   interquartile range = _____

   _____

   _____

   _____

Problem Solving REAL WORLD

3. Brett's history quiz scores are 84, 78, 92, 90, 85, 91, and 0. Decide which measure(s) of center best describes the data set. Explain your reasoning.

   mean = _____ median = _____

   mode = _____

   _____

   _____

   _____

4. Eight students were absent the following number of days in a year: 4, 8, 0, 1, 7, 2, 6, and 3. Decide if the range or interquartile range better describes the data set, and explain your reasoning.

   range = _____ interquartile range = _____

   _____

   _____

   _____

Lesson Check (CC.6.SP.5d)

1. Chloe used two box plots to display some data. The box in the plot for the first data set is wider than the box for the second data set. What does this say about the data?

Ⓐ The first data set has greater values.

Ⓑ The values in the first data set vary more than in the second set.

Ⓒ The data values in the first set are close in value.

Ⓓ The second data set has a greater median.

2. Hector recorded the temperature at noon for 14 days in a row. The temperatures are 20°F, 20°F, 20°F, 23°F, 23°F, 23°F, and 55°F. Which measure of center would best describe the data?

Ⓐ median

Ⓑ mean

Ⓒ mode

Ⓓ interquartile range

Spiral Review (CC.6.SP.4, CC.6.SP.5c, CC.6.SP.5d)

3. By how much does the median of the following data set change if the outlier is removed? **(Lesson 12.7)**

13, 20, 15, 19, 22, 26, 42

Ⓐ It increases by 42.

Ⓑ It decreases by 42.

Ⓒ It increases by 0.5.

Ⓓ It decreases by 0.5.

4. What percent of the people spent at least an hour watching television? **(Lesson 12.8)**

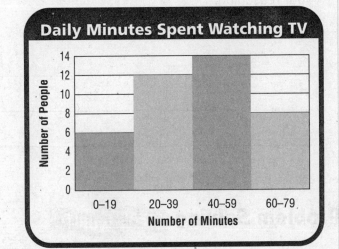

Ⓐ 35%   Ⓒ 20%

Ⓑ 30%   Ⓓ 15%

5. Which data set has a lower quartile of 8? **(Lesson 13.2)**

Ⓐ 4, 9, 8, 5, 8, 10

Ⓑ 12, 9, 10, 8, 7, 12

Ⓒ 10, 11, 6, 5, 8, 8

Ⓓ 16, 8, 9, 13, 17, 12

6. What is the interquartile range of the data shown in the box plot? **(Lesson 13.4)**

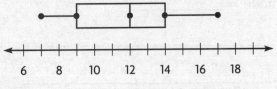

Ⓐ 5   Ⓒ 10

Ⓑ 7   Ⓓ 14

Apply Measures of Center and Variability

COMMON CORE STANDARD CC.6.SP.3
Develop understanding of statistical variability.

Solve.

1. The table shows temperature data for two cities. Use the information in the table to compare the data.

   The mean of City 1's temperatures is ___*less than*___ the mean of City 2's temperatures.

   The ___*interquartile range*___ of City 1's temperatures is ___*less than*___ the ___*interquartile range*___ of City 2's temperatures.

   So, City 2 is typically ___*warmer than*___ City 1, but City 2's temperatures vary ___*more than*___ City 1's temperatures.

Daily High Temperatures (°F)		
	Mean	Interquartile Range
City 1	60	7
City 2	70	15

2. The table shows weights of fish that were caught in two different lakes. Find the median and range of each data set, and use these measures to compare the data.

Fish Weight (pounds)
Lake A: 7, 9, 10, 4, 6, 12
Lake B: 6, 7, 4, 5, 6, 4

_____

_____

_____

_____

Problem Solving REAL WORLD

3. Mrs. Mack measured the heights of her students in two classes. Class 1 has a median height of 130 cm and an interquartile range of 5 cm. Class 2 has a median height of 134 cm and an interquartile range of 8 cm. Write a statement that compares the data.

_____

_____

_____

4. Richard's science test scores are 76, 80, 78, 84, and 80. His math test scores are 100, 80, 73, 94, and 71. Compare the medians and interquartile ranges.

_____

_____

_____

Lesson Check (CC.6.SP.3)

1. Team A has a mean of 35 and a range of 8. Team B has a mean of 30 and a range of 7. Which statement best describes the data?

   (A) Team A has more outliers than Team B.

   (B) Team A and B typically score the same number of points.

   (C) Team A has higher scores, and their scores do not vary as much as Team B's.

   (D) The values in the two data sets have similar amounts of variation, but Team A has higher scores.

2. Jean's test scores have a mean of 83 and an interquartile range of 4. Ben's test scores have a mean of 87 and an interquartile range of 9. Which statement best describes the data?

   (A) Jean's scores are higher and more consistent.

   (B) Ben's scores are higher and more consistent.

   (C) Jean's scores are higher but less consistent.

   (D) Ben's scores are higher but less consistent.

Spiral Review (CC.6.SP.3, CC.6.SP.4, CC.6.SP.5d)

3. Look at the box plots below. What is the difference between the medians for the two groups of data? **(Lesson 13.2)**

   (A) 1   (C) 4

   (B) 2   (D) 6

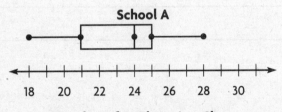

School A

Number of Students in a Class

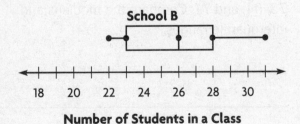

School B

Number of Students in a Class

4. The distances in miles that 6 people drive to get to work are 10, 11, 9, 12, 9, and 27. Which measure of center best describes the data set? **(Lesson 13.5)**

   (A) median

   (B) mode

   (C) range

   (D) mean

5. Which two teams typically practice the same number of hours but have very different variations in their practice times? **(Lesson 13.6)**

Hours of Practice Per Week		
Team	Mean	Range
A	7	1.5
B	10.5	1.5
C	7.5	5
D	10	2

   (A) A and B   (C) B and C

   (B) A and C   (D) B and D

Name _____

Describe Distributions

COMMON CORE STANDARD CC.6.SP.2
Develop understanding of statistical variability.

Chase asked people how many songs they have bought online in the past month. Use the histogram of the data he collected for 1–6.

1. What statistical question could Chase ask about the data?

   <u>Possible answer: What is the median</u>

   <u>number of songs purchased?</u>

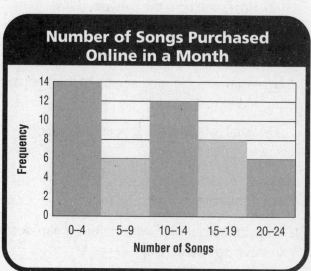

Number of Songs Purchased Online in a Month

2. Describe any peaks in the data.

   _____

   _____

3. Describe any gaps in the data.

   _____

   _____

4. Does the graph have symmetry? Explain your reasoning.

   _____

   _____

Problem Solving REAL WORLD

5. Mr. Carpenter teaches five classes each day. For several days in a row, he kept track of the number of students who were late to class and displayed the results in a dot plot. Describe the data.

   _____

   _____

   _____

   _____

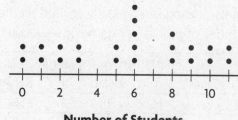

**Number of Students
Late to Class Each Day**

Lesson Check (CC.6.SP.2)

1. The ages of people in a fast-food restaurant are 28, 10, 44, 25, 18, 8, 47, and 30. What statistical question could be asked about the data?

   Ⓐ How much did the 44-year-old's food cost?

   Ⓑ Did the 25-year-old order dessert?

   Ⓒ What was the median age of the people in the restaurant?

   Ⓓ What food did the 8-year-old order?

2. What is the overall shape of the data in the histogram on page P255?

   Ⓐ The data always increases.

   Ⓑ The data always decreases.

   Ⓒ The data decreases, then increases, then decreases.

   Ⓓ The data increases, then decreases, then increases.

Spiral Review (CC.6.SP.2, CC.6.SP.3, CC.6.SP.5c, CC.6.SP.5d)

3. Look at the dot plot. Where does a gap occur in the data? (Lesson 13.1)

   Ⓐ 30   Ⓒ 32

   Ⓑ 31   Ⓓ 33

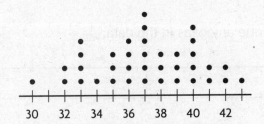

Number of Movies Ordered Per Day

4. Look at the dot plot. Where does a peak occur in the data? (Lesson 13.7)

   Ⓐ 30   Ⓒ 37

   Ⓑ 31   Ⓓ 41

5. Which two teams had similar variations in points earned but typically earned a different number of points per game? (Lesson 13.6)

Points Earned Per Game		
Team	Mean	Range
Red	20	8
Blue	28	8
Green	29	4
Orange	28	4

   Ⓐ Blue, Green   Ⓒ Red, Green

   Ⓑ Blue, Orange   Ⓓ Red, Blue

6. Manny's monthly electric bills for the past 6 months are $140, $165, $145, $32, $125, and $135. Which measure of center best represents the data? (Lesson 13.5)

   Ⓐ mean

   Ⓑ mode

   Ⓒ median

   Ⓓ mean absolute deviation

Name _____

Problem Solving • Misleading Statistics

COMMON CORE STANDARD CC.6.SP.2
Develop understanding of statistical variability.

Mr. Jackson wants to make dinner reservations at a restaurant that has most meals costing less than $16. The Waterside Inn advertises that they have meals that average $15. The table shows the menu items.

Menu Items	
Meal	**Price**
Potato Soup	$6
Chicken	$16
Steak	$18
Pasta	$16
Shrimp	$18
Crab Cake	$19

1. What is the minimum price and maximum price?

   min = _____ $6

   max = _____ $19

2. What is the mean of the prices?

   _____

3. Construct a box plot for the data.

   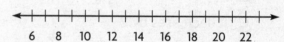

   6   8   10   12   14   16   18   20   22

4. What is the range of the prices?

   _____

5. What is the interquartile range of the prices?

   _____

6. What is the median of the prices?

   _____

7. Does the menu match Mr. Jackson's requirements? Explain your reasoning.

   _____

   _____

   _____

Lesson Check (CC.6.SP.2)

1. Mary's science test scores are 66, 94, 73, 81, 70, 84, and 88. Which of the following is true?

   (A) The mean is greater than the median.

   (B) The interquartile range is 81.

   (C) Half of the scores are less than 70.

   (D) The range is 28.

2. The heights in inches of students on a team are 64, 66, 60, 68, 69, 59, 60, and 70. Which of the following is NOT true?

   (A) Half of the students are taller than 68.5 inches.

   (B) The median is greater than the mean.

   (C) The interquartile range is 8.5 inches.

   (D) The range is 11 inches.

Spiral Review (CC.6.SP.4, CC.6.SP.5c, CC.6.SP.5d)

3. By how much does the median of the following data set change if the outlier is removed? (Lesson 12.7)

   26, 21, 25, 18, 0, 28

   (A) It does not change.

   (B) It increases by 2.

   (C) It decreases by 2.

   (D) It increases by 4.

4. Look at the box plot. What is the interquartile range of the data? (Lesson 13.2)

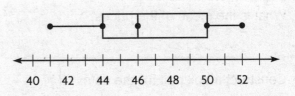

   (A) 6   (C) 46

   (B) 11   (D) 50

5. Erin is on the school trivia team. The table shows the team's scores in the last 8 games. Erin wants to build confidence in her team so that they will do well in the last game. Which measure of center would be best for Erin to use to motivate her teammates? (Lesson 13.5)

   (A) mean

   (B) range

   (C) mode

   (D) median

Trivia Game Results	
Game	Score
Game 1	20
Game 2	20
Game 3	18
Game 4	19
Game 5	23
Game 6	40
Game 7	22
Game 8	19

Name _____

COMMON CORE STANDARDS CC.6.SP.2, CC.6.SP.3, CC.6.SP.4,
CC.6.SP.5c, CC.6.SP.5d

Chapter 13 Extra Practice

Lesson 13.1

Use the dot plot for 1–2.

1. Describe any clusters or gaps.

_____

_____

_____

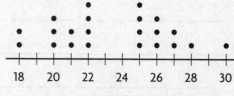

Ages of People in Yoga Class

2. Does the graph have symmetry? Explain.

_____

_____

Lesson 13.2

The heights, in centimeters, of 8 apples are 8, 9, 10, 11, 12, 12, 13, and 13.

3. median = _____

4. lower quartile = _____

5. upper quartile = _____

6. least value = _____

7. greatest value = _____

8. Make a box plot for the data.

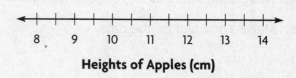

Heights of Apples (cm)

Lessons 13.3 and 13.4

Find the mean absolute deviation of the data.

9. the number of hours Mackenzie spent on homework each week: 4, 8, 7, 6, 8, 8, 5, 10

mean = 7

mean absolute deviation = _____

10. the number of runs scored by the Blasters in 6 games: 8, 0, 0, 3, 3, 4

mean = 3

mean absolute deviation = _____

Lesson 13.5

11. The ages of students in a ballet class are 8, 4, 7, 7, 8, 9, 10, 7, and 9 years. Make a box plot of the data and find the range and interquartile range. Decide which measure better describes the data set and explain your reasoning.

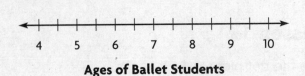

Ages of Ballet Students

_____

_____

_____

_____

range = _____   interquartile range = _____

Lesson 13.6

12. Use the information in the table to compare the data.

_____

_____

_____

Player Scores		
	Mean	Interquartile Range
Player 1	54	4
Player 2	60	9

Lessons 13.7 and 13.8

Ms. Gonzalez is collecting money for a charity. The table shows information about the donations that people made. Use this information for 13–16.

13. What is the range of donations? _____

14. What is the interquartile range of donations? _____

15. Make a box plot for the data.

Statistics for Donations Made	
Lowest Donation	$5
Highest Donation	$150
Lower Quartile Donation	$20
Median Donation	$40
Upper Quartile Donation	$80

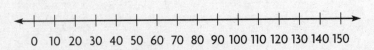

Donation Amounts

16. Ms. Gonzalez hopes that most people donated at least $50. Do the statistics show that this is true? Explain your reasoning.

_____

_____

_____

Name _____

Model Integer Addition

Essential Question How can you use a number line to model addition of integers?

UNLOCK the Problem REAL WORLD

In the first round of a game, Laura lost 5 points. Then she won 9 points in the second round. What is her score after the second round?

- How can you represent a loss of 5 points with an integer? _____
- How can you represent a gain of 9 points with an integer? _____

Find $^-5 + {}^+9$.

STEP 1 Draw a number line.

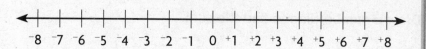

STEP 2 Start at 0. Move 5 units to the

_____ to show $^-5$.

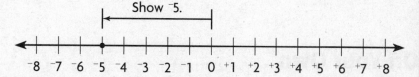

Show $^-5$.

STEP 3 From $^-5$, move 9 units to the

_____ to add $^+9$.

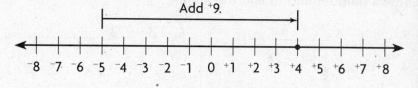

Add $^+9$.

$^-5 + {}^+9 =$ _____

So, Laura's score after the second round is _____.

Math Talk Will $^-5 + {}^+8$ be the same as $^+8 + {}^-5$? **Explain.**

Try This! Tell how to find the sum using a number line.

A. $^+6 + {}^-8$

B. $^-2 + {}^-6$

Share and Show

1. Use the number line to find $^+4 + {}^-7$.

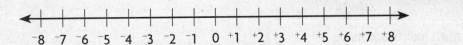

Start at _____.

Move 4 units to the _____. Then move 7 units to the _____.

The sum is _____.

Draw a number line to find the sum.

2. $^-3 + {}^+1$ _____

3. $^-5 + {}^-1$ _____

4. $^+6 + {}^-6$ _____

On Your Own ·

Draw a number line to find the sum.

5. $^-8 + {}^+4$ _____

6. $^-3 + {}^-3$ _____

7. $^+7 + {}^-9$ _____

8. $^+5 + {}^-4$ _____

9. $^-4 + {}^-3$ _____

10. $^-2 + {}^+10$ _____

Problem Solving REAL WORLD

11. In a football game, Jim's team gained 7 yards on the first play, lost 2 yards on the second play, and lost 10 yards on the third play. How many total yards did Jim's team gain or lose after three plays?

_____

12. In the morning the temperature was $^-3°F$. By noon it had risen by $10°F$. What was the temperature at noon?

_____

Model Integer Subtraction

Essential Question How can you use a number line to model subtraction of integers?

🔑 UNLOCK the Problem REAL WORLD

At 6:00 P.M., the temperature was ⁻2°F. By midnight, it had dropped 5°F. What was the temperature at midnight?

> **Math Idea**
> - Move left on a number line to subtract a positive integer.
> - Move right on a number line to subtract a negative integer.

 Find ⁻2 − ⁺5.

STEP 1 Draw a number line.

Start at 0, move 2 units to the

_____ to show ⁻2.

Show ⁻2.

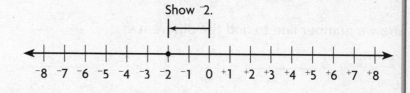

STEP 2 From ⁻2, move 5 units to the

_____ to subtract ⁺5.

⁻2 − ⁺5 = _____

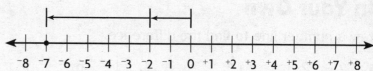

So, the temperature at midnight was ⁻7°F.

EXAMPLE Find ⁺1 − ⁻4.

STEP 1 Draw a number line. Start at 0,

move 1 unit to the _____ to show ⁺1.

Show ⁺1.

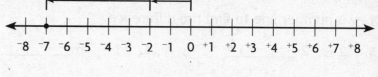

STEP 2 From ⁺1, move 4 units to the right to subtract ⁻4.

So, ⁺1 − ⁻4 = _____.

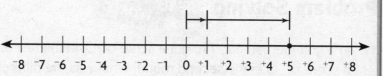

> **Math Talk** Will ⁺1 − ⁻4 be the same as ⁻4 − ⁺1? **Explain.**

Share and Show

1. Use the number line to find $^-3 - ^-3$.

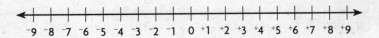

Start at _____.

Move 3 units to the _____.

Move _____ on the number line to subtract $^-3$.

The difference is _____.

Draw a number line to find the difference.

2. $^-3 - ^+4$ _____

3. $^+5 - ^+9$ _____

4. $^+2 - ^-4$ _____

On Your Own . . . .

Draw a number line to find the difference.

5. $^-2 - ^+2$ _____

6. $^+1 - ^-6$ _____

7. $^-7 - ^-7$ _____

8. $^+4 - ^-4$ _____

9. $^+3 - ^+6$ _____

10. $^-8 - ^-3$ _____

Problem Solving REAL WORLD

11. In a golf tournament, Tim got a score of $^+2$ in the first round and a score of $^-3$ in the second round. What was the difference in his scores between the first round and the second round?

_____

12. The high temperature one day was $^-3°F$. The low temperature was $^-7°F$. What was the difference between the high and low temperatures that day?

_____

Name _____

Model Integer Multiplication

Essential Question How can you use a number line to model multiplication of integers?

🔓 UNLOCK the Problem REAL WORLD

Kayla is scuba diving to explore coral reefs. She makes 5 equal descents of 2 meters each. What is Kayla's elevation at the end of her descent?

🔑 **Find ⁻2 × ⁺5.**

By the Commutative Property, ⁻2 × 5 = 5 × ⁻2.

STEP 1 Draw a number line.

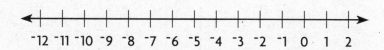

STEP 2 Start at 0. Show five groups of ⁻2.

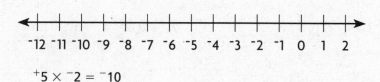

⁺5 × ⁻2 = ⁻10

So, Kayla's elevation at the end of her descent is _____ feet.

> **Math Idea**
> 5 × ⁻2 means 5 groups of ⁻2.

> **Math Talk** What do you notice about the sign of the product when you multiply a positive integer and a negative integer?

Try This! Tell how to find the product using a number line.

A. ⁺3 × (⁻2)

_____

_____

_____

B. ⁻4 × ⁺6

_____

_____

_____

Share and Show

1. Use the number line to find $^+2 \times (^-6)$.

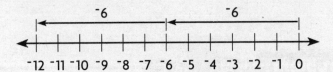

$^-12$ $^-11$ $^-10$ $^-9$ $^-8$ $^-7$ $^-6$ $^-5$ $^-4$ $^-3$ $^-2$ $^-1$ 0

Start at _____.

Show _____ groups of _____.

The product is _____.

Draw a number line to find the product.

2. $^+4 \times (^-1)$ **3.** $^-5 \times {}^+3$ **4.** $^+7 \times (^-2)$

_____   _____   _____

On Your Own

Draw a number line to find the product.

5. $^-4 \times {}^+3$ **6.** $^+3 \times (^-7)$ **7.** $^-2 \times {}^+4$

_____   _____   _____

8. $^+5 \times (^-6)$ **9.** $^-9 \times {}^+2$ **10.** $^+6 \times (^-8)$

_____   _____   _____

Problem Solving REAL WORLD

11. The Milam glacier is changing size at a rate of $^-3$ feet per month. Write a number sentence to show the change in size of the glacier after 3 months.

_____

12. An elevator starts at the lobby of a building and descends into the basement. The elevator's height changes by $^-6$ meters each second. What is the change in the elevator's height after 3 seconds?

_____

Name _____

✔ Checkpoint

Check Concepts and Skills

Draw a number line to find the sum, difference, or product. (pp. P261–P262, P263–P264, P265–P266)

1. $^+4 + (^-2)$

2. $^+5 - (^-1)$

3. $^+6 \times (^-2)$

_____

_____

_____

4. $^-2 - ^+7$

5. $^+7 + (^-2)$

6. $^-3 \times ^+1$

_____

_____

_____

7. $0 - ^+4$

8. $^+3 \times (^-2)$

9. $^-1 + ^+5$

_____

_____

_____

10. $^-3 \times ^+7$

11. $^-6 + ^+8$

12. $^-2 - ^+4$

_____

_____

_____

13. $^+10 + (^-12)$

14. $^-1 - ^+5$

15. $^-6 \times ^+3$

_____

_____

_____

Problem Solving  REAL WORLD

16. The price of a stock increased by $6, then decreased by $8. What integer represents the overall change in the price? (pp. P261)

_____

17. The captain of a boat is 1 meter above sea level. A diver is 8 meters below sea level. What is the difference in elevation between the captain and the diver? (pp. P263)

_____

18. A researcher lowers the temperature of a specimen by 3° each hour for four hours. What integer shows the total change in temperature? (pp. P261)

_____

Choose the letter of the correct answer.

19. When Carlos went to bed, the temperature was ⁻2°F. While he slept, the temperature rose by 5°F. What was the temperature when Carlos woke up? **(pp. P261–P262)**

(A) ⁻7°F

(B) ⁻3°F

(C) 3°F

(D) 7°F

20. To prepare for landing, a jet makes 5 equal descents of 200 meters. Which integer represents the total change in elevation? **(pp. P261–P262)**

(A) ⁻200

(B) ⁻500

(C) ⁻1,000

(D) ⁻2,000

21. The temperature at the base of a mountain is 16°F. The temperature at the summit is ⁻4°F. What is the difference in temperatures between the base of the mountain and the summit? **(pp. P263–P264)**

(A) 20°F

(B) 12°F

(C) ⁻12°F

(D) ⁻20°F

22. In a carnival game, Juan won 11 tickets on his first turn, lost 5 tickets on his second turn, and lost 4 tickets on his third turn. What integer represents the number of tickets Juan has after three turns?
(pp. P265–P266)

(A) 20

(B) ⁻2

(C) 2

(D) ⁻20

23. A submarine sailing 30 meters below sea level rises 20 meters. What integer represents the submarine's new elevation?
(pp. P261–P262)

(A) ⁻50

(B) ⁻10

(C) 10

(D) 20

24. Which of these expressions has the greatest value? **(pp. P261–P266)**

(A) ⁻1 + ⁺7

(B) ⁺2 × (⁻4)

(C) ⁺8 − (⁻3)

(D) ⁻4 + ⁺5

Name _____

Simplify Complex Fractions

Essential Question How can you simplify complex fractions?

A **complex fraction** is a fraction in which the numerator, denominator, or both contain fractions.

UNLOCK the Problem REAL WORLD

Jerrod swam $\frac{1}{2}$ mile in $\frac{1}{4}$ hour. The complex fraction $\frac{\frac{1}{2}}{\frac{1}{4}}$ is a ratio that represents Jerrod's speed in miles per hour.

- What operation does the bar between the numerator and denominator of a fraction represent?

  _____

Simplify the complex fraction that shows Jerrod's speed to find the unit rate.

STEP 1 Write the complex fraction as division.

$$\frac{\frac{1}{2}}{\frac{1}{4}} = \frac{1}{2} \div \frac{1}{4}$$

STEP 2 Use the reciprocal of the divisor to write a multiplication problem. Multiply. Write your answer in simplest form.

$$\frac{1}{2} \div \frac{1}{4} = \frac{1}{\cancel{2}_1} \times \frac{\cancel{4}^2}{1} = 2$$

So, Jerrod's speed was 2 miles per hour.

Math Talk **Explain** how you can use division to simplify a complex fraction.

Example Simplify $\frac{\frac{2}{3}}{\frac{4}{5}}$.

STEP 1 Write the complex fraction as division.

$$\frac{\frac{2}{3}}{\frac{4}{5}} = \frac{2}{3} \div \frac{4}{5}$$

STEP 2 Use the reciprocal of the divisor to write a multiplication problem. Multiply. Write your answer in simplest form.

$$\frac{2}{3} \div \frac{4}{5} = \frac{2}{3}^1 \times \frac{5}{4}_2 = \underline{\hspace{2cm}}$$

So, $\frac{\frac{2}{3}}{\frac{4}{5}} = \underline{\hspace{2cm}}$.

Share and Show

Simplify $\dfrac{\frac{1}{4}}{\frac{3}{5}}$.

1. Write the complex fraction using division: $\dfrac{\frac{1}{4}}{\frac{3}{5}}$ = _____

2. Use the reciprocal of the divisor to write a multiplication problem. Multiply. Write your answer in simplest form.

   $\dfrac{1}{4} \times$ _____ = _____

Simplify the complex fraction. Write your answer in simplest form.

3. $\dfrac{\frac{1}{4}}{\frac{2}{3}}$

4. $\dfrac{\frac{4}{5}}{\frac{1}{5}}$

5. $\dfrac{\frac{1}{2}}{\frac{3}{4}}$

_____

On Your Own

Simplify the complex fraction. Write your answer in simplest form.

6. $\dfrac{\frac{1}{4}}{\frac{2}{5}}$

7. $\dfrac{\frac{1}{6}}{\frac{2}{5}}$

8. $\dfrac{\frac{1}{8}}{\frac{7}{8}}$

_____

9. $\dfrac{\frac{3}{8}}{\frac{3}{4}}$

10. $\dfrac{\frac{2}{9}}{\frac{2}{3}}$

11. $\dfrac{\frac{1}{5}}{\frac{3}{8}}$

_____

Problem Solving REAL WORLD

12. Meg ran $\frac{7}{8}$ mile in $\frac{1}{8}$ hour. What was her running speed in miles per hour?

13. Kareem needs $\frac{3}{4}$ cup of flour to bake a batch of cupcakes. He has $\frac{1}{2}$ cup. What fraction of a batch can Kareem bake?

_____

Name _____

Identify Proportional Relationships

Essential Question How can you identify a proportional relationship?

A **proportional relationship** is a relationship between two quantities in which the ratio of one quantity to the other quantity is constant.

🔓 UNLOCK the Problem REAL WORLD

Kudzu is a fast-growing plant that is found in the southeastern United States. In summer, kudzu grows 12 inches per day. Is the relationship between the length of a kudzu plant and the number of days it has been growing a proportional relationship?

- What operation can you use to find the length of a kudzu plant after a certain number of days?

  _____

🔑 **Find and compare the ratios of the length of a kudzu plant to the number of days it has been growing.**

STEP 1 Make a table of values.

Number of days	1	2	3	4	5
Length (in.)	12	24	36	48	60

STEP 2 Find and compare ratios.

$$\frac{\text{length (in.)}}{\text{number of days}} = \frac{12}{1} = \frac{24}{2} = \frac{36}{3} = \frac{48}{4} = \frac{60}{5} = 12$$

The ratios are constant.
So, the relationship is a proportional relationship.

🔑 Example

Judy drives 150 miles in 3 hours, 250 miles in 5 hours, and 400 miles in 8 hours. Is the relationship between distance and time a proportional relationship? If so, what is the unit rate?

Find and compare ratios: $\frac{\text{distance}}{\text{time}} = \frac{150}{3} = \frac{250}{5} = \frac{400}{8} =$ _____

The ratios are constant.

So, the relationship is a proportional relationship.

The unit rate is the ratio that gives the distance traveled in

one hour. The unit rate is _____ miles per hour.

Math Talk **Describe** the connection between proportional relationships and unit rates.

Share and Show

There are 4 mg of vitamin C in every cup of blueberries. Is the relationship between the amount of vitamin C and the number of cups a proportional relationship?

1. Make a table of values.

Number of cups	1	2	3	4	5
Vitamin C (mg)	4				

2. Find the ratios of the amount of vitamin C to the number of cups of blueberries.

_____

3. Is the relationship a proportional relationship?

_____

On Your Own

4. Each pound of dried cranberries costs $3.50. Is the relationship between cost and the number of pounds a proportional relationship?

_____

5. The equation $y = 2x$ represents the cost y of buying x pounds of cheese. Complete the table and plot the ordered pairs. Tell whether the relationship between y and x is a proportional relationship and describe what you notice about the points you plotted.

Pounds, x	1	2	3	4
Dollars, y				

_____

_____

_____

Cost of Cheese

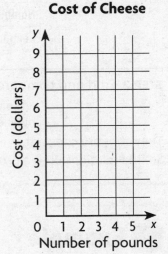

Problem Solving

6. An elevator rises 40 feet in 2 seconds, 100 feet in 5 seconds, and 180 feet in 9 seconds. Is the relationship between distance and time a proportional relationship? If so, what is the unit rate?

_____

7. Drew types 45 words in 1 minute, 120 words in 3 minutes, and 184 words in 4 minutes. Is the relationship between the number of words and time a proportional relationship? If so, what is the unit rate?

_____

Name _____

Analyze Proportional Relationships

Essential Question How can you identify the constant of proportionality in proportional relationships?

A proportional relationship is a relationship between two variables, *x* and *y*, that can be written in the form $y = kx$, or $\frac{y}{x} = k$, where *k* is a nonzero number called the *constant of proportionality*. The graph of a proportional relationship is a straight line through the origin.

 UNLOCK the Problem REAL WORLD

Potato salad costs $3 per pound at a local deli. Write and graph an equation for the proportional relationship. Give the constant of proportionality.

- What operation will you use in your equation for this relationship?

  _____

Analyze the relationship.

STEP 1 Write an equation for the relationship. Let *x* represent the number of pounds of potato salad. Let *y* represent the cost of buying *x* pounds.

Cost = $3 times the number of pounds

$y = 3 \cdot x$

$y = 3x$

STEP 2 Make a table of values. Then graph the relationship by plotting several points and drawing a line through the points and through the origin.

x	y
1	3
2	6
3	9

STEP 3 Identify the constant of proportionality.
The constant of proportionality in $y = 3x$ is 3.

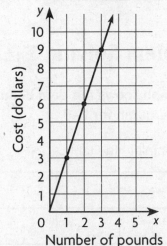

Potato Salad Cost

Math Talk **Explain** why the equation $y = x$ shows a proportional relationship. What is the constant of proportionality?

Share and Show

A shower uses 5 gallons of water per minute. Use this information for 1–3.

1. Let x represent the number of minutes. Let y represent the number of gallons of water used. Write an equation that relates x and y.

_____

2. Give the constant of proportionality.

_____

3. Graph the equation you wrote in Exercise 1.

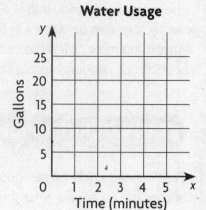

Water Usage

On Your Own

Pencils cost $0.50 each. Use this information for 4–6.

4. Let x represent the number of pencils and let y represent the cost. Write an equation that relates x and y.

_____

5. Give the constant of proportionality. _____

6. Graph the equation you wrote in Exercise 4.

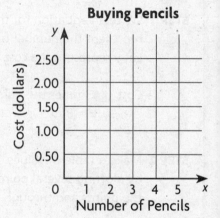

Buying Pencils

Problem Solving REAL WORLD

The graph shows the data about a typical whale's heartbeats. Use the graph for 7–9.

7. Complete the table.

x	1	2	4		
y				140	160

8. Use the table to find the ratio $\frac{y}{x}$. _____

9. Write an equation that relatex x and y.

_____

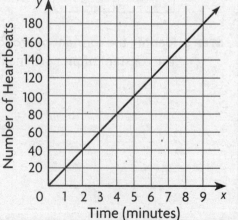

Whale Heartbeat Data

Name _____

Apply Percents

Essential Question How can you solve percent problems involving discounts and sales tax?

A **discount** is a percent of a price that is subtracted from the price. **Sales tax** is a tax that is a percent of a price that is added to the price of an item.

 UNLOCK the Problem REAL WORLD

The regular price of a pair of sneakers is $40. A store is offering a 15% discount on the shoes. What is the sale price?

> • How can you write 15% as a decimal?
>
> _____

Find the discount and sale price of the sneakers.

STEP 1 Find 15% of 40.

$$15\% \text{ of } 40 = \frac{15}{100} \times 40 = 6$$

The discount is $6.

STEP 2 Subtract to find the sale price.

regular price − discount = sale price

$40 − $6 = $34

So, the sale price is $34.

Example

A pair of jeans costs $23 plus tax. The sales tax rate is 8%. What is the sales tax? What is the final cost of the jeans?

STEP 1 Find 8% of 23.

$$8\% \text{ of } 23 = \frac{8}{100} \times 23 = \underline{\hspace{2cm}}$$

The sales tax is $1.84.

STEP 2 Add to find the total cost.

price + sales tax = final cost

$23 + _____ = _____

So, the final cost is _____.

> **Math Talk** How can you use estimation to show that your answer is reasonable?

Share and Show

A video game is on sale for 10% off. The regular price is $29.00.

1. Find the discount.

   10% of 29.00 = _____ × 29 = _____

   The discount is _____.

2. Find the sale price of the game.

   Regular price − discount = sale price

   _____ − _____ = _____

   The sale price is _____.

On Your Own

Find the discount and the sale price.

3. regular price: $50

   discount: 20%

   discount: $ _____

   sale price: $ _____

4. regular price: $56

   discount: 25%

   discount: $ _____

   sale price: $ _____

Find the sales tax and the final cost.

5. price: $75

   sales tax: 6%

   sales tax: $ _____

   final cost: $ _____

6. price: $25

   sales tax: 5%

   sales tax: $ _____

   final cost: $ _____

Problem Solving

7. A sweater that is regularly sold for $35 is on sale for 20% off. What is the sale price of the sweater?

   _____

8. Eileen has a $15 gift card to a music store. She uses the card to pay for a CD that costs $12 + tax. If the tax rate is 5%, how much will be left on the gift card after the purchase?

   _____

Getting Ready for Grade 7

Percent of Change

Essential Question How can you find a percent of change?

A **percent of change** is an amount, stated as a percent, that a number goes up or down. If the number goes up, it is a **percent of increase**. If the number goes down, it is a **percent of decrease**. To find a percent of change, use the following formula:

$$\text{percent of change} = \frac{\text{amount of change}}{\text{original amount}}$$

🔑 UNLOCK the Problem REAL WORLD

The manager of a store raises the price of a pair of shoes from $40 to $42. What is the percent of change in the price?

> • What clue word tells you that this problem involves a price increase?
>
> _____

🔑 **Use the formula to find the percent of change.**

STEP 1 The change is an increase. Find the amount of increase: $42 - 40 = 2$.

STEP 2 Find the percent of increase.

$\text{percent of change} = \dfrac{\text{amount of change}}{\text{original amount}}$	Write the formula.
$= \dfrac{2}{40}$	Substitute.
$= 0.05 = 5\%$	Divide. Write the quotient as a percent.

So, the percent of change is a 5% increase.

🔑 Example Find the percent of change when the amount of water in a storage tank drops from 640 gallons to 512 gallons.

STEP 1 The change is a decrease. Find the amount of decrease: $640 - 512 = 128$.

STEP 2 Find the percent of change.

$\text{percent of change} = \dfrac{\text{amount of change}}{\text{original amount}}$	Write the formula.
$= \dfrac{128}{640}$	Substitute.
$= \underline{\hspace{1cm}} = \underline{\hspace{1cm}}$	Divide. Write the quotient as a percent.

So, the percent of change is a 20% decrease.

> **Math Talk** **Explain** what it means when a price increases by 100%.

Share and Show

Use these steps to find the percent of change for the prices in the advertisement at right.

Model Train Set
Original Price: $50
Now reduced to $29!

1. Tell whether the change is an increase or decrease. Then find the amount of change.

   _____

2. Substitute values in the formula and divide.

   _____

3. Write the quotient as a percent.

   _____

Find the percent of change. Label the change as increase or decrease.

4. 60 is increased to 75.

   _____

5. 1,200 is decreased to 1,176.

   _____

On Your Own

Find the percent of change. Label the change as increase or decrease.

6. 85 is increased to 119.

   _____

7. 5 is decreased to 4.

   _____

8. 35 is decreased to 21.

   _____

9. 22 is increased to 44.

   _____

10. 18 is increased to 26.1.

    _____

11. 700 is increased to 777.

    _____

Problem Solving

12. The owner of a boutique buys necklaces from a jewelry maker for $25 each. Then the boutique owner sells the necklaces for $40 each. What is the percent of change in the price?

    _____

13. On Saturday, 400 people attended a school festival. On Sunday, 366 people attended the festival. What is the percent of change in the attendance for the festival from Saturday to Sunday?

    _____

Name _____

Check Concepts and Skills

Simplify the complex fraction. Write your answer in simplest form. (pp. P269–P270)

1. $\dfrac{\frac{1}{4}}{\frac{2}{3}}$

_____

2. $\dfrac{\frac{1}{6}}{\frac{2}{3}}$

_____

3. $\dfrac{\frac{3}{5}}{\frac{7}{10}}$

_____

Bananas cost $0.30 each. Use this information for 4-6. (P271–P274)

4. Let x represent the number of bananas. Let y represent the cost. Write an equation that relates x and y.

_____

5. Give the constant of proportionality.

_____

6. Graph the equation you wrote in Exercise 4.

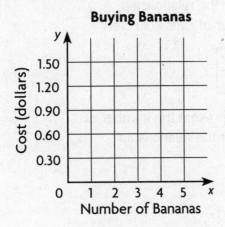

Buying Bananas

Problem Solving REAL WORLD

7. Joelle made 3 bracelets in 15 minutes, 4 bracelets in 20 minutes, and 6 bracelets in 30 minutes. Is the relationship between the number of bracelets and time a proportional relationship? If so, what is the unit rate? **(pp. P271–P272)**

_____

8. A calculator that normally sells for $45 is on sale for 20% off. What is the amount of the discount? **(pp. P275–P276)**

_____

9. The number of members in the Service Club rose from 18 to 27. What is the percent of change in the membership? **(pp. P277–P278)**

_____

Choose the letter of the correct answer.

10. A box contains $\frac{5}{6}$ pound of cereal. Each serving of cereal is $\frac{1}{12}$ pound. How many servings are in the cereal box? **(pp. P269–P270)**

    (A) $\frac{5}{72}$ serving

    (B) $\frac{5}{2}$ servings

    (C) 6 servings

    (D) 10 servings

11. Kaylin reads 96 pages in 3 hours, 128 pages in 4 hours, and 192 pages in 6 hours. Which statement is correct? **(pp. P271–P272)**

    (A) The relationship is a proportional relationship. The unit rate is 32 pages per hour.

    (B) The relationship is a proportional relationship. The unit rate is 96 pages per hour.

    (C) The relationship is a proportional relationship. The unit rate is 192 pages per hour.

    (D) The relationship is not a proportional relationship.

12. To attend a school Movie Night, students are asked to donate canned goods. The table below shows data for the relationship between the number of people and the number of cans collected.

People	10	20	40	100
Cans	20	40	80	200

    Let x represent the number of people and y represent the number of cans. What is the constant of proportionality for the relationship? **(pp. P273–P274)**

    (A) 2

    (B) 10

    (C) 20

    (D) 100

13. What is the total cost of a cell phone if the price of the cell phone is $60 and the sales tax rate is 5%? **(pp. P275–P276)**

    (A) $60

    (B) $63

    (C) $65

    (D) $66

14. After exercising, Ellen's heart rate went from 120 beats per minute to 84 beats per minute. What is the percent of change in her heart rate? **(pp. P277–P278)**

    (A) 36% decrease

    (B) 30% decrease

    (C) 20% decrease

    (D) 16% decrease

Name _____

Add Algebraic Expressions

Essential Question How can you add algebraic expressions?

🔓 UNLOCK the Problem REAL WORLD

During track practice, Steven runs laps and then runs cross-country. The expression $3x + 2$ represents the distance in miles he ran on Monday, where x is the length in miles of each lap. The expression $4x + 3$ represents the distance in miles he ran on Tuesday. Write and simplify an expression to show the total distance in miles Steven ran on both days.

> **Math Idea**
>
> Is $3x + 2 = 5x$? Explain.
>
> _____
>
> _____
>
> _____

Day	Laps	Cross-Country Distance (mi)
Monday	3	2
Tuesday	4	3

🔑 **Write and simplify an algebraic expression for the total distance.**

STEP 1 Write the algebraic expression for the total distance.

    Monday   Tuesday

    $(3x + 2) + (4x + 3)$

STEP 2 Use the Associative Property of Addition to remove the parentheses.

    $3x + 2 + 4x + 3$

STEP 3 Simplify the expression by combining like terms.

Use the Commutative Property of Addition to reorder the terms.

    $3x + 4x + 2 + 3$

Use parentheses to group like terms.

    $(3x + 4x) + (2 + 3)$

Combine like terms.

    $7x + 5$

So, the simplified expression $7x + 5$ represents the total distance in miles. Steven ran $7x + 5$ miles on Monday and Tuesday.

> **Math Talk** Explain how you can identify like terms in an algebraic expression.

Share and Show

Find the sum of the expressions $(5y + 29)$ and $(8 + 6y)$.

1. Write the algebraic expression for the total.

   _____

2. Use the Associative Property of Addition to remove the parentheses.

   _____

3. Use the Commutative Property of Addition to reorder the terms.

   _____

4. Use parentheses to group like terms.

   _____

5. Combine like terms.

   _____

Find the sum of the expressions.

6. $(x + 12) + (11 + 2x)$

   _____

7. $(4s + 1) + (8s + 14)$

   _____

8. $(1 + 41y) + (6y + 2)$

   _____

On Your Own

Find the sum of the expressions.

9. $(10t + 7) + (8 + 3t)$

   _____

10. $(8 + 3x) + (11 + 17x)$

    _____

11. $(9 + 19c) + (18c + 4)$

    _____

12. $(16y + 0) + (y + 23)$

    _____

13. $(45t + 27) + (23t + 32)$

    _____

14. $(35 + 6x) + (6 + x)$

    _____

Problem Solving REAL WORLD

15. Zoe orders 3 books for her friend Amelia and 4 books for her friend Edward. She pays an additional shipping charge of $5 for Amelia's order and $7 for Edward's order. Simplify the expression $(3c + 5) + (4c + 7)$, where c represents the cost of each book, to find the total Zoe spent on both orders.

    _____

16. Molly works 4 hours on Saturday and earns an additional $22 in tips. On Sunday, she works 6 hours and earns an additional $15 in tips. Simplify the expression $(4h + 22) + (6h + 15)$, where h represents the amount she is paid per hour, to find the total she earned over the weekend.

    _____

Name _____

Solve Two-Step Equations

Essential Question How do you solve two-step equations?

 UNLOCK the Problem REAL WORLD

Olivia orders 5 sets of beads. She pays $7 for shipping, and the total cost of the order is $52. Solve the equation $5p + 7 = 52$ to find the price p in dollars of each set of beads.

> **Math Idea**
>
> Suppose Olivia had a coupon. What operation would this indicate?
>
> _____

🔑 **Solve the equation to find the price of each set of beads.**

STEP 1   Write the equation.

$$5p + 7 = 52$$

STEP 2   Use the Properties of Equality and inverse operations to get the variable by itself on one side. First undo addition or subtraction, and then undo multiplication or division.

Undo the addition. Subtract 7 from both sides.

$$5p + 7 - 7 = 52 - 7$$
$$5p = 45$$

Undo the multiplication. Divide both sides by 5.

$$\frac{5p}{5} = \frac{45}{5}$$
$$p = 9$$

So, the price of each set of beads is $9.

Math Talk **Explain** how you know that your answer is correct.

Try This! Tell how to solve the equation for x.

A. $6x - 9 = 15$

_____

_____

_____

_____

Share and Show

1. Solve the equation $\frac{1}{4}c + 6 = 18$.

   First undo the _____ by using _____.

   Then undo the _____ by using _____.

   $c =$ _____

Solve the equation.

2. $12x + 2 = 38$

   _____

3. $\frac{1}{3}y - 5 = 3$

   _____

4. $3 + 7p = 52$

   _____

On Your Own

Solve the equation.

5. $23 + 4t = 59$

   _____

6. $2x - 8 = 64$

   _____

7. $5r + 30 = 105$

   _____

8. $\frac{1}{2}p + 15 = 29$

   _____

9. $3c + 58 = 97$

   _____

10. $6y - 37 = 29$

   _____

Problem Solving REAL WORLD

11. Lee started a round on a game show with 65 points. He answered all 5 questions during the round correctly. Lee's score at the end of the round was 105 points. Solve the equation $65 + 5p = 105$ to find the number of points p that Lee earned for each correct answer.

   _____

12. To repair a bike, a shop charges a fee of $11, plus $13 for each hour that the mechanic works on the bike. Minh paid $63 to have his bike fixed. Solve the equation $11 + 13h = 63$ to find the number of hours h the mechanic worked on Minh's bike.

   _____

Name _____

Solve Inequalities

Essential Question How can you solve inequalities?

Solving inequalities is much like solving equations. To solve an inequality, get the variable on one side by itself using the Properties of Inequality and inverse operations.

Addition and subtraction properties of inequality	
You can add or subtract the same number on both sides of an inequality, and the inequality will still be true.	$3 + 2 < 8$ $3 + 2 - 2 < 8 - 2$ $3 + 0 < 6$ $3 < 6$

Multiplication and division properties of inequality	
You can multiply or divide both sides of an inequality by the same positive number, and the inequality will still be true.	$2 \times 4 > 6$ $\frac{2 \times 4}{2} > \frac{6}{2}$ $1 \times 4 > 3$ $4 > 3$

🔑 UNLOCK the Problem REAL WORLD

A person must be at least 50 inches tall to be allowed to ride a roller coaster. Belinda is 38 inches tall. The inequality $38 + n \geq 50$ can be used to find the number of inches n Belinda must grow to be able to ride the roller coaster. Solve the inequality. Explain what the solution means.

Math Idea

Inequalities may have more than one solution. *Any* value of n that when added to 38 totals more than 50 is a solution for the inequality $38 + n \geq 50$.

 Solve the inequality.

STEP 1 Write the inequality.

$$38 + n \geq 50$$

STEP 2 Use the Properties of Inequality and inverse operations to get the variable by itself on one side.

$$38 - 38 + n \geq 50 - 38$$
$$n \geq 12$$

Undo the addition. Subtract 38 from both sides.

So, the solution of the inequality is $n \geq 12$.

This means that Belinda must grow 12 or more inches before she is able to ride the roller coaster. Any amount of growth she experiences that is 12 inches or more will allow her to ride the roller coaster.

Math Talk Describe the inverse operation you would use to solve $3x < 18$.

Share and Show

1. Solve the inequality $2s \leq 6$.

   Use the Properties of Inequality and inverse operations to get the variable by itself on one side.

   Undo the multiplication by _____.

   The solution is _____.

Solve the inequality.

2. $x + 3 < 4$

   _____

3. $n - 12 > 10$

   _____

4. $\dfrac{p}{3} \geq 9$

   _____

On Your Own

Solve the inequality.

5. $n + 5 < 9$

   _____

6. $x - 1 \leq 0$

   _____

7. $7c > 7$

   _____

8. $\dfrac{m}{2} \geq 2$

   _____

9. $a + 16 > 26$

   _____

10. $y - 5 \geq 19$

   _____

Problem Solving REAL WORLD

11. An elephant weighs more than 30 times what a tiger weighs. An average elephant weighs 12,000 pounds. The inequality $30w < 12,000$ can be used to find the possible weight w in pounds of the tiger. Solve the inequality and explain what the solution means.

    _____

    _____

12. The inequality $m + 12 \leq 20$ can be used to find the amount of money m in dollars that Nolan can spend at a circus. Solve the inequality and explain what the solution means.

    _____

    _____

    _____

    _____

Name _____

Vertical Angles

Essential Question How can you find the unknown measure
of vertical angles?

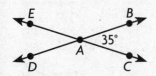 **UNLOCK the Problem** REAL WORLD

Vertical angles are formed when two lines or line
segments intersect. Vertical angles are
opposite congruent angles.

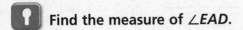

- What is true about congruent angles?

_____

- What is the measure of
a straight angle?

_____

- ∠*EAB* and ∠*DAC* are vertical angles.
- ∠*BAC* and ∠*EAD* are vertical angles.

🔑 **Find the measure of ∠*EAD*.**

    THINK: Vertical angles are congruent.

- ∠*BAC* and ∠*EAD* are vertical angles, so the measure of
  ∠*BAC* = the measure of ∠*EAD*.
- The measure of ∠*BAC* is 35°.

So, the measure of ∠*EAD*, written m∠*EAD*, is _____.

🔑 **Find the measure of ∠*EAB* and ∠*DAC*.**

    THINK: A straight angle is 180°.

- Together, ∠*EAB* and ∠*BAC* make up a straight angle, ∠*EAC*.

- Subtract the measure of ∠*BAC* from _____ to find the   .

    measure of ∠*EAB*. 180° − _____ = _____

Since ∠*EAB* and ∠*DAC* are vertical angles and the measure of

∠*EAB* is _____, the measure of ∠*DAC* is _____.

Try This!

Materials ■ protractor

- Draw two intersecting lines. Use a protractor to measure one angle.
- Find and label the measure of the other three angles using what you know
  about vertical angles and straight angles.

Share and Show

For 1–3, use the drawing to find the measure of the angle.

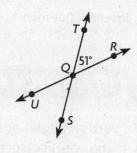

1. m∠SQR = 180° − 51° = _____

2. m∠UQS = _____

3. m∠UQT = _____

On Your Own

For 4–6, use the drawing to find the measure of the angle.

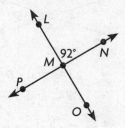

4. m∠PMO =

5. m∠LMP =

6. m∠NMO =

_____   _____   _____

For 7–9, use the drawing to find the measure of the angle.

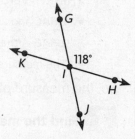

7. m∠HIJ =

8. m∠JIK =

9. m∠KIG =

_____   _____   _____

Problem Solving REAL WORLD

10. Two intersecting lines form vertical angles that are not obtuse or acute. Describe the angles that are formed and make a sketch of the lines.

_____

11. The figure at the right shows three lines intersecting to form an isosceles right triangle. How many acute angles are formed? **Explain** why they all are congruent.

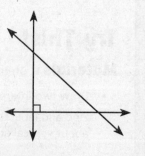

_____

_____

_____

Name _____

Complementary and Supplementary Angles

Essential Question How can you find the unknown measure of complementary or supplementary angles?

When the sum of the measures of two angles equals 90°, the angles are **complementary angles**. The angles do not need to be adjacent in order to be complementary. For example, ∠MNO and ∠PQR are complementary, and each angle is the complement of the other.

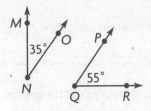

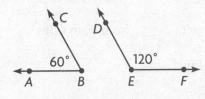

$$35° + 55° = 90°$$

When the sum of the measures of two angles is 180°, the angles are called **supplementary angles**. You can show that ∠ABC and ∠DEF are supplementary by adding their measures.

$$60° + 120° = 180°$$

🔓 UNLOCK the Problem   REAL WORLD

The figure shows the support beams of a half-pipe skateboard ramp. Find m∠TQG.

∠TQY is a right angle, so it measures _____.

∠TQG and ∠GQY together form ∠TQY, so they are _____ angles.

🔑 **Find the measure of the unknown angle.**

STEP 1 The sum of the measures of complementary angles is 90°.

STEP 2 Substitute the measures of the angles.

STEP 3 Solve the equation by using Properties of Equality.

Simplify.

So, the m∠TQG is 35°.

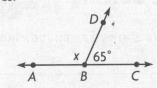

$$m∠TQG + m∠GQY = 90°$$

$$x + 55° = 90°$$

$$x + 55° − 55° = 90° − 55°$$

$$x = 35°$$

Math Talk Explain whether it is possible for two angles to be both congruent and complementary.

Try This! Find m∠ABD.

∠ABC is a straight angle so it measures _____, ∠ABD and ∠CBD together form ∠ABC, so they are _____ angles.

$$m∠ABD + m∠CBD = \underline{\hspace{1cm}}$$

$$x + \underline{\hspace{1cm}} = \underline{\hspace{1cm}}$$

$$x + \underline{\hspace{1cm}} − \underline{\hspace{1cm}} = \underline{\hspace{1cm}} − \underline{\hspace{1cm}}$$

$$x = \underline{\hspace{1cm}}$$

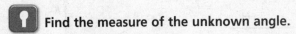

So, m∠ABD = _____.

Share and Show

1. Find the unknown angle measure.

STEP 1 The angles are _____.

STEP 2 Substitute the measures of the angles.

STEP 3 Solve the equation by using Properties of Equality.

    Subtract _____ from both sides.

    Simplify.

So, m∠SQR is _____.

$m\angle PQS + m\angle SQR =$ _____

_____ $+ x =$ _____

_____ $-$ _____ $+ x =$ _____ $-$ _____

$x =$ _____

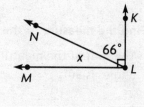

Find the unknown angle measure.

2.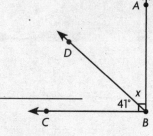

3.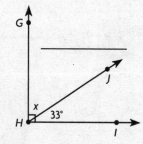

4.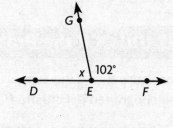

On Your Own

Find the unknown angle measure.

5.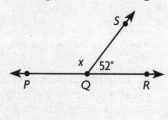

6.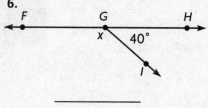

7.

8.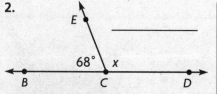

9.

10.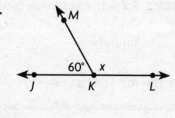

Problem Solving REAL WORLD

11. The figure shows a ramp meeting a wall. Find m∠CBD.

_____

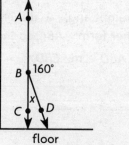

Name _____

Parts of a Circle

Essential Question How can you identify and draw the parts of a circle?

A **circle** is a closed figure made up of points that are the same distance from a point called the **center**. A circle is named by its center point. Other parts of a circle include:

- A **radius** is a line segment with one endpoint at the center of the circle and the other endpoint on the circle.
- A **chord** is a line segment that has both of its endpoints on the circle.
- A **diameter** is a chord that passes through the center of the circle.

Use a compass to draw and label the parts of a circle.

🔓 Activity

Materials  compass, straightedge

A Draw circle *O* with radius $\overline{OP}$ that measures 5 centimeters.

- Draw and label center point *O*. Place the compass point on it.
- Open the compass to 5 centimeters and draw the circle.
- Label point *P* on the edge of the circle.
- With a straightedge, draw the radius $\overline{OP}$.

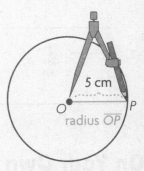

B Draw chord $\overline{QR}$ on circle *O*.

- Label points *Q* and *R* on the circle.
- Use a straightedge to connect *Q* and *R* to create chord $\overline{QR}$.

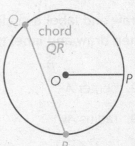

C Draw diameter $\overline{QT}$ on circle *O*.

- Draw a line segment that includes point *Q* and passes through the center.
- Label point *T* where the line segment meets the other side of the circle.

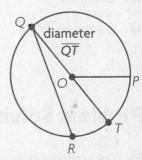

Math Talk How is the length of the diameter related to the length of the radius?

Share and Show

Draw and label a circle with a radius of 4 cm.
Then draw and label the following.

1. center *O*

2. radius $\overline{OB}$

3. chord $\overline{CD}$

4. diameter $\overline{BE}$

Identify each part of the circle shown below.

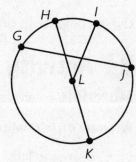

5. the center

_____

6. a radius

_____

7. a chord

_____

8. a diameter

_____

On Your Own ·

Draw and label a circle with a radius of 6 cm.
Then draw and label the following.

9. center *A*

10. radius $\overline{AY}$

11. chord $\overline{MN}$

12. diameter $\overline{XY}$

Problem Solving REAL WORLD

13. Dave needs to buy steel to replace 5 broken spokes on his
    bicycle wheel. Each spoke is equal to the length of the radius
    of the wheel. The diameter of the wheel is 24 inches. How
    many inches of steel does Dave need to make 5 spokes?

_____

Name _____

Estimate Circumference

Essential Question How does the diameter of a circle relate to the circumference?

The **circumference** is the distance around a circle. You can use a ruler and string to estimate the circumference of a circle.

🔑 Activity

In this Activity, you will explore the relationship between the diameter and the circumference of a circle.

Materials: compass, centimeter ruler, string, and calculator

> **Math Idea**
>
> A diameter is a line segment that passes through the center and has both endpoints on the circle.

STEP 1 Use a compass to draw a circle. Mark the center of the circle. Use a ruler to draw a diameter through the center of the circle.

STEP 2 Measure the diameter of the circle to the nearest millimeter. Record your measurement.

STEP 3 Lay the string around the circle. Mark the string where it meets itself.

STEP 4 Use the ruler to measure the string from its end to the mark you made. Measure to the nearest millimeter. Record your measurement.

STEP 5 Use a calculator to divide the circumference of your circle by the diameter. Record your result.

STEP 6 Display your results on the board with those of other students in the class by making a table like the one below.

Circumference (C)	Diameter (d)	C ÷ d

- Compare your results with those of other students. What appears to be the approximate ratio $\frac{C}{d}$ for any circle?

_____

Share and Show

Use a compass to draw a circle with radius 4 cm. Use the circle to answer Exercises 1–4.

1. What is the diameter of this circle? _____

2. Use a string to measure the circumference of the circle, as you did in the activity. What is an estimate of the circumference? _____

3. What is an estimate for the ratio of the circumference to the diameter of the circle? _____

4. If you know the diameter of a circle, how can you use the ratio you found to estimate the circumference? _____

Estimate the circumference of the circle.

5. radius = 8 cm _____

6.
6 yd
_____

7.
5.4 m
_____

8.
18 mm
_____

On Your Own

Estimate the circumference of the circle.

9.
$9\frac{1}{2}$ ft
_____

10.
25 in.
_____

11.
$\frac{1}{2}$ in.
_____

12.
14 in.
_____

13.
7.2 cm
_____

14.
9 yd
_____

Problem Solving REAL WORLD

15. The diameter of the clock on the face of Big Ben in London is 23 feet. Estimate the circumference.

_____

16. The Cevahir clock at a shopping mall in Turkey may be the world's largest clock. The diameter of its face is 118 feet. A football field is 100 yd long. How does the circumference of the Cevahir clock compare with the length of a football field?

_____

_____

Name _____

Check Concepts and Skills

Solve the equation. (pp. P283–P284)

1. $\frac{x}{7} - 8 = 0$

_____

2. $13p + 19 = 97$

_____

3. $3c - 42 = 15$

_____

Solve the inequality. (pp. P285–P286)

4. $8y - 55 < 129$

_____

5. $21 + 16k \geq 101$

_____

6. $82 + \frac{p}{4} > 96$

_____

For 7–9, use the drawing to find the measure of the angle. (pp. P287–P288, P289–P290)

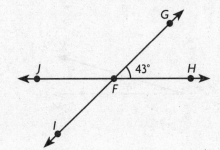

7. m∠JFG

_____

8. m∠JFI

_____

9. m∠IFH

_____

For 10–12, use the drawing to identify the parts of the circle. (pp. P291–P292)

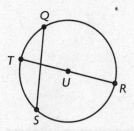

10. the center

_____

11. a radius

_____

12. a chord

_____

Estimate the circumference of the circle. (pp. P293-P294)

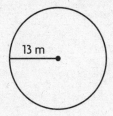

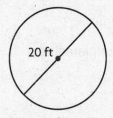

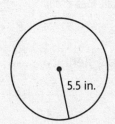

13. _____

14. _____

15. _____

Choose the letter of the correct answer.

16. On Thursday, Gia took two aerobics classes and walked for an additional 20 minutes on the treadmill. On Friday, she took 1 aerobics class and walked for an additional 35 minutes. Simplify the expression $(2m + 35) + (3m + 15)$, where m represents the length in minutes of each class, to show the total number of minutes Gia exercised on those two days. (pp. P281–P282)

Ⓐ $5m + 20$

Ⓑ $5m + 50$

Ⓒ $6m + 20$

Ⓓ $6m + 50$

17. Hank and his friend are drawing a big circle as a boundary for their game. Hank holds one end of a rope and stands at what will be the center of the circle. His friend holds the other end and stands 10 feet away at what will be the edge of the circle. The 10-foot rope is the radius of the circle. What will be its estimated circumference? (pp. P293–P294)

Ⓐ 20 ft

Ⓑ 30 ft

Ⓒ 40 ft

Ⓓ 60 ft

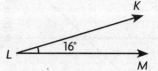

18. Kyle drew ∠KLM and has been asked to draw an angle that is complementary. What should be the measure of the new angle?
(pp. P289–P290)

Ⓐ 64°

Ⓑ 74°

Ⓒ 164°

Ⓓ 174°

19. Carmen has a $30 gift card for her favorite online store. She is hoping to buy 4 bracelets. She knows the bracelets will be priced the same but also knows she needs to allow for the $6 shipping fee. Use the inequality $4p + 6 \leq 30$, where p represents the cost of each bracelet, to find the maximum price she can afford to pay per bracelet. (pp. P285–P286)

Ⓐ $p \leq \$5$

Ⓑ $p \leq \$6$

Ⓒ $p \leq \$8$

Ⓓ $p \leq \$9$

20. Emma looked at the way one of the painted parking lot lines met the curb. She incorrectly described the angles formed as vertical angles. Which term below would describe the two angles correctly?
(pp. P287–P288, P289–P290)

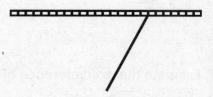

Ⓐ acute

Ⓑ complementary

Ⓒ equal

Ⓓ supplementary

Name _____

Samples and Surveys

Essential Question How can you learn about a population by taking a sample?

A **survey** is a method of gathering information about a group. Surveys are usually made up of questions or other items that require responses. You can survey a population, which is the entire group of individuals or objects. If the population is large, you can survey a part of the population, called a **sample**.

UNLOCK the Problem REAL WORLD

Ron surveys students at his school about their favorite pizza toppings. He surveys the first 25 students to walk into school on Monday morning. What sampling method does he use?

> **Math Idea**
>
> Underline the sentence that tells you what you are trying to find.

Identify the sampling method.

A **sampling method** is a way to choose a sample of a population. The table summarizes some sampling methods.

Sampling Method	Definition	Example
Random Sampling	Every individual or object has an equal chance of being chosen for the survey.	Assign a number to every student in the school. Then use a computer to randomly select numbers.
Convenience Sampling	Individuals or objects that are easily available are chosen for the survey.	Choose a convenient location, such as the library, and survey students as they enter.
Systematic Sampling	Choose a random individual or object as the starting point and then use a pattern to choose additional individuals or objects.	Randomly choose a name from a list of all students and then choose every 10th name after that.

Describe how Ron chooses the sample for his survey.

_____

So, Ron uses _____ sampling.

> **Math Talk** Describe why someone might use a convenience sample rather than a random sample.

Try This!

Meg takes a similar survey. She chooses one name at random from a list of all students at the school. Then she chooses every 15th name after that. What sampling method does she use?

_____

Share and Show

Identify the sampling method.

1. Brianna randomly chooses 20 names from a database of all students at her school.

   Every student has an equal chance of being chosen. So, Brianna's method is

   _____

2. Jorge randomly chooses one name from a phone list of all employees at his company. Then he chooses every 10th name after that.

   _____

On Your Own ·

Identify the sampling method.

3. Mitchell stands at the exit of a train station and surveys 25 commuters as they leave the station.

   _____

4. Marie wants to survey owners of pet stores in her city. She chooses the name of a pet store from the phone book. Then she chooses every 3rd pet store after that.

   _____

5. A caterer randomly chooses 20 names from a list of clients and surveys them to see if they are satisfied with his service.

   _____

6. Ray wants to know how many books people in his town read each month. He surveys the first 50 people that walk into a grocery store.

   _____

Problem Solving

7. A manager wants to know how many of the light bulbs that a factory produces might be defective. She randomly chooses and tests 30 light bulbs produced at the factory. Identify the sampling method the manager used.

   _____

8. Lashonda wants to know the favorite type of music of teens in her town. She surveys 10 students sitting near her at lunch. Identify the sampling method she used.

   _____

Name _____

Make Predictions from Samples

Essential Question How can you use a sample to make a prediction about a population?

You can use equivalent ratios to make predictions about samples.

UNLOCK the Problem REAL WORLD

There are 90 sixth graders at Webb Middle School. In a randomly selected sample of 25 sixth graders at the school, 20 said that they spend more than 3 hours per week exercising. Based on the sample, predict how many of the sixth graders at Webb Middle School spend more than 3 hours exercising per week.

Find equivalent ratios by using a unit rate.

STEP 1

Write ratios that compare the number of students that exercise more than 3 hours per week to total number of students.

$$\frac{20}{25} = \frac{\boxed{}}{90}$$

STEP 2

90 is not a multiple of 25.
Write the known ratio as a unit rate.

$$\frac{20 \div \boxed{}}{25 \div 25} = \frac{\boxed{}}{90}$$

$$\frac{\boxed{}}{1} = \frac{\boxed{}}{90}$$

STEP 3

Write an equivalent rate by multiplying the _____
and the _____ by the same value.

Think: Multiply 1 by _____ to get 90.

So, multiply the numerator by _____ also.

$$\frac{0.8 \cdot \boxed{}}{1 \cdot \boxed{}} = \frac{\boxed{}}{90}$$

So, based on the sample, _____ students out of the 90 sixth graders at Webb Middle School are predicted to spend more than 3 hours per week exercising.

Math Talk **Explain** how you know that your prediction is reasonable.

Share and Show

1. There are 80 children registered for a swimming contest. In a randomly selected sample of 15 children, 3 were over the age of 12. Based on the sample, predict how many contestants are over the age of 12.

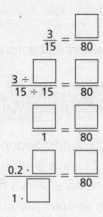

$$\frac{3}{15} = \frac{\square}{80}$$

$$\frac{3 \div \square}{15 \div 15} = \frac{\square}{80}$$

$$\frac{\square}{1} = \frac{\square}{80}$$

$$\frac{0.2 \cdot \square}{1 \cdot \square} = \frac{\square}{80}$$

_____

2. A comic book store carries 80 different titles. In a randomly selected sample of 10 titles, 2 had been published in the last year. Based on the sample, predict how many titles in the store had been published in the last year.

_____

3. Annita has 300 songs on her computer. In a randomly selected sample of 12 songs, 4 songs were rock. Base on the sample, predict how many rock songs Annita has.

_____

On Your Own

4. A car dealership has 200 cars in the parking lot. In a randomly selected sample of 25 cars, 6 cars were white. Based on the sample, predict how many cars at the dealership are white.

_____

5. There are 480 pages in a sixth grade math book. In a randomly selected sample of 40 pages, 15 had color pictures on them. Based on the sample, predict how many pages in the entire book have color pictures.

_____

Problem Solving

6. There are 170 students at Riverdale Middle School. In a randomly selected sample of 30 students, 12 said that they would attend the play. Based on the sample, predict how many students at Riverdale Middle School will attend the play.

_____

7. The Widget Factory produces 500 widgets in one hour. In a randomly selected sample of 20 widgets, 2 were found to be defective. Based on the sample, predict how many widgets produced in one hour are defective.

_____

Name _____

Probability and Likelihood

Essential Question How can you use probability to describe the likelihood of an event?

An **experiment** is an activity involving chance where the results are observed or measured, such as spinning a spinner. A possible result of an experiment is an **outcome**.

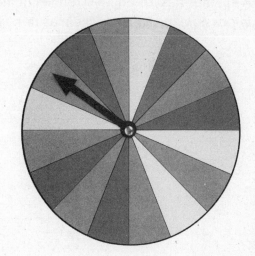

The **sample space** of an experiment is the set of all possible outcomes.

An **event** is a set of one or more outcomes. The **probability** of an event measures the likelihood that the event will occur. Probabilities range from 0 (the event is impossible) to 1 (the event is certain).

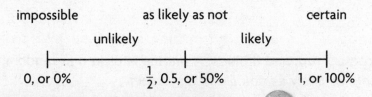

impossible   as likely as not   certain

    unlikely   likely

0, or 0% $\frac{1}{2}$, 0.5, or 50%   1, or 100%

🔑 UNLOCK the Problem REAL WORLD

A number cube used in a board game has faces labeled 1 to 6. Describe each event as *impossible, unlikely, as likely as not, likely,* or *certain.*

A. Evelyn rolls the number cube and gets a 6.

_____

B. James rolls the number cube and gets an even number.

_____

C. Stefan rolls the number cube and gets a number

greater than 0. _____

> **Math Idea**
> When rolling a six-sided number cube, an impossible event would be rolling a 9.

> **Math Talk** Give an example of an event that is certain to happen.

Try This! According to a weather forecast, the probability that it will rain on Monday is 70%. Describe the likelihood of rain on Monday as impossible, unlikely, as likely as not, likely, or certain.

_____

Share and Show

A spinner has 10 equal-sized sections that are numbered 1–10. Describe each event as *impossible, unlikely, as likely as not, likely,* or *certain.*

1. spinning a 4 or 5

_____

2. spinning a number greater than 2

_____

3. spinning an even number

_____

4. spinning a number less than 9

_____

On Your Own

A jar contains 10 marbles. There are 1 green, 1 red, and 8 blues. A marble is picked at random. Describe each event as *impossible, unlikely, as likely as not, likely,* or *certain.*

5. picking a blue

_____

6. picking a yellow

_____

Describe each event as *impossible, unlikely, as likely as not, likely,* or *certain.*

7. The probability that Jack throws a paper ball into a wastebasket is 16%.

_____

8. There is a 50% chance of snow on Tuesday.

_____

Problem Solving

9. The probability that Marguerite will win a game is 20%. Describe the event of Marguerite winning as impossible, unlikely, as likely as not, or certain.

_____

10. A spinner has 5 equal-sized sections. The sections are numbered 1–5. If Jeff spins the spinner, describe the likelihood that he spins a number less than 5.

_____

Name _____

Write Probabilities

Essential Question How can you write the probability of an event?

You can write the probability of an event as a fraction, decimal, or percent.

🔓 UNLOCK the Problem REAL WORLD

A restaurant is having a prize giveaway. The probability that a customer will win a prize is $\frac{1}{8}$. Write this probability as a decimal and as a percent.

STEP 1 Write the probability as a decimal. Divide the numerator by the denominator.

$$\frac{1}{8} = 1 \div 8$$

$$
\begin{array}{r}
 \\
8\overline{)1.000} \\
\underline{8} \\
20 \\
\underline{16} \\
40 \\
\underline{40} \\
\end{array}
$$

$$\frac{1}{8} = 1 \div 8 = \underline{\hspace{2cm}}$$

STEP 2 Write the probability as a percent. Multiply the decimal by 100, and include a percent sign.

$$0.125 = \underline{\hspace{2cm}}$$

STEP 3 Check that 12.5% is correct.

$$12.5\% = \frac{12.5}{100} = \frac{125}{\boxed{}} = \frac{\boxed{}}{\boxed{}}$$

Math Talk Describe the likelihood that a customer will win a prize.

Try This! Write the probability in two different ways.

A. The probability of rain on Wednesday is 85%.

Fraction: $\frac{85}{100} = \dfrac{\boxed{}}{\boxed{}}$

Decimal: _____

B. The probability of scoring a point is 0.625.

Fraction: $\dfrac{\boxed{}}{\boxed{}}$ Percent: _____

Share and Show

Write the probability in two different ways.

1. The probability of a light bulb being defective is 15%.

   Fraction: $\dfrac{\boxed{}}{100} = \dfrac{\boxed{}}{\boxed{}}$

   Decimal: _____

2. The probability of a thunderstorm occurring today is 0.66.

   Fraction: $\dfrac{\boxed{}}{100} = \dfrac{\boxed{}}{\boxed{}}$

   Percent: _____

On Your Own

Write the probability in two different ways.

3. Sarah randomly chooses a cookie from a jar. The probability that the cookie is peanut butter is $\frac{3}{5}$.

   Decimal: _____

   Percent: _____

4. The probability that a player wins a prize at a carnival is 5%.

   Decimal: _____

   Fraction: _____

5. The probability that Jan makes a free throw is 0.94.

   Percent: _____

   Fraction: _____

6. The probability that Max wins a competition is $\frac{9}{20}$.

   Decimal: _____

   Percent: _____

Problem Solving

Write the probability in two different ways.

7. A teacher will randomly choose a student to help with decorations for an upcoming dance. The probability that Raymond will be chosen is 0.08.

   _____

8. Melvin tries to throw a ball into a cup. The probability that he makes the shot is $\frac{27}{40}$.

   _____

Name _____

Experimental Probability

Essential Question How can you calculate the experimental probability of an event?

A **trial** is one performance of an experiment. The **experimental probability** of an event is the ratio of the number of times the event occurs to the total number of trials of the experiment.

Each time an experiment is performed is called a **trial**.

> **Experimental Probability**
>
> $P(\text{event}) = \dfrac{\text{number of times that the event occurs}}{\text{total number of trials}}$

🔓 UNLOCK the Problem   REAL WORLD

A spinner has 16 sections that are red, orange, yellow, or green. Cara spins the pointer 20 times and records her results in the table. Write each probability as a fraction, decimal, and percent. What color is the most likely result of a spin?

Color	Frequency
Red	2
Orange	11
Yellow	4
Green	3

 Write each probability as a fraction, decimal, and percent.

$P(\text{red}) = \dfrac{2}{20} = \dfrac{1}{10}$ or 0.1 or 10% $P(\text{orange}) = \dfrac{11}{20}$ or _____ or _____

$P(\text{yellow}) = \dfrac{\square}{20} = \dfrac{1}{\square}$ or _____ or _____ $P(\text{green}) = \dfrac{\square}{\square}$ or _____ or _____

So, _____ is the most likely result of a spin because this color has the greatest experimental probability.

Math Talk Explain how you compared the experimental probabilities.

Try This! Amirah and Scott each roll a number cube at the same time, and they record the sum. They performed 50 trials, and rolled a sum of 5 seven different times. Find the experimental probability of rolling a sum of 5.

$P(5) =$ _____ out of _____, or _____%

Share and Show

Dylan randomly selects a marble from a bag and replaces it. He does this a total of 40 times and records his results in the table. Use the table to find the experimental probability. Write the probability as a fraction, decimal, and percent.

Color	Red	Blue	Green
Frequency	12	20	8

1. P(red)

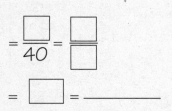

$= \dfrac{\square}{40} = \dfrac{\square}{\square}$

$= \square = \underline{\hspace{2cm}}$

2. P(blue)

_____

_____

3. P(green)

_____

_____

On Your Own

A spinner has 10 sections, labeled 1–10. Trey spins the spinner and records his results each time. Use the results in the table to find the experimental probability. Write the probability as a percent.

4. spinning a 4

_____

5. spinning a 1

_____

6. spinning a 7

_____

7. spinning a 9 or 10

_____

9	2	3	10	8
3	2	6	5	8
1	4	9	3	4
1	10	2	1	6

Problem Solving

8. Ling tossed two coins, at the same time, 5 times. Her results were TT, TH, TH, HH, and HT. What is her experimental probability of flipping two tails? Express your answer as a decimal, fraction, and percent.

_____

9. The letters R, A, N, D, O, and M are written on cards and placed in a bag. Jack randomly chooses and replaces a card several times. Find the experimental probability of picking an N. Express your answer as a percent.

Letter	R	A	N	D	O	M
Frequency	0	2	3	1	2	4

_____

Name _____

✔ Checkpoint

Check Concepts and Skills

Identify the sampling method. (pp. P297–P298)

1. Sam wants to know which genre of movie is the favorite among his classmates. He randomly chooses 15 names from a list of the students in his class.

_____

2. Shaelun is interested in finding the number of students in her school who like math. She asks the people on her team in gym class.

_____

Write the probability in two different ways. (pp. P303–P304)

3. The probability of precipitation is 30%.

Fraction: _____   Decimal: _____

4. The probability of picking a diamond from a standard deck of cards is $\frac{1}{4}$.

Decimal: _____   Percent: _____

5. The probability that Jiho will select a blue marble from a bag is 0.19.

Fraction: _____   Percent: _____

6. The probability that the pointer will land on red when Yvette spins a prize wheel is $\frac{1}{20}$.

Decimal: _____   Percent: _____

Problem Solving REAL WORLD

Valerie places some cards in a bag. Each card shows a color.
She randomly chooses and replaces a card 20 times. Use the
results in the table to find the experimental probability indicated.
Express your answer as a percent. (pp. P305–P306)

Color	Red	Yellow	Blue	Green	Orange	Purple	Black	Brown
Frequency	2	5	3	0	2	2	3	3

7. What is the experimental probability of choosing an orange card?

_____

8. What is the experimental probability of choosing a yellow card?

_____

Choose the letter of the correct answer.

9. The probability that Jordan will make a free throw shot in his basketball game is 50%. Which term describes the likelihood of Jordan making a free throw? (pp. P301–P302)

Ⓐ impossible   Ⓒ as likely as not

Ⓑ unlikely   Ⓓ certain

10. There are 25 students in Winnie's class. In a randomly selected sample of 10 classmates, 4 have dogs. Based on the sample, predict how many students in Winnie's class who have dogs. (pp. P299–P300)

Ⓐ 4   Ⓑ 8   Ⓒ 10   Ⓓ 12

11. There are 140 students enrolled at Madame LaComtesse's Dance School. In a random sample of 30 students, 6 said they would be interested in the new hip-hop class. Based on the sample, how many students out of 140 are interested in the hip-hop class? (pp. P299–P300)

Ⓐ 6   Ⓑ 18   Ⓒ 24   Ⓓ 28

12. Kyran has 6 socks in a bag. There are 4 white socks and 2 blue socks. Which term describes the event of picking a white sock from the bag? (pp. P301–P302)

Ⓐ certain   Ⓒ as likely as not

Ⓑ likely   Ⓓ unlikely

13. The probability that Yvette wins a game is 15%. Which of the following shows this probability written in two different ways? (pp. P303–P304)

Ⓐ 0.15 and $\frac{3}{10}$ Ⓒ 0.15 and $\frac{3}{20}$

Ⓑ 1.5 and $\frac{3}{10}$ Ⓓ 15.0 and $\frac{3}{20}$

14. Nika has a bag of cards, each showing a shape. She randomly chooses and replaces a card 12 times. Use the results in the table to find the experimental probability that Nika will choose a card showing a heart. (pp. P305–P306)

Ⓐ 25%   Ⓒ 0.20

Ⓑ $\frac{3}{10}$ Ⓓ $\frac{1}{3}$

Shape	Frequency
Square	2
Heart	3
Diamond	5
Triangle	2

15. Use the results in the table to find the experimental probability that Nika will choose a card that does NOT show a triangle.

Ⓐ $\frac{1}{6}$ Ⓒ $\frac{7}{12}$

Ⓑ $\frac{5}{12}$ Ⓓ $\frac{5}{6}$